Requirements for Certification

Requirements for Certification

of Teachers, Counselors, Librarians, Administrators

for Elementary and Secondary Schools

Eighty-Fourth Edition, 2019–2020

Edited by
Colleen M. Frankhart

The University of Chicago Press
Chicago and London

The University of Chicago Press, Chicago 60637

© 2020 by The University of Chicago

All rights reserved. No part of this book may be used or reproduced in any manner whatsoever without written permission, except in the case of brief quotations in critical articles and reviews. For more information, contact the University of Chicago Press, 1427 E. 60th St., Chicago, IL 60637.

Eighty-fourth edition 2020

Published annually since 1935

International Standard Book Number-13: 978-0-226-66628-0 (cloth)

International Standard Book Number-13: 978-0-226-66810-9 (e-book)

DOI: https://doi.org/10.7208/chicago/9780226668109.001.0001

International Standard Series Number: 1047-7071

Library of Congress Catalog Card Number: A43-1905

♾ This paper meets the requirements of ANSI/NISO Z39.48-1992 (Permanence of Paper).

Contents

Introduction to the Eighty-Fourth Edition
2019–2020

Why do we need a book of requirements for educator certification in our electronic age? This volume provides a concise, accessible summary of relevant information that is simply not consistently available on the websites of individual state certification offices. The goal of our compilation is to provide a "balcony view" of state certification regulations that enables readers to access and compare information either about different positions within a single state or about a single position in one or more states.

Interestingly, states present the material on their certification websites in a variety of formats and levels of accessibility. While some are carefully designed to be user-friendly and intuitively clear to navigate, others are the electronic version of a procedures manual for staff. With an array of online application forms, automated certification systems, and literally hundreds of pages of state legislative regulations reproduced verbatim, it can be a significant challenge to unearth a clear, consistent overview of the field one is exploring, along with suggestions on where to dive in more deeply when full detail is required. We aim to provide exactly that service.

What we present in *Requirements for Certification* is that much-needed survey of current information on certification requirements for all fifty states and the District of Columbia. Updated annually and presented in a clear, concise outline format, the book provides a fresh overview of certification information for teachers, counselors, librarians, and administrators, as well as those who aspire to join their ranks. As this volume moves into its eighty-fourth year of continuous publication, it provides an essential service to both the public and the professionals who consult it.

Requirements for Certification had its inception in the Board of Vocational Guidance and Placement (now Career Advancement) at the University of Chicago. The original study was made by Robert C. Woellner, professor of education and head of the Board, and M. Aurilla Wood, placement counselor. The digest continued under the direction of Elizabeth H. Woellner until her retirement in 1983. Produced only in mimeograph form its first year, the digest was published and made available for sale by the University of Chicago Press in 1935 and has appeared in annual editions since that time.

The publication of this volume would not be possible without the cheerful and generous help of Mary Beth Leone-Getten and the state certification officers who go above and beyond to help us ensure that this book is accurate and complete. We trust that these efforts, by helping to make the requirements for educator certification as widely available as possible throughout the United States and its possessions and territories, will bear fruit both for the certification professionals and for those who seek access to their knowledge.

Alabama

Stages and Titles of Teaching Certificates

I. Class B Professional Educator Certificate (valid 5 ycars*)
   A. Issued on basis of a bachelor's degree and completion of all other requirements for issuance
II. Class A Professional Educator Certificate (valid 5 years*)
   A. Issued on basis of a master's degree and completion of all other requirements for issuance
III. Class AA Professional Educator Certificate (valid 5 years*)
   A. Issued on basis of completion of an approved, planned sixth-year program of at least 30 semester hours of post-master's graduate credit, which may result in an education specialist degree, and completion of all other requirements for issuance
IV. Class A Professional Leadership Certificate (valid 5 years*)
   A. Issued on basis of a master's degree and completion of all other requirements for issuance
V. Class AA Professional Leadership Certificate (valid 5 years*)
   A. Issued on basis of completion of an approved, planned sixth-year program of at least 30 semester hours of post-master's graduate credit, which may result in an education specialist degree, and all other requirements for issuance

*Valid from the date of issuance through the remainder of the same scholastic year, and thereafter, for the next 5 consecutive scholastic years.

Requirements for Teaching Certificates

I. Teaching certificates available include:
   A. Pre-Kindergarten (Birth–Age 4)
   B. Early childhood education (P–3)
   C. Early childhood special education (P–3)
   D. Elementary education (K–6)
   E. Collaborative special education teacher (K–6)
   F. Middle level (4–8)
   G. High school (6–12)
   H. Collaborative special education teacher (6–12)
   I. Elementary-secondary (P–12)
   J. Special education (P–12 for hearing impairment, visual impairment, or gifted)
II. Certificates are endorsed in specific teaching field(s).
III. The Educator Certification Chapter of the Alabama Administrative Code adopted March 10, 2016, contains all current information applicable to earning a certificate in

Alabama and is accessible via the following links: https://www.alsde.edu/sec/ec/Pages/home.aspx (click on "SBOE Administrative Code")

or

If the link does not work, go to www.alsde.edu and click on Department Offices: Educator Certification: SBOE Administrative Code.

IV. Specific Teaching Certificates and Their Requirements

  A. Class B Professional Educator Certificate

   1. Earn a bachelor's degree from a regionally accredited senior institution,
      and

   2. Meet academic requirements in teaching field for which certification is sought through 1 of the following options:

      a. Alabama State Board of Education–approved program,
         or

      b. Valid professional educator certificate issued by another state, the District of Columbia, a US territory, or the Department of Defense Education Activity (DoDEA) at the bachelor's degree level,
         or

      c. Educator preparation program in another country,
         or

      d. Valid certification by the National Board for Professional Teaching Standards (NBPTS) in a teaching field in which Alabama offers comparable certification; see Rule 290-3-2-.27 in document accessible via link at III, directly above.

  B. Class A Professional Educator Certificate

   1. Earn a master's degree from a regionally accredited senior institution,
      and

   2. Meet academic requirements in teaching field for which certification is sought through 1 of the following options:

      a. Alabama State Board of Education–approved program,
         or

      b. Valid professional educator certificate issued by another state, the District of Columbia, a US territory, or DoDEA at the master's degree level,
         or

      c. Educator preparation program in another country,
         or

      d. Valid NBPTS Certification in a teaching field in which Alabama offers comparable certification; see Rule 290-3-2-.27 in document accessible via link at III, directly above.

  C. Class A Professional Educator Certificate: Alternative Class A Approved Program

   1. Meet Alabama State Board of Education–approved program requirements specified in Rule 290-3-3-.44 of the Educator Preparation Chapter of the Alabama Administrative Code accessible via link at III, directly above. If the link does not work, go to www.alsde.edu and click on Department Offices: Educator Preparation: ALSBE Admin Code.

D. Class AA Professional Educator Certificate
1. Complete an approved, planned sixth-year program of at least 30 semester hours of post-master's graduate credit with a regionally accredited senior institution, *and*
2. Meet academic requirements in teaching field for which certification is sought through 1 of the following options:
    a. Alabama State Board of Education–approved program, *or*
    b. Valid professional educator certificate issued by another state, the District of Columbia, a US territory, or DoDEA at the sixth-year level, *or*
    c. Educator preparation program in another country, *or*
    d. Valid NBPTS Certification in a teaching field in which Alabama offers comparable certification; see Rule 290-3-2-.27 in document accessible via link at III, directly above.

Administrative/Supervisory Certificates and Their Requirements

I. Class A Professional Leadership Certificate
A. Earn a master's degree from a regionally accredited senior institution, *and*
B. Meet requirements in administration through 1 of the following options:
1. Alabama State Board of Education–approved program in Instructional Leadership (note: prior to admission to the program, the applicant must have had at least 3 full years of full-time, acceptable professional educational experience in a P–12 setting, to include at least 1 full year of full-time P–12 classroom teaching experience) (Instructional Leadership certification allows one to serve as an administrator and/or supervisor), *or*
2. Valid professional educator certificate in administration issued by another state, the District of Columbia, a US territory, or DoDEA at the master's degree level, and 3 full years of full-time acceptable professional educational experience in a P–12 setting, to include at least 1 full year of full-time P–12 classroom teaching experience.
C. Meet requirements in supervision through a valid professional educator certificate in supervision issued by another state, the District of Columbia, a US territory, or DoDEA at the master's degree level, and 3 full years of full-time acceptable professional educational experience in a P–12 setting, to include at least 1 full year of full-time P–12 classroom teaching experience.
II. Class AA Professional Leadership Certificate
A. Complete an approved, planned sixth-year program of at least 30 semester hours of post-master's graduate credit with a regionally accredited senior institution, *and*

B. Meet requirements in administration through 1 of the following options:
  1. Alabama State Board of Education–approved program in Instructional Leadership (Instructional Leadership certification allows one to serve as an administrator and/or supervisor),
    or
  2. Valid professional educator certificate in administration issued by another state, the District of Columbia, a US territory, or DoDEA at the sixth-year level, and 3 full years of full-time acceptable professional educational experience in a P–12 setting, to include at least 1 full year of full-time P–12 classroom teaching experience.
C. Meet requirements in supervision through a valid professional educator certificate in supervision issued by another state, the District of Columbia, a US territory, or DoDEA at the sixth-year level, and 3 full years of full-time acceptable professional educational experience in a P–12 setting, to include at least 1 full year of full-time P–12 classroom teaching experience.

Support Services Certificates and Their Requirements

I. Class A Certificate for Library Media, School Counselor, School Psychometrist, or Sport Manager
  A. Earn a master's degree from a regionally accredited senior institution,
    and
  B. Meet academic requirements in support area for which certification is sought through 1 of the following options:
    1. Alabama State Board of Education–approved program,
      or
    2. Valid professional educator certificate issued by another state, the District of Columbia, a US territory, or DoDEA at the master's degree level,
      or
    3. Valid certification by the NBPTS in the support area.
      a. See Rule 290-3-2-.27 in document accessible via link at Requirements for Teaching Certificates, III, above.
    4. For school counseling, verify compliance with the Council for Accreditation of Counseling and Related Educational Programs (CACREP) approach.
      a. See Rule 290-3-2-.22 in document accessible via link at Requirements for Teaching Certificates, III, above.
  C. Demonstrate 2 full years of full-time acceptable professional educational experience in a P–12 school system. Applicants through the CACREP approach do not have to meet this requirement.
II. Class A Speech-Language Pathology
  A. Earn a master's degree from a regionally accredited senior institution,
  B. Meet academic requirements in speech-language pathology through completion of a master's degree–level speech-language pathology program that was accredited by the Council on Academic Accreditation (CAA) of the American Speech-Language-Hearing Association (ASHA) at the time of program completion,

    C.   Verify satisfactory performance on the CAA-prescribed Praxis subject test(s), *and*

    D.   Verify a valid speech-language pathology license issued by any state's board of examiners in speech-language pathology.

III. Class AA Certificate for Library Media or School Counselor

    A.   Complete an approved, planned sixth-year-level program of at least 30 semester hours of post-master's graduate credit from a regionally accredited senior institution, *and*

    B.   Meet academic requirements in support area for which certification is sought through 1 of the following options:

        1.   Alabama State Board of Education–approved program, *or*

        2.   Valid professional educator certificate issued by another state, the District of Columbia, a US territory, or DoDEA at the sixth-year level, *or*

        3.   Valid certification by the NBPTS in the support area.

            a.   See Rule 290-3-2-.27 in document accessible via link at Requirements for Teaching Certificates, III, above.

    C.   Demonstrate 2 full years of full-time acceptable professional educational experience in a P–12 school system.

IV. Class AA Certificate for School Psychologist

    A.   Complete an approved, planned sixth-year-level program of at least 30 semester hours of post-master's graduate credit from a regionally accredited senior institution, *and*

    B.   Meet academic requirements in school psychology through 1 of the following options:

        1.   Alabama State Board of Education–approved program, *or*

        2.   Valid school psychologist professional educator certificate issued by another state, the District of Columbia, a US territory, or DoDEA at the sixth-year level, *or*

        3.   Verification of compliance with the Nationally Certified School Psychologist (NCSP) approach.

            a.   See Rule 290-3-2-.28 in document accessible via link at Requirements for Teaching Certificates, III, above.

    C.   Demonstrate 2 full years of full-time acceptable professional educational experience in a P–12 school system. Applicants through the NCSP approach do not have to meet this requirement.

Alabama Educator Certification Assessment Program

I. Applicants for an Alabama professional educator certificate, professional leadership certificate, or alternative approach certificate must meet the requirements of the Alabama Educator Certification Assessment Program (AECAP) as a precondition for certification.

A. AECAP consists of basic skills assessments (measuring fundamental skills in mathematics, reading, and writing), subject area assessments, and, beginning in Fall 2018, a performance assessment.
   1. Basic skills assessments are the Praxis Core Academic Skills for Educators, administered by the Educational Testing Service (ETS).
   2. Subject area assessments consist of Alabama State Board of Education–approved tests from the Praxis Subject Assessment series, administered by ETS.
   3. The performance assessment, beginning in Fall 2018, will be Educative Teacher Performance Assessment (edTPA), administered by Pearson Education, Inc.

Out-of-State Reciprocity

I. Professional educator and professional leadership certification in Alabama is not offered reciprocally on the basis of educator preparation programs completed at non-Alabama institutions.

II. Alabama professional educator and professional leadership certification is only considered reciprocally on the basis of holding a valid professional educator or professional leadership certificate issued by another state, the District of Columbia, a US territory, or DoDEA, and if Alabama offers comparable certification.

Alaska

Initial Teacher Certificates

I. Initial/2- and 3-Year Teacher Certificate (valid 2 years; not renewable, but may be extended to a third year if Alaska studies and Alaska multicultural coursework are turned in before interim deadline)
   A. Requirements for Initial 2-Year Certification—Candidate:
      1. Has completed a bachelor's degree from a regionally accredited university;
      2. Has completed a state-approved teacher preparation program;
      3. Has passing scores on an approved basic competency exam (BCE) (for details, consult https://education.alaska.gov/teachercertification/praxis);
      4. Has passing scores on an approved Content Area Exam (for details, consult https://education.alaska.gov/teachercertification/contentareaexams);
      5. Has never held an Initial or Provisional Alaska teacher certificate;
      6. Is not eligible for reinstatement of a Professional or Master teacher certificate; *and*
      7. Has completed the 4 mandatory trainings during the 5 years prior to receipt of application.
      8. For the 1-year extension, official transcripts—showing the completion of 3 semester hours of an approved Alaska studies course and the completion of 3 semester hours of an approved Alaska multicultural course—must be received by the Teacher Certification office prior to the expiration date of the Initial certificate.
         a. An applicant who has satisfied the Alaska studies and Alaska multicultural coursework requirements at the time of application will be issued an Initial/3-Year teacher certificate.
II. Initial/Out-of-State Teacher Certificate (valid 1 year; may be extended twice for a total of 3 full years; end dates of extensions are June 30 and December 31 of the given year)
   A. Requirements—Candidate:
      1. Has completed a bachelor's degree from a regionally accredited university;
      2. Has never held an Alaska teacher certificate; *and*
      3. Holds a current, valid out-of-state teacher certificate at the time the applicant's contract for instructional services begins in an Alaska public school district.
         a. Out-of-country certificates will not be accepted.
      4. To extend the 1-year certificate for an additional year, the applicant must obtain passing scores on an approved basic competency exam.
      5. To extend the 2-year certificate for an additional year, the applicant must:
         a. Complete 3 semester hours of an approved Alaska studies course; *and*
         b. Complete 3 semester hours of an approved Alaska multicultural course.

6. Endorsements placed on an Initial/Out-of-State teacher certificate will reflect the endorsements on the applicant's out-of-state certificate.
   a. If an applicant holds more than 1 valid out-of-state certificate, the applicant must choose which out-of-state certificate to submit with the Initial application.

III. Initial/Program Enrollment Teacher Certificate (valid 1 year; may be reissued twice for a total of 2 1-year extensions)
   A. Requirements—Candidate:
   1. Has completed a bachelor's degree from a regionally accredited university;
   2. Is enrolled in a state-approved teacher preparation program;
      a. Program enrollment may not be used for individuals enrolled in special education programs; rather, they must complete their program prior to applying for the Initial certificate.
   3. Has been offered a certified teaching position by an Alaska public school district;
   4. Has obtained passing scores on an approved basic competency exam (for details, consult https://education.alaska.gov/teachercertification/praxis);
   5. Has obtained passing scores on an approved content area exam;
   6. Has included the Proof of Program Enrollment form in the application packet, completed by the correct university official;
      and
   7. Has obtained from the hiring district a completed District Request & Assurance form, signed by the district superintendent or human resources director, attesting to the applicant's 5 years of subject matter experience (can include undergraduate coursework).
   8. For the first 1-year extension, the certificate holder must submit the following items to the Teacher Certification office prior to expiration date of the Initial Proof of Program Enrollment teaching certificate:
      a. An updated Proof of Program Enrollment form;
         and
      b. An updated transcript showing progress toward the completion of a state-approved teacher preparation program.
   9. For the second 1-year extension, the certificate holder must submit the following:
      a. A State-Approved Program Verification form;
      b. Official transcripts showing 3 semester hours of an approved Alaska studies course and 3 semester hours of an approved Alaska multicultural course.
         and
      c. Transcripts showing completion of the teacher preparation program.

IV. Initial/Reemployment Teacher Certificate (valid 1 year; nonrenewable and not eligible for extension)
   A. Requirements—Candidate:
   1. Has never held a Reemployment teacher certificate in Alaska;
      and

2. Has held an Alaska teacher certificate that was valid for at least 2 years.
3. The most recent Alaska teacher certificate held by candidate must have expired more than 1 year prior to the date of application.
4. Endorsements placed on an Initial/Reemployment certificate will reflect the endorsements on the applicant's previous Alaska teacher certificate. No endorsements may be added or removed during the life of the Reemployment certificate.
5. An applicant who has held a Reemployment certificate is no longer eligible for another Initial certificate, but must apply for a Professional teacher certificate to continue teaching.
6. An applicant is eligible to apply only for the Professional 5-year certificate and will not qualify for another Initial certificate unless the applicant meets every requirement for the Professional *except* 2 full years of certified, full-time equivalent (FTE) teaching experience. Under that circumstance, the applicant must apply for the Second Initial certificate.

B. Additional Requirements
1. Special Education—applicants who wish to teach special education to children with disabilities must, in addition to meeting other requirements for teacher certification, secure an endorsement based upon completion of an approved teacher-training program in special education.
   a. Preschool Special Education—those who wish to teach preschool children with special needs and who are not eligible for an endorsement in preschool special education must have completed at least 6 semester hours in early childhood special education in addition to holding a teaching certificate with a special education endorsement. This does not constitute an endorsement in Early Childhood Special Education.
2. Gifted—applicants who wish to teach gifted children must, in addition to meeting requirements for teacher certification, have completed at least 6 semester hours in gifted education. This does not constitute an endorsement.
3. Vocational Education—applicants who wish to teach vocational trades must have an endorsement in vocational education or a Type M Limited Certificate.

V. Second Initial Teacher Certificate (valid 3 years; nonrenewable)
A. Requirements—Candidate:
1. Has held an Initial or Provisional teacher certificate;
2. Has passing scores on an approved basic competency exam (for details, consult https://education.alaska.gov/TeacherCertification/praxis.html);
3. Has completed a teacher preparation program as verified by a State-Approved Program Verification form;
   and
4. Presents official transcripts showing 3 semester hours of approved Alaska studies coursework; 3 semester hours of approved Alaska multicultural coursework; and 6 semester hours of coursework completed in the 5 years prior to application (recency credit).
5. If the applicant has held a Professional or regular Type A teacher certificate, the certificate must have expired more than 1 year prior to the date of application.

Professional and Master Teacher Certificates

I. Professional Teacher Certificate (valid 5 years; renewable)
   A. Requirements—Candidate:
      1. Has completed a bachelor's degree from a regionally accredited university;
      2. Has completed a state-approved teacher preparation program;
      3. Has passing scores on an approved basic competency exam (BCE) (for details, consult https://education.alaska.gov/teachercertification/praxis);
      4. Has passing scores on an approved Content Area Exam;
      5. Has completed 3 semester hours of an approved Alaska studies course;
      6. Has completed 3 semester hours of an approved Alaska multicultural course;
      7. Has completed 6 semester hours of college coursework within the 5 years prior to application;
      8. Has 2 years of teaching experience in a state-approved or accredited school while holding a teaching certificate;
         and
      9. Has completed the 4 mandatory trainings during the 5 years prior to receipt of application.
   B. Renewal requirements: Prior to the expiration date of the certificate, applicant must:
      1. Earn 6 semester hours of renewal credit taken during the life of the certificate being renewed, of which, a minimum of 3 semester hours must be upper-division or graduate credit;
      2. Present verification of current employment in an Alaska public school district in a position requiring a certificate;
         a. If an applicant is not employed in this capacity at the time of renewal, a fingerprint card will be required.
         and
      3. Complete application and pay all fees; fees are nonrefundable.
      4. The 6 renewal credits earned must be:
         a. Related to the certificated person's employment at the time of renewal, if that employment requires a certificate;
         b. Related to the certificated person's endorsements;
            or
         c. A required element of a program that will lead to an endorsement under 4 AAC 12.395 that the certificated person seeks to acquire.
   C. Additional Requirements—See Initial Teacher Certificates, IV, B, 1–3, above.
II. Master Teacher Certificate (valid 10 years; renewable)
   Note: All endorsements for which an applicant was eligible on a Professional teacher certificate can be added to this certificate, in addition to the endorsement for National Board Certification.
   A. Requirements—Candidate must:
      1. Meet all requirements for the Professional certificate;
      2. Hold a current Initial or Professional certificate;
      3. Hold current National Board Certification issued by National Board for Professional Teaching Standards (NBPTS);

4. Complete application and pay all fees, all of which are nonrefundable;
    and
5. Have completed the 4 mandatory trainings during the 5 years prior to receipt of application (for applications on and after June 30, 2017).

B. Renewal requirements—Candidate must:
1. Hold a current, renewed National Board Certification;
2. Have completed 6 semester hours of renewal credit taken during the life of the Master certificate being renewed, of which a minimum of 3 semester hours must be upper-division or graduate credit;
3. Present verification of employment in an Alaska public school district in a position requiring a certificate;
    a. If an applicant is not employed in this capacity at the time of renewal, fingerprint cards will be required.
    and
4. Complete application and pay all fees; fees are nonrefundable.
5. The 6 renewal credits earned must be:
    a. Related to the certificated person's employment at the time of renewal, if that employment requires a certificate;
    b. Related to the certificated person's endorsements;
        or
    c. A required element of a program that will lead to an endorsement under 4 AAC 12.395 that the certificated person seeks to acquire.
6. If the requirements to renew a Master certificate have not been met, an applicant must meet all current renewal requirements for the Professional certificate.

C. Additional Requirements—See Initial Teacher Certificates, IV, B, 1–3, above.

Administrative Certificates

I. Type B Administrative Certificate (valid 5 years; renewable)
A. Requirements—Candidate:
1. Has at least 3 years of experience as a certificated teacher or special service provider;
2. Has completed an approved teacher-education program in school administration;
3. Has completed a master's or higher degree from a regionally accredited institution;
4. Has completed a state-approved, university-based educator preparation program;
5. Has completed 6 semester hours or 9 quarter hours of credit earned during the 5-year period preceding the date of application;
    a. See Provisional Type B Administrator certificate, directly below.
6. Has completed 3 semester hours of approved Alaska studies and 3 semester hours of approved multicultural education/cross-cultural communications;
    a. See Provisional Type B Administrator certificate, directly below.
7. Has completed application packet, which includes a signed and notarized application, the State-Approved Program Verification form, official transcripts,

2 sets of completed fingerprint cards, and processing fees, all of which are nonrefundable;
and

8. Has completed the 4 mandatory trainings during the 5 years prior to receipt of application (for applications on and after June 30, 2017). Note: Trainings are not required under the reemployment option for this certificate.

B. Renewal Requirements: Prior to the expiration date of the certificate, applicant must:

1. Have completed 6 semester hours of renewal credit taken during the life of the certificate being renewed, of which a minimum of 3 semester hours must be upper-division or graduate credit;

2. Present verification of current employment in an Alaska public school district in a position requiring a certificate;

    a. If an applicant is not employed in this capacity at the time of renewal, a fingerprint card will be required.

    and

3. Complete application and pay all fees; fees are nonrefundable.

4. The 6 renewal credits earned must be:

    a. Related to the certificated person's employment at the time of renewal, if that employment requires a certificate;

    b. Related to the certificated person's endorsements;

    or

    c. A required element of a program that will lead to an endorsement under 4 AAC 12.395 that the certificated person seeks to acquire.

II. Provisional Type B Administrator Certificate (valid 2 years; nonrenewable)

A. This certificate is for applicants meeting all other requirements for certification, but who lack 6 semester hours of credit earned during the 5-year period preceding the date of application, or who lack 3 semester hours of credit in Alaska studies and/or 3 semester hours of credit in multicultural education or cross-cultural communications.

B. In order to avoid a lapse in certification, the Provisional Type B Administrator certificate holder must submit official transcripts to the Teacher Certification office showing the completion of 3 semester hours of approved Alaska studies coursework and the completion of 3 semester hours of approved Alaska multicultural coursework prior to the expiration date of the Provisional certificate.

1. In addition, prior to the expiration date of their certificate, the Provisional certificate holder must apply for the 5-year Regular Type B Administrative certificate.

C. Candidates must have completed the 4 mandatory trainings during the 5 years prior to receipt of application.

III. Superintendent Endorsement

A. Requirements—Candidate:

1. Has completed a State-Approved Program Verification form showing completion of an approved superintendency program from a regionally accredited university;

2. Has at least 5 years of employment as a classroom teacher or administrator;

    a.   At least 3 years must have been satisfactory employment as a teacher with a teaching certificate or comparable certificate issued by another state; and at least 1 year must have been satisfactory employment as an administrator with a Type B certificate or comparable certificate from another state.
    and

3. Has completed the 4 mandatory trainings during the 5 years prior to receipt of application.

IV. Special Education Administrator Endorsement
  A. Requirements—Candidate:
    1. Has completed a State-Approved Program Verification form showing completion of an approved special education administrative program from a regionally accredited university;
    2. Has at least 3 years of employment as a certified special education teacher or school psychologist, with a teaching or special services certificate or comparable certificate issued by another state;
      and
    3. Has completed the 4 mandatory trainings during the 5 years prior to receipt of application.

V. Director of Special Education
  A. Requirements for applicants who wish to be employed solely as the administrator or director of special education and are not eligible for a special education administrator endorsement:
    1. Possess both a Type B certificate and a teaching certificate endorsed for special education or for a related services specialty. (This does not constitute an endorsement.)
      a. To be assigned as a classroom teacher in Alaska, applicant must have a valid teacher certificate (Initial, Professional, or Master), since the Type B certificate does not allow the holder to be a classroom teacher.
      b. Applicants who currently hold a valid Alaska teaching certificate and are applying for a Type B certificate are considered an initial applicant for the Type B.
    2. Have completed the 4 mandatory trainings during the 5 years prior to receipt of application (for applications on and after June 30, 2017).

VI. Type C Special Services Certificate (valid 5 years; renewable)
  A. Requirements—Candidate:
    1. Has completed a program in a special service area;
    2. Has a bachelor's or higher degree;
    3. Has completed a state-approved, university-based preparation program;
    4. Has completed 6 semester hours or 9 quarter hours of credit taken within the past 5 years;
    5. Has completed 3 semester hours of approved Alaska studies and 3 semester hours of Alaska multicultural education/cross-cultural communications;
    6. Has completed an application packet, which includes a signed and notarized application, a State-Approved Program Verification form, official transcripts, a fingerprint card, and fees, all of which are nonrefundable;

and

7. Has completed the 4 mandatory trainings during the 5 years prior to receipt of application. Note: Trainings are not required under the reemployment option for this certificate.

B. Renewal Requirements: Prior to the expiration date of the certificate, applicant must:
1. Have completed 6 semester hours of renewal credit taken during the life of the certificate being renewed, of which a minimum of 3 semester hours must be upper division or graduate credit;
2. Present verification of current employment in an Alaska public school district in a position requiring a certificate;
   a. If an applicant is not employed in this capacity at the time of renewal, a fingerprint card will be required.

   and
3. Complete application and pay all fees; fees are nonrefundable. (For Advanced Type C renewal applicants, a completed application includes a copy of the certificate showing renewed National Board Certification. The expiration date of the renewed Advanced Type C certificate will be the same as the National Board Certification expiration date.)
4. The 6 renewal credits earned must be:
   a. Related to the certificated person's employment at the time of renewal, if that employment requires a certificate;
   b. Related to the certificated person's endorsements;
      or
   c. A required element of a program that will lead to an endorsement under 4 AAC 12.395 that the certificated person seeks to acquire.

VII. Provisional Type C Special Services Certificate (valid 2 years)
A. This certificate is for applicants meeting all other requirements for certification, but who lack 6 semester hours of credit earned during the 5-year period preceding the date of application; or who lack 3 semester hours of credit in Alaska studies and/or 3 semester hours of credit in multicultural education or cross-cultural communications.
B. In order to avoid a lapse in certification, the Provisional Type C Special Services certificate holder must submit official transcripts to the Teacher Certification office showing the completion of 3 semester hours of approved Alaska studies coursework and the completion of 3 semester hours of approved Alaska multicultural coursework prior to the expiration date of the Provisional certificate.
1. In addition, prior to the expiration date of their certificate, the Provisional certificate holder must apply for the 5-year regular Type C Special Services certificate.
C. Candidates must have completed the 4 mandatory trainings during the 5 years prior to receipt of application.

VIII. Initial Special Services (Type C) Endorsements
A. Endorsements under a Type C certificate include Audiology, Occupational Therapy, Physical Therapy, School Nursing, School Psychology, School

Psychometry, School Social Work, Speech Pathology, School Counselor, and Library Science-Media.

1. School Psychology Endorsement Requirements
   a. Candidate must also hold a master's or higher degree in school psychology; be recommended by an institution whose school psychology program has been approved by the National Association of School Psychologists (NCATE) or the American Psychological Association; and have completed a 1200-hour internship (with 600 of the hours in a school setting);
   or
   Be certified under the certification system of the National Association of School Psychologists.

2. Speech, Language, or Hearing Endorsement Requirements
   a. Candidate must hold either a master's or higher degree with a major emphasis in speech-language pathology, audiology, or speech-language and hearing science;
   or
   Possess certification of clinical competence from the American Speech-Language-Hearing Association.
   b. Candidate must also be recommended for endorsement by an institution with a program approved by NCATE or the American Speech-Language-Hearing Association.

3. Other Special Service Endorsement Requirements
   a. Candidates who wish to be employed to provide such services as speech or language pathology, school psychology, school counseling, orientation and mobility, psychometry, library and/or media services, or school nursing, must have a Type C Special Services Certificate endorsed in the field of employment.
   b. A Type C certificate does not qualify the holder for assignment as a classroom teacher or school administrator.

IX. Reemployment Certificate—Type B and C (valid 1 year, effective the date the complete application packet is received in the office of Teacher Education and Certification; nonrenewable)
   A. Applicants who held a certificate that has been expired for over 12 months may be eligible for the Reemployment Certificate. During the year of validity, the applicant must complete all current requirements for the Regular 5-year certificate and submit an application.
      1. See Administrative Certificates, I, Type B Administrative Certificate; and VI, Type C Special Services Certificate, above, for details.
   B. After holding a Reemployment certificate, applicants are only eligible to apply for the Regular 5-year certificate and will not qualify for Provisional certification.
   C. The endorsements on the Reemployment certificate will be the same as those on the applicant's expired administrative or special services certificate.
   D. During the life of the Reemployment certificate no endorsements may be added or removed.

Other Certificates

For details, consult https://education.alaska.gov/teachercertification/certification.

  I.   Retired (Lifetime) Certificate
 II.   Type E Early Childhood Certificate
III.   Type M Limited Certificate
 IV.   Vocational / Technical

Arizona

Standard Professional Teaching Certificates

I. Standard Professional Teaching Certificates (valid for 12 years; may be renewed)
   A. Early Childhood (Birth–Grade 3 or Age 8)
   B. Elementary (K–8)
   C. Secondary (6–12)
   D. Mild/Moderate Disabilities (K–12)
   E. Moderate/Severe Disabilities (K–12)
   F. Hearing Impaired (Birth–Grade 12)
   G. Visually Impaired (Birth–Grade 12)
   H. Early Childhood Special Education (Birth–Grade 3 or Age 8)
   I. PreK–12 Arts Education (Art, Dance, Dramatic Arts, or Music)
   J. PreK–12 Physical Education

II. Specific information on coursework and exam requirements for Standard Professional Teaching Certificates may be downloaded at http://www.azed.gov/educator-certification/forms-and-information/certificates/.

III. The requirements for a Standard Professional Teaching Certificate are:
   A. A valid Arizona Department of Public Safety IVP fingerprint clearance card
   B. A bachelor's or more advanced degree from an accredited institution
   C. One of the following:
      1. Completion of a teacher preparation program in the specified certification area from an accredited institution or a Board-approved teacher preparation program; or
      2. Completion of the specified Board-approved or accredited teacher education coursework or trainings and 2 years of full-time teaching experience in the specified certificate area.
   D. A passing score on the required Arizona Professional Knowledge Exam or qualification for an exam waiver. The Professional Knowledge Exam requirement may be waived with 1 of the following:
      1. A passing score on a substantially similar Professional Knowledge Exam from another state; or
      2. A National Board for Professional Teaching Standards certificate in the appropriate area; or
      3. Three years of full-time teaching experience in any state in the comparable area of certification.
   E. A passing score on the required Arizona Subject Knowledge Exam or qualification for an exam waiver. For Secondary Certificates: If an exam is not offered in the subject area, 24 semester hours of coursework in the subject is required. The Subject Knowledge Exam requirement may be waived with 1 of the following:

1. A passing score on a substantially similar subject knowledge exam from another state or agency; or
2. A National Board for Professional Teaching Standards certificate in the appropriate area; or
3. A bachelor's, master's, or doctoral degree in the subject area; or
4. Three years of full-time teaching experience in any state in the appropriate subject area; or
5. Experience teaching courses relevant to the appropriate subject area for the last 2 consecutive years, and for a total of at least 3 years, at 1 or more accredited postsecondary institutions; or
6. Demonstration of expertise in the appropriate subject area through 5 years of relevant work experience.
7. If a Subject Knowledge Exam is not offered in a foreign language, a passing score of Advanced Low on the American Council for the Teaching of Foreign Languages (ACTFL) speaking and writing exams may substitute for 24 semester hours of coursework.
8. Verification of Native American Language proficiency from an official designated by the tribe may substitute for 24 semester hours of coursework.

F. The Standard Professional Visually Impaired Special Education, Birth–Grade 12 Certificate also requires demonstration of proficiency in Braille.

G. The Standard Professional Elementary Certificate also requires completion of 45 hours of training or a 3-semester-hour course in research-based systematic phonics within 3 years from date of issuance.

H. All Standard Professional Teaching Certificates require a class or exam covering the provisions and principles of the constitutions of Arizona and the United States within 3 years of date of issuance of the certificate, unless the applicant is certified to teach an academic course on history, government, social studies, citizenship, law, or civics. In that case, the requirement must be completed in 1 year.

I. Educators who hold a valid comparable out-of-state teaching certificate and who are in good standing in their state may qualify for the equivalent Standard Professional Teaching Certificate under reciprocity rules. Teachers who qualify under reciprocity are exempt from all requirements except for the requirement to hold a valid Arizona Department of Public Safety IVP fingerprint clearance card and to complete the Arizona and US Constitutions requirements within the allowable time frame.

Additional Secondary Teaching Certificates

I. All certificates require a valid Arizona Department of Public Safety IVP fingerprint clearance card.

II. Specialized Secondary Certificate—Science, Technology, Engineering, or Mathematics (STEM), Grades 6–12 (valid for 12 years; may be renewed)
  A. Demonstration of expertise in a STEM subject through 1 of the following:
    1. A bachelor's, master's, or doctoral degree and 24 semester hours of relevant coursework in an academic subject that is specific to science, technology, engineering, or mathematics; or

2.   Teaching experience in science, technology, engineering, or mathematics for the last 2 consecutive years, and for a total of 3 years, at 1 or more accredited postsecondary institutions; or

B.   Five years of verified work experience in science, technology, engineering, or mathematics.

III.   Subject Matter Expert Standard Teaching Certificate, Grades 6–12 (valid for 12 years; may be renewed)

A.   A bachelor's degree.

B.   One of the following:

1.   Experience teaching the subject area of certification for the last 2 consecutive years, and for a total of 3 years, at 1 or more accredited postsecondary institutions; or

2.   A bachelor's, master's, or doctoral degree from an accredited institution in the specific subject area of certification; or

3.   Verification of expertise in the subject area of certification through 5 years of work experience relevant to the subject area.

C.   The Subject Matter Expert Standard Teaching Certificate requires passing the Arizona Professional Knowledge Secondary Exam, or qualification for an exam waiver, within 2 years from date of issuance of the certificate. Individuals who qualify with postsecondary teaching experience are exempt from this requirement.

Other Teaching Certificates

I.   All certificates require a valid Arizona Department of Public Safety IVP fingerprint clearance card.

II.   Detailed information on requirements to qualify for and maintain these certificates may be downloaded on the certification website at http://www.azed.gov/educator-certification/forms-and-information/certificates/.

III.   Substitute Certificate, PreK–12 (valid for 6 years; may be renewed).

A.   The requirement is:

1.   A bachelor's degree

IV.   Emergency Substitute Certificate, PreK–12 (valid for 1 school year or part thereof; nonrenewable)

A.   The certificate authorizes the holder to substitute teach only in the district that verifies that an emergency employment situation exists.

B.   The requirements are:

1.   A high school diploma, GED, or associate degree

2.   Verification from a district superintendent that an emergency employment situation exists

V.   Emergency Teaching Certificate, PreK–12 (valid for 1 school year or part thereof; nonrenewable)

A.   The certificate authorizes the holder to enter into a teaching contract only in the district that verifies an emergency employment situation exists.

B.   The requirements are:

1.   A bachelor's degree

        2.   Verification from a district superintendent or charter school administrator that an emergency employment situation exists

VI.   Alternative Teaching, PreK–12 (valid for 2 years; may be extended yearly for no more than 2 consecutive years)
    A.   The certificate entitles the holder to enter into a teaching contract while completing the requirements for an Arizona teaching certificate.
    B.   The requirements are:
        1.   A bachelor's degree
        2.   Verification of enrollment in an Arizona Board of Education–approved alternative path to certification program or a Board-approved educator preparation program

VII. Standard Adult Education Certificate (valid for 12 years; may be renewed)
    A.   The certificate requires a bachelor's degree.

VIII. Junior Reserve Officer Training Corps Teaching Certificate, Grades 9–12 (valid for 12 years; may be renewed). The requirements are:
    A.   Verification from a school district that it offers an approved Junior Reserve Officer Training Corps program of instruction in which the applicant will be teaching
    B.   Verification by the district that the applicant meets the work experience required through military service

IX.   Athletic Coaching Certificate, Grades 7–12 (valid for 12 years; may be renewed). The requirements are:
    A.   Valid certification in first aid and CPR
    B.   Completion of required training or coursework
    C.   Verification of 250 hours of verified coaching experience in the sport to be coached

X.   International Teaching Certificate (valid for the length of the certificate holder's visa, not to exceed 12 years)
    A.   The certificate is issued to teachers who are contracted through the foreign teacher exchange program.
    B.   The requirements are:
        1.   Verification that the applicant has completed teacher preparation in the home country or country of legal residence that is comparable to the requirements to qualify for an Arizona teaching certificate.
        2.   A valid non-immigrating visa issued by the United States Department of State or United States Citizenship and Immigration Services for international teachers.
        3.   Verification that the applicant has been contracted by an Arizona school through a foreign teacher program.

XI.   Native American Language Certificate, PreK–12 (valid for 12 years; may be renewed)
    A.   The certificate requires verification of proficiency in a Native American language by a person, persons, or entity designated by the appropriate tribe.

XII. Student Teaching Intern Certificate, PreK–12 (valid for 1 year; may be extended for 1 year)
    A.   The certificate is optional and entitles the holder to perform teaching duties under the supervision of a program supervisor.
    B.   The requirements are:

1. Verification of enrollment in the culminating student teaching capstone experience of an Arizona Board of Education–approved educator preparation program (EPP). The program must have a Board-approved written supervision plan for student teachers.
2. A request for issuance of the Student Teaching Intern Certificate from the district or charter school superintendent and EPP
3. Verification that the applicant has completed coursework with a minimum GPA of 3.0 on a 4.0 scale, or the equivalent
4. A passing score on the required Arizona Professional Knowledge Exam
5. A passing score on the required Arizona Subject Knowledge Exam

XIII. Classroom-Based Standard Teaching Certificate (valid for 12 years; may be renewed). The requirements are:

A. A bachelor's degree
B. Successful completion of an Arizona Board of Education–approved classroom-based alternative preparation program
C. Verification of satisfactory progress and achievement with students
D. Demonstration of subject knowledge proficiency by passing the required Arizona Subject Knowledge Exam or qualifying for a waiver of the exam requirement
E. Demonstration of professional knowledge proficiency by passing the required Arizona Professional Knowledge Exam requirement or qualifying for a waiver of the exam requirement

Endorsements

I. Endorsements are posted to valid educator certificates. Each is automatically renewed with the certificate on which it is posted.
II. Applicants who hold a valid, comparable endorsement from another state and are in good standing in that state may qualify to add the equivalent endorsement in Arizona under the rules of reciprocity.
III. Detailed information on the requirements for endorsements may be downloaded from the certification website at http://www.azed.gov/educator-certification/forms-and -information/endorsements/.
IV. Special subject endorsements, PreK–12
   A. Special subject endorsements are issued in the areas of art, computer science, dance, dramatic arts, music, or physical education.
   B. The requirements are:
      1. An Elementary, Secondary, or Special Education Certificate
      2. One course in methods of teaching the subject at the elementary level and 1 course in methods of teaching the subject at the secondary level
      3. A passing score on the appropriate Arizona Subject Knowledge Exam, qualification for a waiver of the Subject Knowledge Exam requirement, or completion of 30 semester hours of coursework in the subject area which may include the methods courses
V. Mathematics Endorsement, K–8. The requirements are:
   A. An Elementary or Special Education Certificate

B. Three years of full-time teaching
C. Completion of 6 semester hours of specified mathematics education coursework
D. One of the following:
1. Eighteen semester hours of specified mathematics content coursework; or
2. A passing score on the Arizona Subject Knowledge Middle Grades Mathematics Exam or qualification for an exam waiver
VI. Reading Endorsements, K–8. The requirements are:
A. An Elementary, Special Education, or Early Childhood Certificate
B. Three years of full-time teaching experience
C. Three semester hours of a supervised field experience or practicum in reading for grades K–8
D. One of the following:
1. Twenty-one semester hours of specified reading coursework; or
2. A passing score on the Arizona Subject Knowledge Reading Endorsement K–8 Exam or qualification for an exam waiver
VII. Reading Endorsement, 6–12. The requirements are:
A. An Elementary, Secondary, or Special Education Certificate
B. Three years of full-time teaching experience
C. Three semester hours of a supervised field experience or practicum in reading completed for grades 6–12
D. One of the following:
1. Twenty-one semester hours of specified reading coursework; or
2. A passing score on the Arizona Subject Knowledge Reading Endorsement 6–12 Exam or qualification for an exam waiver
VIII. Reading Endorsement, K–2. The requirements are:
A. An Elementary, Secondary, Special Education, or Early Childhood Certificate
B. Three years of full-time teaching experience
C. Three semester hours of supervised field experience or practicum in reading for grades K–5
D. Three semester hours of supervised field experience or practicum for grades 6–12
E. One of the following:
1. Completion of 24 semester hours of specified reading coursework; or
2. A passing score on the Arizona Subject Knowledge Reading Endorsement K–8 and Reading Endorsement 6–12 Exams, or qualification for a waiver of the exam requirement
IX. Elementary Foreign Language Endorsement, K–8. The requirements are:
A. An Elementary, Secondary, or Special Education Certificate
B. Verification of proficiency in speaking, reading, and writing a language other than English, verified by an accredited institution. Native American language proficiency shall be verified by an official designated by the appropriate tribe.
C. Three semester hours of courses in the methods of teaching a foreign language at the elementary level
X. Provisional Bilingual Endorsement, PreK–12
A. The Provisional Bilingual endorsement is valid for 3 years and is nonrenewable.
B. The requirements are:

1. An Arizona Elementary, Secondary, Supervisor, Principal, Superintendent, Special Education, Early Childhood, Arts Education, or Career and Technical Education (CTE) Certificate; and
2. Proficiency in a spoken language other than English

XI. Bilingual Endorsement, PreK–12. The requirements are:
   A. An Arizona Elementary, Secondary, Supervisor, Principal, Superintendent, Special Education, Early Childhood, Arts Education, or CTE Certificate
   B. Proficiency in a spoken language other than English
   C. Completion of a bilingual education program from an accredited institution or 18 semester hours of specified bilingual education courses
   D. A practicum in a bilingual program or 2 years of bilingual teaching experience

XII. Provisional English as a Second Language (ESL) Endorsement, PreK–12
   A. The Provisional ESL endorsement is valid for 3 years and is nonrenewable.
   B. The requirements are:
      1. An Elementary, Secondary, Supervisor, Principal, Superintendent, Special Education, Early Childhood, Arts Education, or CTE Certificate
      2. Six semester hours of ESL courses, including at least 1 course in methods of teaching ESL students

XIII. English as a Second Language (ESL) Endorsement, PreK–12. The requirements are:
   A. An Elementary, Secondary, Supervisor, Principal, Superintendent, Special Education, Early Childhood, Arts Education, or CTE Certificate
   B. Completion of an ESL education program from an accredited institution or 18 semester hours of specified ESL coursework
   C. Three semester hours of practicum or 2 years of verified ESL or bilingual teaching experience
   D. Second-language learning experience. For requirements, please refer to http://www.azed.gov/educator-certification/forms-and-information/endorsements/.

XIV. Provisional Gifted Endorsement, PreK–12
   A. The Provisional Gifted Endorsement is valid for 3 years and is nonrenewable.
   B. The requirements are:
      1. A valid Elementary, Secondary, Early Childhood, or Special Education Certificate
      2. One of the following:
         a. Two years of teaching experience in which most students were gifted; or
         b. Ninety clock hours of verified in-service training in gifted education; or
         c. Six semester hours of courses in gifted education

XV. Gifted Endorsement, PreK–12. The requirements are:
   A. An Elementary, Secondary, Early Childhood, or Special Education Certificate
   B. Completion of 9 semester hours of upper division or graduate coursework in an academic discipline
   C. Two of the following:
      1. Three years of verified teaching experience in gifted education as a teacher, resource teacher, specialist, or similar position
      2. A minimum of 135 clock hours of verified in-service training in gifted education

3. Twelve semester hours of courses in gifted education. Up to 6 semester hours of coursework may be waived with district in-service training.
4. Completion of 6 semester hours of practicum or 2 years of teaching experience in which most students were gifted

XVI. Provisional Early Childhood Endorsement, Birth–Age 8 or Grade 3
    A. The Provisional Early Childhood Endorsement is valid for 3 years and is nonrenewable.
    B. The requirements are:
       1. An Elementary or Special Education Certificate
       2. A passing score on the Arizona Subject Knowledge Early Childhood Education Exam or qualification for a waiver of the exam requirement

XVII. Early Childhood Endorsement, Birth–Age 8 or Grade 3. The requirements are:
    A. An Elementary or Special Education Certificate
    B. A passing score on the Arizona Subject Knowledge Early Childhood Education Exam or qualification for a waiver of the exam requirement
    C. One of the following:
       1. Completion of 21 semester hours of specified coursework; 4 semester hours of practicum or 1 year of teaching in Birth–PreK; and 4 semester hours of student teaching or 1 year of teaching in K–3
       2. A passing score on the Arizona Professional Knowledge Early Childhood Exam or qualification for an exam waiver; 4 semester hours of practicum or 1 year of teaching in Birth–PreK; and 4 semester hours of practicum or 1 year of teaching in K–3
       3. Three years of teaching experience in Birth–Grade 3 or Age 8

XVIII. Library Media Specialist Endorsement, K–12. The requirements are:
    A. An Arizona Elementary, Secondary, Early Childhood, or Special Education Certificate
    B. A passing score on the Arizona Subject Knowledge Library Media Specialist Exam or qualification for a waiver of the Subject Knowledge Exam
    C. One year of teaching experience

XIX. Driver's Education endorsement. The requirements are:
    A. An Arizona teaching certificate
    B. An Arizona driver's license
    C. A 3-semester-hour course or 45 hours of training in safety education
    D. A 3-semester-hour course or 45 hours of training in driver and highway safety education
    E. A 3-semester-hour course or 45 hours of training in driver education laboratory experience
    F. A driving record with less than 7 violation points and no revocation or suspensions within 2 years preceding the application

XX. Cooperative Education
    A. A Provisional or Standard CTE Certificate
    B. A course in CTE

Administrative Certificates

I.   All certificates require a valid Arizona Department of Public Safety IVP fingerprint clearance card.

II. An applicant who holds a valid, comparable administrative certificate from another state and is in good standing with that state may qualify for the equivalent Arizona certificate under reciprocity rules.

III. The Arizona Administrator Exam requirements may be waived with 1 of the following:
    A. A passing score on a substantially similar administrator exam from another state; or
    B. Three years of full-time experience as an administrator in any state, including Arizona

IV. Standard Professional Supervisor Certificate, PreK–12 (valid for 12 years; may be renewed). The requirements are:
    A. A valid Arizona Early Childhood, Elementary, Secondary, Special Education, Career and Technical Education certificate or other professional certificate
    B. A master's or more advanced degree from an accredited institution
    C. Three years of verified full-time teaching or related education services experience in PreK–12
    D. Completion of a program in educational administration consisting of a minimum of 18 graduate semester hours of educational administration courses teaching the knowledge and skills described in Arizona's Professional Administrative Standards (R7-2-603, available at http://azsbe.az.gov/sites/default/files/media/Item4GCloseArticle6.pdf), and 3 semester hours of school law and 3 semester hours of school finance
    E. A practicum in educational administration or 2 years of verified educational administrative experience in grades PreK–12
    F. A passing score on the Arizona Supervisor, Principal, or Superintendent Exam or qualification for a waiver of the exam requirement

V.   Standard Professional Principal Certificate, PreK–12 (valid 12 years; may be renewed). The requirements are:
    A. A master's or more advanced degree from an accredited institution
    B. Three years of verified full-time teaching experience in grades PreK–12
    C. Completion of a program in educational administration for principals including at least 30 graduate semester hours of educational administration courses teaching the knowledge and skills described in Arizona's Professional Administrative Standards (R7-2-603, available at http://azsbe.az.gov/sites/default/files/media/Item4GCloseArticle6.pdf) and 3 semester hours of school law and 3 semester hours of school finance
    D. A practicum as a principal or 2 years of experience as a PreK–12 principal or assistant principal under the supervision of a certified principal
    E. A passing score on either the Principal or Superintendent portion of the Arizona Educator Proficiency Assessments (AEPA) or qualification for a waiver of the exam requirement

VI. Superintendent Certificate, PreK–12 (valid 12 years; may be renewed). The requirements are:

A. A master's or higher degree, including at least 60 graduate semester hours from an accredited institution

B. Completion of a program in educational administration for superintendents including at least 36 graduate semester hours of educational administrative courses teaching the knowledge and skills described in Arizona's Professional Administrative Standards (R7-2-603, available at http://azsbe.az.gov/sites/default/files/media/Item4GCloseArticle6.pdf) and 3 semester hours of school law and 3 semester hours of school finance

C. Three years of verified full-time teaching or related education services experience in PreK–12

D. A practicum as a superintendent or 2 years of verified experience as a superintendent, assistant superintendent, or associate superintendent in grades PreK–12

E. A passing score on the Arizona Superintendent Exam requirement or qualification for a waiver of the exam requirement

VII. Arizona issues Interim Supervisor, Interim Principal, and Interim Superintendent Certificates to individuals who are enrolled in Board-approved administrator preparation programs and are working under the direct supervision of a certified administrator or county school superintendent. Interim administrative certificates are valid for 1 year and may be extended yearly for no more than 2 consecutive years. Specific requirements for these certificates may be downloaded at http://www.azed.gov/educator-certification/forms-and-information/certificates/.

Professional Non-Teaching Certificate (PreK–12)

I. All certificates require a valid Arizona Department of Public Safety IVP fingerprint clearance card.

II. An applicant who holds a valid, comparable professional non-teaching certificate in another state and is in good standing in that state may qualify for the equivalent Arizona professional non-teaching certificate under reciprocity rules.

III. Standard School Psychologist Certificate, PreK–12 (valid for 12 years; may be renewed). The requirements are:

A. A master's or more advanced degree from an accredited institution

B. One of the following:
1. Completion of a graduate program in school psychology, consisting of at least 60 graduate semester hours; or
2. Completion of a doctoral program in psychology and completion of a retraining program in school psychology from an accredited institution or a Board-approved program with a letter of institutional endorsement from the head of the school psychology program; or
3. Five years of experience as a full-time school psychologist within the last 10 years; or
4. A Nationally Certified School Psychologist Credential; or
5. Diploma in school psychology from the American Board of School Psychology

C. One of the following:
1. A letter from a university department head or designee verifying completion of

       a supervised internship of at least 1,200 clock hours with a minimum of 600 of those hours in a school setting; or

    2. A letter from a district superintendent, personnel director, or designee verifying 3 years of experience as a certified school psychologist within the last 10 years

IV. Standard School Counselor Certificate, PreK–12 (valid for 12 years; may be renewed). The requirements are:

  A. A master's or more advanced degree

  B. Completion of a graduate program in guidance and counseling

  C. One of the following:

    1. Completion of a supervised counseling practicum in school counseling (official transcript[s] required); or

    2. Two years of verified full-time experience as a school guidance counselor; or

    3. Three years of verified full-time teaching experience

V. Standard Speech-Language Pathologist Certificate, PreK–12 (valid for 12 years; may be renewed). The requirements are:

  A. A master's or more advanced degree in speech pathology or communication disorders

  B. A minimum of 250 clinical clock hours supervised by a university or a speech-language pathologist with a certificate of clinical competence

  C. A certificate of clinical competence, a passing score on the national exam in speech pathology, or a passing score on the Arizona Speech and Language Impaired Exam

VI. Standard School Social Worker, PreK–12 (valid for 12 years; may be renewed). The requirements are:

  A. A master's or more advanced degree in social work

  B. Completion of 6 semester hours of practicum in social work in a school setting or 1 year of full-time experience as a social worker in a setting which primarily serves children in PreK–12.

Career and Technical Education Certificates

I. Career and Technical Education (CTE) Certificates are issued in the areas of Agriculture, Business and Marketing, Education and Training, Family and Consumer Sciences, Health Careers, and Industrial and Emerging Technologies.

II. All certificates require a valid Arizona Department of Public Safety IVP fingerprint clearance card.

III. Standard Career and Technical Education Certificates, Grades K–12 (valid for 12 years; may be renewed). The requirements are:

  A. One of the following:

    1. A bachelor's degree and 240 clock hours of work experience in the CTE area; or

    2. A valid Arizona Provisional or Standard Teaching Certificate, verification of 1 year of teaching with satisfactory performance, completion of specified coursework, and 240 clock hours of work experience in the CTE area; or

    3. Six thousand (6,000) clock hours of work experience in the CTE area; or

    4. A bachelor's degree, completion of a teacher preparation program in the CTE area, and 240 clock hours of work experience in the CTE area

B. A course or examination covering the provisions and principles of the Arizona and US Constitutions must be completed within 3 years from date of issuance.

C. A passing score on the required Arizona Professional Knowledge Secondary Exam, or qualification for an exam waiver, must be completed within 3 years from date of issuance.

D. Completion of specified CTE professional knowledge coursework must be completed within 3 years from date of issuance.

E. An applicant who holds a valid, comparable CTE certificate from another state and is in good standing with that other state may qualify for the Standard CTE Certificate under reciprocity rules. Applicants who qualify under reciprocity are exempt from all requirements except for the requirements to hold a valid IVP fingerprint clearance card and to complete the Arizona and US Constitutions requirements within 3 years.

IV. Standard Specialized Career and Technical Education (CTE) Certificates, Grades K–12 (valid for 12 years; may be renewed). The requirements are:

A. Demonstration of expertise in the specified CTE area through 1 of the following:
1. A bachelor's or more advanced degree in the specified CTE area; or
2. A bachelor's or more advanced degree and completion of 24 semester hours of coursework in the specified CTE area; or
3. An associate degree in the specified CTE area; or
4. An industry certification, license, or credential in the specified CTE area approved by the Arizona Department of Education CTE Program Specialist or Program Services Director

B. Individuals who qualify for the Specialized CTE Certificate are exempt from the Arizona and US Constitutions and Professional Knowledge Exam requirements.

V. Detailed information on the requirements to qualify for and maintain a CTE Certificate may be downloaded at http://www.azed.gov/educator-certification/forms-and -information/certificates/.

Arkansas

Types of Licenses

I. Standard License (valid 5 years; renewable)
  A. Prerequisites
     1. Bachelor's or higher degree from an accredited institution
     2. Successful completion of the following tests:
        a. Praxis II: Content test for all parts required
        b. Praxis II: Principles of Learning and Teaching or World Languages Pedagogy
     3. Criminal background check by the Arkansas State Police and the FBI
     4. Child Maltreatment Central Registry Check
     5. Novice teachers must successfully complete Arkansas Department of Education (ADE) induction program.
     6. Completion of 7 hours of Preservice Professional Development
  B. Renewal Requirements
     1. Accrue 36 professional development hours during each year of the 5-year renewal cycle
        a. One 3-hour college credit course may count as 15 hours of professional development.
II. Alternative Route Licensure
  A. These programs are designed to give talented and highly motivated applicants with college degrees in fields other than education an opportunity to obtain the proper credentials and become educators in Arkansas public schools.
     1. Prerequisites: See Standard License, I, A, 1, 2b, 3–6 above.
     2. Complete application and supporting documents
     3. Successful personal interview
     4. Ethics training

Levels and Areas of Licensure

I. Levels of Licensure are defined as the grade-age-level parameters of the educator license and include the following:
  A. Birth–Kindergarten: Integrated
  B. Kindergarten/Young Adulthood: Grades K–12
  C. Elementary (K–6)
  D. Middle Childhood/Early Adolescence: Grades 4–8
  E. Adolescence/Young Adulthood: Grades 7–12
  F. Postsecondary: Above Grade 12
II. Teacher Licensure Competency Areas are defined as the particular content field(s) of the teaching license.

A. Areas include adult education; agriculture sciences technology (7–12); art (K–12); business technology (4–12); chemistry (7–12); coaching education (K–12); drama/speech (K–12); early childhood instructional specialist (birth–K); early childhood special education (birth–K); educational examiner (K–12); English-language arts/social studies (4–8); English-language arts (7–12); ESL education (K–12); family and consumer science (7–12); foreign language (K–12); gifted and talented education (K–12); industrial technology (K–12); library media specialist (K–12); life science (7–12); marketing technology (7–12); mathematics/science (4–8); mathematics (7–12); music-instrumental (K–12); music-vocal (K–12); physical science (7–12); physical education/health (K–12); physics (7–12); reading specialist (K–12); speech-language pathologist (K–12); school counseling (K–12); school psychology specialist (K–12); social studies (7–12); special education (K–12); teachers of hearing-impaired students; teachers of visually impaired students (K–12).

B. Exception areas include special education; added endorsements; educational leadership and supervision; ancillary student services; and professional and technical.

   1. Applicants cannot test out of exception areas but must complete the program of study and the required Praxis assessment.

III. Adding Areas of Licensure

Note: Questions about adding additional licensure areas may be directed to the Office of Educator Licensure (see Appendix 1). Speak only with a supervisor who works with adding areas of licensure. Be sure to document with whom you spoke and what was said.

A. Prerequisites

   1. Hold a valid Standard Arkansas teaching license. See Types of Licenses, I, A and B, above.

B. To add non-exception teaching areas within the same level of licensure or 1 grade-level span above or below initial level of licensure, an applicant must pass the State Board–required specialty area assessment(s).

C. To add exception areas:

   1. Complete an approved performance-based program of study, *and*

   2. Pass the State Board–required assessment(s).

D. Teachers may test out of licensure areas within their level of licensure and 1 level above or below their initial level of licensure.

E. To add an area of licensure or endorsement for which there is not a State Board–required specialty area assessment:

   1. Successfully complete an approved performance-based program of study, *and*

   2. Complete the State Board–required pedagogical assessment.

F. Special Situations

   1. The non-instruction student services areas of school psychology specialist and speech-language pathology shall have completed a master's degree in the area from an accredited program and the State Board–required assessment to be licensed.

2. Teachers or administrators adding elementary (K–6), all middle school areas, or secondary social studies to their valid standard license shall have completed a 3-credit-hour course in Arkansas history.

3. Elementary (K–6) and special education (K–12) teachers must pass the Foundations of Reading exam.

4. Additional areas/levels of licensure or endorsement shall be added to a valid standard license upon receiving documentation that all requirements have been met and upon receiving an application requesting the additional licensure area or endorsement.

Administrative Licensure

I. Levels of Licensure
   A. Building Level Administrator—Principal, assistant principal, or vice principal (P–12)
   B. Curriculum/Program Administrator—A school leader responsible for program development and administration, and/or employment evaluation decisions. Each Curriculum/Program Administrator License is limited to 1 of the following areas:
      1. Special Education (P–12)
      2. Gifted and Talented Education (P–12)
      3. Career and Technical Education (P–12)
      4. Content Area Specialist (P–12)
      5. Curriculum Specialist (P–12)
      6. Adult Education (Post-secondary)
   C. District Level Administrator—Superintendent, assistant superintendent, or deputy superintendent (P–12)

II. Types of Licensure
   A. Standard License
      1. Have 3 years of experience in classroom teaching, in counseling, or in library media
      2. Hold a graduate degree that includes a program of study with an internship
         a. For candidates holding a graduate degree in an area other than educational leadership, the Arkansas institution of higher education will review their credentials to determine their individual needs.
      3. Participate in a mentoring experience upon first employment
         a. The mentor provided should have relevant experience sought by the new administrator, at least 3 years of administrator experience, hold a standard teaching license, and have completed the mentorship training.
         b. Districts shall submit their administrator mentoring plans to the Arkansas State Department of Education for approval.
      4. Successfully complete the School Leaders Licensure Assessment (SLLA) with a minimum cut-score of 163
   B. District Administrator License
      1. Hold a standard teaching license
      2. Have 3 years of classroom teaching experience and be licensed as a Building-

Level Administrator or Curriculum/Program Administrator with at least 1 year of experience

3. Hold an advanced degree, or complete an advanced program of study above the master's degree, based on individual needs inclusive of an internship and portfolio development based on the Standards for District Level Administrator licensure

4. Successfully complete the School Superintendent Assessment (SSA) with a score of 156 or higher

Reciprocity

I. Eligibility to apply:
   A. Hold a valid or expired teaching license from another state,
      or
   B. Hold a degree from an institution that holds regional or national accreditation recognized by the United States Department of Education (USDOE). The education program must also hold national accreditation recognized by the USDOE or be state approved.

II. A 3-hour Arkansas history course will be required for Arkansas licensure when the licensure area is elementary, middle school social studies, or secondary social studies.

III. For full details on exceptions to eligibility requirements as well as information on candidates from other countries, contact the Office of Professional Licensure (see Appendix 1).

California

All multiple and single subject professional teacher preparation programs require candidates to pass an assessment of teaching performance in order to earn a teaching credential. For full details about the Teaching Performance Assessment (TPA), consult the website (see Appendix 1).

Teaching Credentials

I. Multiple Subject Teaching Credential—Commonly used in elementary school service
II. Single Subject Teaching Credential—Commonly used in secondary school service
III. Education Specialist Instruction Credential—Commonly used in special education settings
IV. Five-Year Preliminary Multiple Subject and Single Subject Teaching Credential (nonrenewable)
    A. Requirements for California-Trained Teachers
        1. Bachelor's or higher degree from regionally accredited college or university, except in professional education
        2. Teacher preparation program, including student teaching, completed at California college or university with a Commission-approved program
        3. California's basic skills requirement (BSR)*
        4. US Constitution (course or examination)
        5. Subject-matter competence by obtaining passing score on appropriate subject-matter examination or obtaining letter from California college or university with approved subject-matter program
        6. Completion of course in developing English language skills, including reading
        7. Completion of course in foundational uses of computers in educational settings
        8. Multiple Subject Teaching Credential only: all California-prepared applicants must pass Reading Instruction Competence Assessment (RICA)
    B. Requirements for Teachers Trained in Other States or US Territories
        1. Bachelor's or higher degree from regionally accredited college or university
        2. Possession of comparable teaching credential (does not have to be valid at time of application)
        3. Prior to or within first year of issuance of credential, candidate must satisfy the BSR*: see IV, A, 3, directly above.
            a. Unless the BSR* is satisfied within 1 year of issuance date of credential, credential will not be valid for employment in California's public schools until requirement is met.
        4. There are 3 different routes under which an out-of-state-trained teacher may qualify for certification, and each route has specific renewal requirements.
            a. Route 1: Less than 2 years of out-of-state, full-time teaching experience
            b. Route 2:

    i. Two or more years of full-time teaching experience in a public or regionally accredited private school, *and*

    ii. Photocopies of performance evaluations from 2 separate years of the verified out-of-state teaching experience on which the candidate received ratings of "satisfactory" or better

  c. Route 3: Possess National Board for Professional Teaching Standards (NBPTS) Certificate (results in issuance of clear credential)

 C. Requirements for Teachers Trained Outside of the United States

  1. The equivalent of a bachelor's or higher degree from a regionally accredited college or university located in the United States

  2. Completion of a comparable teacher preparation program, including student teaching, that is equivalent to a teacher preparation program from a regionally accredited college or university located in the United States

  3. Possession of, or eligibility for, a comparable teaching credential issued by the country in which the program was completed

  4. Prior to or within first year of issuance of credential, candidate must satisfy the BSR*

   a. See B, 3, a, above.

  5. Individuals trained outside of the United States must have their foreign transcripts evaluated by a Commission-approved agency prior to submission of their application packet.

V. Five-Year Clear Multiple Subject and Single Subject Teaching Credential (renewable every 5 years)

 A. Requirements for California-Trained Teachers

  1. See IV, A, 1–8, above.

  2. Completion of Commission-approved induction program with subsequent formal recommendation to the Commission for the credential by induction program sponsor

 B. Requirements for Teachers Trained in Other States or US Territories

  1. See IV, B, 1–4

  2. Complete renewal requirements associated with route under which preliminary teaching credential was issued

   a. Route 1:

    i. Complete Commission-approved induction program with subsequent formal recommendation by induction program sponsor

    ii. Earn a California English learner authorization

   b. Route 2:

    i. Earn a master's degree (or the equivalent in units) from a regionally accredited college or university, *or*

     Complete 150 clock hours of professional activities under the California Standards for the Teaching Profession

    ii. Earn a California English learner authorization

        c.   Route 3: Individuals who qualify based on NBPTS Certification are issued clear credentials.

   C.   Requirements for Teachers Trained Outside of the United States

      1.   See IV, C, 1–5, above.

      2.   Completion of a course in developing English language skills, including reading (or passage of RICA for holders of Multiple Subject credentials only)

      3.   US Constitution course or examination

      4.   Subject-matter competence by obtaining a passing score on appropriate subject-matter examination or obtaining letter from California college or university with Commission-approved subject-matter program

      5.   Commission-approved induction program with subsequent final recommendation by induction program sponsor

      6.   CPR training for adults, infants, and children

   D.   Clear credentials are renewable every 5 years via the Commission's online renewal system or by paper application.

VI.   Authorization for Service for Multiple Subject and Single Subject Teaching Credential

   A.   Teacher authorized for multiple subject instruction may be assigned to teach in any self-contained classroom in preschool and grades K–12 and in classes organized primarily for adults.

   B.   Teacher authorized for single subject instruction may be assigned to teach any subject in authorized fields in any grade level (preschool, grades K–12) and in classes organized primarily for adults.

      1.   Statutory subjects available: agriculture, art, business, English, foundational-level general science, foundational-level mathematics, health science, home economics, industrial and technology education, mathematics, music, physical education, science (in 1 of these areas: biological sciences, chemistry, geosciences, or physics), specialized science (in 1 of the 4 science areas immediately prior), and social science, world language: English language development, world languages: languages other than English (specify)

VII.   Five-Year Clear Specialist Instruction Credential—Covers specialist areas requiring advanced professional preparation or special competencies, including agriculture, early childhood education, gifted education, mathematics, reading and language arts, and health science

   A.   Requirements

      1.   Valid prerequisite California teaching credential

      2.   Professional preparation program in specialist area

      3.   Recommendation of California college or university with specific, Commission-approved specialist program

          a.   Applicants trained outside of California who meet requirements in VII, A, 1 and 2, directly above, may still be certified. Student teaching must have been completed, and applicant must provide photocopy of out-of-state credential listing a comparable authorization.

          b.   Applicants for Mathematics Instructional Leadership Specialist Credential who trained out of state must apply through and be recommended by

California college or university with Commission-accredited program, possess an English learner authorization, and verify 3 years of experience.

   B. Authorization for Service

      1. Credential authorizes holder to teach in area of specialization in preschool and grades K–12 classes and in classes organized primarily for adults.

VIII. Five-Year Preliminary or Level I Education Specialist Instruction Credential—Available in following specialization areas: mild/moderate disabilities, moderate/severe disabilities, deaf and hard of hearing, visual impairments, physical and health impairments, early childhood special education, and language and academic development

   A. Requirements for California-Trained Teachers

      1. Bachelor's or higher degree from regionally accredited college or university

      2. Professional preparation program in education specialist category completed at California college or university with Commission-approved program

      3. BSR*

      4. US Constitution course or examination

      5. Completion of course in developing English-language skills, including reading

      6. Passage of RICA

         a. RICA passage is not required for category of early childhood special education, nor is it required of those who hold a valid California teaching credential issued based upon possession of a bachelor's degree and completion of a teacher preparation program including student teaching.

      7. Verification of subject-matter competence, as aligned with core academic subjects (see IV, A, 5, above)

         a. Verification of subject-matter competence is not required for category of early childhood special education, nor is it required of those who hold a valid California clear or life general education teaching credential based upon possession of a bachelor's degree and completion of a teacher preparation program including student teaching.

      8. Formal recommendation of California college or university with Commission-approved program

   B. Requirements for Teachers Trained in Other States, US Territories, or outside of the United States

      1. See IV, B and C, above, with the addition to IV, B, 4, b, i, that the 2 or more years of full-time teaching experience in a public or regionally accredited private school must be in special education.

   C. Contact Commission on Teacher Credentialing (see Appendix 1) for full information on Preliminary, Level I, Clear, or Level II Education Specialist Instruction Credential requirements.

IX. Authorization of Service for Education Specialist Instruction Credential

   A. Authorizes holder to teach in area of specialization and at level listed on credential in following settings: special schools, home/hospital settings, correctional facilities, nonpublic schools and agencies, and resource rooms, special education settings, state hospitals, development centers, and alternative and nontraditional settings

Services Credentials

I. Five-Year Preliminary Administrative Services Credential (nonrenewable)
    A. Requirements for Individuals Prepared in California
        1. Possession of valid clear California credential, which may be in teaching; designated-subjects teaching (if bachelor's or higher degree, conferred by a regionally accredited college or university, is held); pupil personnel services; librarian; health services school nurse; clinical or rehabilitative services; or speech-language pathology
        2. Five years of successful, full-time experience in public or private schools of equivalent status in any of areas listed directly above in A, 1
        3. Approved program of specialized and professional preparation in administrative services
            or
            Passing score on the California Preliminary Administrative Credential Examination (CPACE; valid for 10 years)
            or
            Approved administrative internship program from California college or university
        4. BSR*
        5. Recommendation of program sponsor with Commission-approved administrative services program
        6. California-trained applicants must have offer of employment in administrative position from California school district, nonpublic school or agency, or county office of education,
            or
            May apply for Certificate of Eligibility.
    B. Common Requirements for Individuals Prepared in Other States or US Territories (see I, C, 1 and 2, below, for additional requirements)
        1. Verify completion of bachelor's or higher degree from regionally accredited college or university
        2. BSR*
            a. The 1-year nonrenewable credential is available to an administrator, at the request of an employing agency, who prepared out of state if all requirements except the BSR* are complete.
        3. Complete administrative preparation program in which candidate was issued, or qualified for, administrative services credential based upon that program
    C. There are 2 different routes under which out-state-prepared administrators may qualify for preliminary certification.
        1. Route 1: 5 or more years of out-of-state teaching experience
            a. Candidates who meet common requirements (see I, B, 1–3, above) and the additional requirements listed below will be academically eligible for the Preliminary Administrative Services Credential.
                i. Completion of a teacher preparation program in another state

          ii.   Possession of or eligibility for the equivalent of a professional-level teaching credential issued by another state

          iii. Verification of 5 years of successful, full-time teaching experience in a public or private school of equivalent status located in another state

   2.   Route 2: Less than 5 years of out-of-state teaching experience

      a.   Candidates who meet common requirements (see I, B, 1–3, above) and the additional requirements listed below will be academically eligible for the Preliminary Administrative Services Credential or Certificate of Eligibility.

          i.   Possession of a clear or life teaching or services credential in California

          ii.   Verification of 5 years of successful, full-time teaching and/or services experience in a public or private school of equivalent status located in California and/or another state

          iii. Verification of an offer of employment in an administrative position from a California employing agency (candidates who do not have an offer of employment in an administrative position may apply for a Certificate of Eligibility)

II. Five-Year Clear Administrative Services Credential

   A.   Requirements for California-trained Candidates

      1.   Preliminary credential (see I, A, 1–6, above)

      2.   Two years of successful full-time experience in position requiring preliminary credential

      3.   Completion of a Commission-approved induction program and subsequent formal recommendation to the Commission for the clear credential by the program sponsor

   B.   Requirements for out-of-state-prepared administrators

      1.   Possession of a preliminary credential (see I, C, 1 and 2, above)

      2.   Two years of successful, full-time experience while holding the preliminary credential

      3.   Completion of a Commission-approved induction program and subsequent formal recommendation to the Commission for the clear credential by the program sponsor

      4.   Candidates who qualify for a preliminary credential under Route 2 (see I, C, 2, above) must also maintain possession of a California clear or life teaching or services credential.

   C.   Candidates prepared outside of California may earn a clear credential without first holding a preliminary credential by:

      1.   Meeting common requirements (see I, B, 1–3, above)

      2.   Completing a teacher preparation program in another state

      3.   Possessing a professional-level teaching credential issued by another state

      4.   Verifying 5 years of successful, full-time teaching experience in a public or private school of equivalent status located in another state

      5.   Verifying 3 years of successful, full-time administrative experience in a public or regionally accredited private school located in another state

6. Submitting photocopies of performance evaluations from the last 2 years of verified out-of-state administrative experience with ratings of "satisfactory" or better
   a. Possessing a California teaching or services credential and verifying employment in an administrative position in California are not required of candidates who qualify via this option.

D. The 1-year nonrenewable credential is available, at the request of the employing agency, to administrators who prepared out of state if all requirements except the BSR* are complete.

III. Authorization for Service

A. An Administrative Services Credential authorizes the holder to provide various duties that may allow the holder to serve in a number of positions, including superintendent, associate superintendent, deputy superintendent, principal, assistant principal, dean, supervisor, consultant, coordinator, or in equivalent or intermediate-level administrative positions.

IV. Clear Teacher Librarian Services Credential

A. Requirements
   1. Bachelor's degree from regionally accredited college or university
   2. Valid prerequisite California teaching credential (if it is a clear full-time designated-subjects teaching credential, the individual must also possess a baccalaureate degree from a regionally accredited institution and satisfy the BSR*)
   3. Completion of:
      a. Commission-approved teacher librarian services program and recommendation of California college or university where program was completed
         or
      b. Out-of-state teacher librarian services program consisting of 30 graduate semester units approved by appropriate state agency in state where program was completed
   4. BSR*
      a. The 1-year nonrenewable credential is available, at the request of an employing agency, to an individual who prepared out of state if all requirements except the BSR* are complete.
   5. Possession of an English learner authorization

B. An individual who holds NBPTS Certification in the area of Early Childhood through Young Adulthood—Library Media may be issued a Clear Teacher Librarian Services Credential if the following requirements are also met:
   1. Possession of a valid prerequisite California teaching credential (if it is a clear full-time designated-subjects teaching credential, the individual must also possess a baccalaureate degree from a regionally accredited institution and satisfy the BSR*)
   2. Possession of an English learner authorization

C. Authorization for Service

1. Teacher Librarian Services Credential authorizes holder to assist and instruct pupils in choice and use of library materials; to plan and coordinate school library programs with instructional programs of school district; to select materials for school and district libraries; to conduct planned course of instruction for those pupils who assist in operation of school libraries; to supervise classified personnel assigned to school library duties; and to develop procedures for and management of school and district libraries.

2. The Special Class Authorization authorizes the holder to provide departmentalized instruction in information literacy, digital literacy, and digital citizenship to students in grades 12 and below, including preschool, and in classes organized primarily for adults. Individuals must satisfy all of the following requirements:

    a. Hold a valid prerequisite California teaching credential as follows:
        i.   A valid 1-year nonrenewable, Clear, or Life Teacher Librarian or Library Media Services Credential
        ii. Library Services Credential
        iii. Standard Elementary, Secondary, Early Childhood Education, or Junior College Teaching Credential with a specialized preparation minor in Librarianship
        iv. General Credential in Librarianship

    b. Completion of a Commission-approved Special Class Authorization program of professional preparation

    c. Recommendation from a Commission-approved Teacher Librarian Services program

V. Pupil Personnel Services Credential
    A. Authorization for Services
        1. Credential available in 4 different areas: school counseling, school social work, school psychology, and child welfare and attendance services
    B. Requirements for School Counseling Authorization
        1. A baccalaureate degree or higher, except in professional education, from a regionally accredited college or university
        2. Post-baccalaureate study consisting of 48 semester units (30 semester units for out-of-state prepared) specializing in school counseling, including a supervised field experience
        3. BSR*
            a. The 1-year nonrenewable credential is available, at the request of an employing agency, to an individual who prepared out of state if all requirements except the BSR* are complete.
        4. Recommendation of a California college or university with a Commission-approved School Counseling program
            a. Individuals who trained out of state must:
                i. Verify possession of, or eligibility for, the equivalent authorization in the state where the program was completed,
                    and

       ii. Provide written verification from the college or university where the program was completed that the program included supervised field experience with school-age children in school counseling.

C. An individual who holds NBPTS Certification in the area of Early Childhood to Young Adulthood—School Counseling may apply directly to the Commission for a Clear Pupil Personnel Services Credential in School Counseling and is exempt from BSR* satisfaction and all other credential requirements.

D. Requirements for School Social Work Authorization

  1. A baccalaureate degree or higher, except in professional education, from a regionally accredited college or university

  2. Post-baccalaureate study consisting of 45 semester units specializing in school social work, including a supervised field experience

  3. BSR*

    a. The 1-year nonrenewable credential is available, at the request of an employing agency, to an individual who prepared out of state if all requirements except the BSR* are complete.

  4. Recommendation of a California college or university with a Commission-approved School Social Work program

    a. Individuals who trained out of state must:

       i. Verify possession of, or eligibility for, the equivalent authorization in the state where the program was completed,
and

       ii. Provide written verification from the college or university where the program was completed that program included supervised field experience with school-age children in school social work.

E. Requirements for School Psychology Authorization

  1. A baccalaureate degree or higher, except in professional education, from a regionally accredited college or university

  2. Post-baccalaureate study consisting of 60 semester units specializing in school psychology, including a practicum and supervised field experience

  3. BSR*

    a. The 1-year nonrenewable credential is available, at the request of an employing agency, to an individual who prepared out of state if all requirements except the BSR* are complete.

  4. Recommendation of a California college or university with a Commission-approved School Psychology program

    a. Individuals who trained out of state must:

       i. Verify possession of, or eligibility for, the equivalent authorization in the state where the program was completed,
and

       ii. Provide written verification from the college or university where the program was completed that the program included a supervised field experience with school-age children in school psychology.

F. Child Welfare and Attendance Authorization. Contact the Commission (see Appendix 1) for full information

VI.   For detailed information on credentials in speech-language pathology and clinical or rehabilitative services, consult the website (see Appendix 1).

*Unless otherwise noted, for initial issuance all applicants must satisfy the BSR. This requirement does not apply to applicants who are having their credentials renewed, reissued, or upgraded. Applicants who prepared out of state may be issued a 1-year, nonrenewable credential pending satisfaction of the BSR if a California public school employer cannot find a fully credentialed person to fill the position and offers employment to the credential applicant.

Colorado

Applying for an Initial License

I. Initial License (valid 3 years; renewable). Requirements for applicant include:
  A. Hold an earned bachelor's or higher degree from a regionally accredited institution of higher education;
  B. Complete an approved teacher preparation program at a regionally accredited institution of higher education or a state-approved alternative teacher preparation program;
  C. Pass a fingerprint-based criminal history background check via the Colorado Bureau of Investigation;
  D. Submit a complete application for licensure, including copies of official transcripts, an approved program verification form, associated fees, and other supporting documentation, to the Colorado Department of Education (CDE) Licensure Office (see Appendix 1);
     and
  E. Demonstrate subject matter knowledge necessary for teaching in the endorsement area.
     1. All elementary education teachers, including special education generalist teachers, must pass a Colorado State Board of Education (CSBE)–approved elementary education content exam.
     2. All special education generalist teachers must also pass the CSBE-approved special education exam.
     3. Teachers of all middle school (grades 6–8), secondary (grades 7–12), K–12, and endorsement areas for ages 0–8, must hold an earned bachelor's or higher degree in the endorsement area;
        or
        Demonstrate 24 semester hours of applicable coursework as determined by a transcript review;
        or
        Pass the CSBE-approved assessment of content knowledge relevant to the area of endorsement.
II. Available Endorsement Areas for Colorado Educator Licenses
  A. Colorado issues 4 types of licenses—administrator, principal, special services provider, and teacher—with endorsements that indicate the age or grade level(s), subject area(s), or other areas of specialization that are appropriate to the applicant's preparation, training, and experience. They are typically granted in the major areas of specialization and only in those areas which constitute approved programs. Available endorsements include:
     1. Administrator (Grades K–12)

      a.   Administrator (superintendent), Director of Special Education, Director of Gifted Education

  2. Principal (Grades K–12)

      a.   School Principal

  3. Special Services Provider (Ages 0–21)

      a.   School Audiologist; School Counselor; School Nurse; School Occupational Therapist; School Orientation and Mobility Specialist; School Physical Therapist; School Psychologist; School Social Worker; School Speech-Language Pathologist

  4. Teacher

      a.   Elementary Education, Grades K–6; Early Childhood Education, Ages 0–8; Early Childhood Special Education, Ages 0–8; Special Education Generalist, Ages 5–21

      b.   Grades K–12 include: Culturally & Linguistically Diverse Education;* Culturally & Linguistically Diverse–Bilingual Education Specialist;* Dance; Drama/Theater Arts; Health; Instructional Technology Specialist;* Instructional Technology Teacher; Music; Physical Education; Visual Arts; World Language (American Sign Language, French, German, Italian, Japanese, Latin, Mandarin Chinese, Russian, Spanish)

      c.   Middle School (Grades 6–8) includes: Middle School Mathematics

      d.   Secondary (Grades 7–12) includes: Agriculture and Renewable Natural Resources; Business Education; Business and Marketing Education; English Language Arts; Family and Consumer Sciences; Marketing; Mathematics; Science; Social Studies; Speech; Technology Education (Industrial Arts); Trade and Industry Education

      e.   Endorsements requiring graduate-level courses or a master's degree (depending on endorsement area sought) include: Early Childhood Special Education Specialist, Ages 0–8; Gifted Education Core, Grades PK–12; Gifted Education Specialist, Grades PK–12;* Reading Specialist, Grades K–12;* Reading Teacher, Grades K–12;* Special Education Specialist, Ages 5–21;* Special Education Specialist: Visually Impaired, Ages 0–21; Special Education Specialist: Deaf/Hard of Hearing, Ages 0–21; Teacher Librarian, Grades K–12*

         *This endorsement cannot be issued as a stand-alone endorsement. It may only be added to an existing valid license.

III. Applying for an Initial Special Services Provider License

  A. Meet all requirements for applying for an initial license, I, A–E, above, except that the approved preparation program must be for the special services area of specialization.

  B. Meet additional requirements for specific special services licenses, including:

    1. School Audiologist

      a.   Hold a doctor of audiology degree (AuD) or PhD in audiology;

      b.   Complete a minimum 8-week full-time practicum or internship in audiology in a school setting;
         and

    c.   Pass the CSBE-approved audiology exam.

2.   School Counselor

    a.   Option 1:

        i.   Hold a master's degree in school counseling;

        ii.   Complete a Council for Accreditation of Counseling and Related Educational Programs (CACREP)–accredited school counseling program;

        iii.   Complete a minimum 100-clock-hour practicum and a minimum 600-clock-hour internship in a school setting;
            and

        iv.   Pass the CSBE-approved school counselor exam;

        or

    b.   Option 2:

        i.   Hold a master's degree in a clinical counseling domain;
            and

        ii.   Hold a valid Colorado Department of Regulatory Agencies-issued LPC license;
            and

        iii.   Have 3 or more years' full-time, licensed clinical counseling experience.

        iv.   Applicants who meet all 3 requirements in i.–iii., directly above, and who have been hired in a school counseling role may be issued an interim authorization valid for 1 year. During this year, they must complete an approved induction program and take and pass the CSBE-approved school counselor exam. Upon completion of the year under the interim authorization, the induction program, and the test, the candidate may then apply to advance to a professional SSP license (school counselor).

3.   School Nurse

    a.   Option 1:

        i.   Hold a bachelor of science or higher degree in nursing from an accepted institution of higher education;
            and

        ii.   Hold a valid Colorado registered nurse (RN) license issued by the Colorado Department of Regulatory Agencies or a compact state;

        or

    b.   Option 2:

        i.   Hold a valid Colorado RN license issued by the Department of Regulatory Agencies or a compact state;
            and

        ii.   Have 3 or more years of practical experience working with school-aged children;
            and

        iii.   Have completed an RN or bachelor of science in nursing (BSN) program recognized by the US Secretary of Education and a specialized accrediting agency, such as the Commission on Collegiate Nursing Education (CCNE) or the Accreditation Commission for Education in Nursing (ACEN).

4. School Occupational Therapist
    a. Hold a bachelor's degree;
    b. Complete an American Occupational Therapy Association (AOTA)–accredited occupational therapy program;
    c. Complete an internship or supervised field experience;
    d. Pass the national exam through the National Board for Certification in Occupational Therapy (NBCOT);
        and
    e. Hold a valid Colorado occupational therapist license issued by the Colorado Department of Regulatory Agencies.

5. School Orientation and Mobility Specialist
    a. Hold a bachelor's degree;
    b. Complete approved preparation program for school orientation and mobility specialists;
    c. Complete a minimum 320-clock-hour full-time practicum in a school setting;
    d. Pass the Academy for Certification of Vision Rehabilitation and Education Professionals (ACVREP) exam;
        and
    e. Hold ACVREP orientation and mobility certificate.

6. School Physical Therapist
    a. Hold a bachelor's degree;
    b. Complete an American Physical Therapy Association (APTA)–accredited physical therapy program;
    c. Complete a practicum;
        and
    d. Hold a valid Colorado physical therapist license issued by the Colorado Department of Regulatory Agencies.

7. School Psychologist
    a. Complete a state-approved sixth-year specialist program (60 graduate semester hours) or doctoral program for school psychologist, serving children birth–21;
    b. Complete a practicum;
    c. Complete a minimum 1200-clock-hour internship or supervised field experience;
        and
    d. Pass the CSBE-approved school psychologist exam or hold National Association of School Psychologists (NCSP) certification.

8. School Social Worker
    a. Hold a master's degree in social work (MSW), including coursework in school and special education law, functional behavior assessment, and the development of behavioral intervention plans;

      b.   Complete a minimum 900-clock-hour practicum, including 1 placement with school-aged children; *and*

      c.   Pass the Association of Social Work Boards (ASWB) clinical or advanced generalist exam.

   9.   School Speech-Language Pathologist

      a.   Hold a master's or higher degree in communication disorders or speech-language pathology;

      b.   Complete an American Speech-Language-Hearing Association (ASHA)–accredited speech-language pathology program accredited by the Council on Academic Accreditation (CAA) in audiology and speech-language pathology of the ASHA;

      c.   Complete a minimum 8-week full-time practicum; *and*

      d.   Hold ASHA certification or have passed the CSBE-approved speech-language pathology exam.

IV.   Applying for an Initial Principal License

   A.   Meet all requirements for applying for an initial license, I, A–E, above, except that the approved preparation program must be for principals.

   B.   Meet additional requirements for principal license, including:

      1.   Provide documented evidence of 3 or more years of full-time successful experience working as a licensed or certificated professional in a public or nonpublic elementary or secondary school in the United States; *and*

      2.   Achieve a passing score on the CSBE-approved principal exam.

V.   Applying for an Initial Administrator License

   A.   Meet all requirements for applying for an initial license, I, A–E, above, except that the approved preparation program must be for administrators.

   B.   Meet additional requirements for specific administrator licenses, including:

      1.   Initial Administrator (Superintendent) License

        a.   Complete an approved graduate program for school district administration at an accepted, regionally accredited institution of higher education; *and*

        b.   Have a passing score on the CSBE-approved administrator exam.

      2.   Initial Administrator (Director of Special Education) License

        a.   Hold a master's or higher degree in special education from a regionally accredited institution of higher education;

        b.   Have a minimum of 2 years of experience working with students with disabilities; *and*

        c.   Complete an approved program for the preparation of special education directors, including a supervised field-based experience, or complete an approved administrator preparation program.

      3.   Initial Administrator (Director of Gifted Education) License

    a. Hold a master's or higher degree in gifted education from a regionally accredited institution of higher education;

    b. Have a minimum of 2 years of experience working with gifted students; *and*

    c. Complete an approved program for the preparation of gifted education directors, including a supervised field-based experience, or complete an approved administrator preparation program.

Moving from an Initial License to a Professional License

I. Professional License (valid 5 years; renewable). Requirements include:
  A. Complete a CSBE-approved induction program.
    1. Approved induction programs are provided by Colorado school districts and Boards of Cooperative Education Services (BOCES), and include supervision by mentor teachers, ongoing professional development, ethics training, and performance evaluations.
  B. Complete and submit an online license application.
    1. Upload a copy of original induction certificate of completion into the application.
  C. See more at http://www.cde.state.co.us/cdeprof/Licensure_provtoprof_faq.asp.

Connecticut

To access Connecticut's most recent certification requirements changes, consult "Certification News and Alerts" at https://portal.ct.gov/SDE/Certification/Bureau-of-Certification.

Three-Tier Certification System Overview

I. Initial Educator Certificate (valid 3 years)
   A. Issued to applicants who meet all eligibility requirements and who have fewer than 3 full school years of appropriate successful teaching experience in the past 10 years.
II. Provisional Educator Certificate (valid 8 years)
   To qualify for the provisional educator certificate, an applicant must complete 1 of the following:
   A. Ten months of successful appropriate experience under the initial educator certificate or interim initial educator certificate in a Connecticut public school and the teacher induction/mentoring program, as made available by the Connecticut State Board of Education;
      or
   B. Thirty months of successful appropriate experience within 10 years in a public school system, approved nonpublic school, or nonpublic school approved by the appropriate governing body in another state.
III. Professional Educator Certificate (valid 5 years)
   To qualify for the professional educator certificate, an applicant must complete the following requirements:
   A. Thirty school months of successful appropriate experience in a Connecticut public or approved nonpublic school under the provisional educator certificate;
      and
   B. Any person who is issued a Connecticut educator certificate for the first time on or after July 1, 2018, will be required to complete a master's degree in an appropriate subject matter area in order to advance their provisional educator certificate to the professional educator certificate;
      or
   C. Additional course requirements, as prescribed by current Connecticut certification regulations. Specific course work requirements vary depending on endorsement.
      1. For certificate-specific requirements, consult https://portal.ct.gov/-/media/SDE/Certification/regulations.pdf?la=en, as well as the "Guide to Assessments for Educator Certification in Connecticut" at https://portal.ct.gov/-/media/SDE/Certification/guides/assess_for_cert.pdf?la=en.
IV. Interim Educator Certificate (valid 3 calendar years)
   A. The interim educator certificate may be issued at the initial or provisional level.

B. A nonrenewable interim certificate may be issued with test deferrals and in some cases with a deficiency for the required special education course.

C. A renewable interim educator certificate may be issued with specific course deficiencies for vocational certificates only, as provided by certification regulations.

First-Time Connecticut Certification

I. Requirements include:

A. Successfully complete a state-approved planned program of general academic and professional education at a regionally accredited college or university; *and*

B. Pass subject-specific tests, if applicable to the endorsement requested.

    1. For certificate-specific requirements, consult https://portal.ct.gov/-/media/SDE/Certification/regulations.pdf?la=en, as well as the "Guide to Assessments for Educator Certification in Connecticut" at https://portal.ct.gov/-/media/SDE/Certification/guides/assess_for_cert.pdf?la=en.

II. Eligibility Based on Teaching Experience

A. Educators who have completed the equivalent of 2 school years of full-time teaching in the grade level and subject appropriate to the endorsement requested may waive the planned program requirement. However, all course work, degree, testing and any experiential requirements must still be met. To obtain such certification, educators must:

    1. Document no fewer than 20 school months of successful, appropriate full-time teaching experience in the same approved nonpublic school or an out-of-state public school under a valid certificate;

    2. Pass subject-specific tests for those endorsements where a test is required; *and*

    3. Successfully complete all required general academic and professional education course work for the endorsement areas sought.

        a. All course work must result in college-level credit awarded to official transcripts from regionally accredited colleges or universities.

    4. For certificate-specific requirements, consult https://portal.ct.gov/-/media/SDE/Certification/regulations.pdf?la=en, as well as the "Guide to Assessments for Educator Certification in Connecticut" at https://portal.ct.gov/-/media/SDE/Certification/guides/assess_for_cert.pdf?la=en.

    5. All candidates applying for a Connecticut educator certificate which requires completion of a bachelor's degree from a regionally accredited institution must submit official transcripts verifying completion of the degree, regardless of the basis of their certification.

        a. Only course work resulting in credit awarded to an official transcript of a regionally accredited college or university can be accepted to meet certification requirements.

III. Out-of-State Educators

A. Connecticut participates in the National Association of State Directors of Teacher

Education and Certification (NASDTEC) Interstate Agreement (NIA). Under this agreement, to waive specific course work requirements, Connecticut may accept:

1. Completion of a state-approved educator preparation program at a regionally accredited college or university from another US state;
   or
2. A minimum of 30 months of successful full-time experience under the other state's valid educator certificate (at least equivalent to a Connecticut initial educator certificate), appropriate to the subject area being requested.
   a. To be considered, the experience must be completed within 10 years of the date of application for Connecticut certification.
3. The interstate agreement does not exempt candidates from degree, testing and/or experiential requirements applicable to the requested certification endorsement.
   a. For certificate-specific requirements, consult https://portal.ct.gov/-/media/SDE/Certification/regulations.pdf?la=en, as well as the "Guide to Assessments for Educator Certification in Connecticut" at https://portal.ct.gov/-/media/SDE/Certification/guides/assess_for_cert.pdf?la=en.
4. Candidates who do not qualify for Connecticut certification under the terms of the interstate agreement must meet all of Connecticut's requirements for the endorsement requested, including course work.
5. Connecticut does not participate in the interstate agreement for administrative endorsements.
6. Assessment Exemptions. Effective July 1, 2009, amended as of July 1, 2013, educators may be exempt from Board-approved assessment requirements, including Praxis II subject knowledge tests, Connecticut Foundations of Reading Test, Reading Specialist Test, Early Childhood Test, and/or ACTFL OPI and WPT, if they meet the following criteria:
   a. Hold a valid certificate in another state that is equivalent to at least a Connecticut initial educator certificate and have 1 of the following:
      i. Have 3 years of successful appropriate experience in the endorsement area requested, under a valid certificate, within the past 10 years;
         or
      ii. Hold a master's degree in the academic subject area for which Connecticut certification is being requested. Pedagogical degrees in the subject area, such as those for elementary education, special education or physical education, do not meet the requirements of the exemption.
7. Assessment Deferral
   a. Out-of-state applicants who meet all certification criteria except Connecticut assessment requirements may be issued a 3-year, nonrenewable interim certificate with a deferral for testing.
   b. To maintain certification and obtain subsequent certificates, the applicant must complete all required tests before the expiration date of the certificate.
   c. All applicants who are eligible for a deferral of testing requirements will automatically be issued an interim certificate once all requirements other than testing have been met.

IV. Foreign credentials for certification
   A. Applicants who completed any education required for certification outside of the United States must have their credentials evaluated by an agency currently approved by the Connecticut State Department of Education and meet current certification requirements, including course work and assessments, as appropriate.
      1. To access a list of approved agencies, consult https://portal.ct.gov/SDE/ Certification/Foreign-Credentials.
   B. In addition to credential evaluations, applicants must submit:
      1. Original course-by-course analysis, completed by 1 of the approved agencies, of all college- or university-level course work including general academic, subject area and program preparation course work completed outside of the United States;
         and
      2. ED 126 Statement of Successful Professional Experience, verifying completion of K–12 teaching/service completed within the past 10 years in foreign public schools or approved nonpublic schools, along with a copy of the certificate or license authorizing this service.
         a. Foreign experience must be verified by the superintendent or head of the school district, or by the ministry of education or other authorized agency.
         b. If the verification of teaching experience or the teaching license or authorization is printed in a language other than English, the original document must be accompanied by a notarized translation.

Delaware

In Delaware, educators are required to hold both a License and a Certificate.

Licensure

I. Initial License (valid 4 years; issued to applicants with 0 – 4 years of teaching experience)
   A. In-State Requirements
      1. Bachelor's degree from regionally accredited college or university
      2. Complete 1 of the following:
         a. An approved student teaching program
         b. An approved alternative route to licensure and certification program
         c. Ninety-one days "in lieu of student teaching" of long-term teaching experience in 1 assignment in a Delaware public/charter school within the same academic year before application for licensure, with supporting evidence of satisfactory performance evaluations
            NOTE: The first certificate under this option may not be in a core content area (math, English/language arts, social studies, science, or elementary).
      3. Disclose any criminal conviction history
      4. Educators with less than 1 year of licensed and certified teaching experience must achieve a qualifying score on an approved performance assessment (PPAT or edTPA) within the first 2 years of teaching.
   B. Out-of-State or Lapsed Requirements
      1. Out-of-State: Department of Education may issue:
         a. Initial License to an applicant who is currently licensed as an educator in another jurisdiction with less than 4 years of credentialed teaching experience. The applicant must also meet requirements for certification.
         b. Continuing License to an applicant who has 4 years of verified teaching experience under a full and valid out-of-state credential with attestation/proof of a minimum of 2 satisfactory summative evaluations during that license period.
      2. Lapsed: An applicant who previously held a Delaware Initial License that has been expired for more than 5 years will be treated as a new applicant and must meet all current requirements in law and regulation. In addition to an Initial License, applicants must also apply for a Standard Certificate in the appropriate area; see Standard Certificate below. This may apply for both the Initial License and the Continuing License.
   C. Preparations for Continuing License Application
      Before expiration of Initial License, applicant must:
      1. Complete 90 professional development hours and mentoring activities
      2. Receive 2 out of 3 satisfactory evaluations

      3.   Disclose any criminal conviction history

II. Continuing License (valid 5 years; renewable and extendable upon proof of exigent circumstances for up to 3-year leave of absence)

    A. General Requirements

      1. Successfully complete requirements for Initial License (see I, A, directly above)

      2. Receive no more than 1 unsatisfactory annual evaluation, as defined by the Delaware Performance Appraisal System, during period of Initial License

      3. Hold current and valid educator license in another jurisdiction with evidence of completing 4 or more years of successful teaching experience and 2 successful summative evaluations

    B. Delaware Certificates issued prior to July 2, 2001

      1. Continuing License may be issued to educator who holds a Delaware Certificate issued prior to July 13, 1971, or who previously held a valid Delaware Standard or Professional Status Certificate that has expired.

      2. As a condition of maintaining the original license, the educator shall successfully complete 1 year of an approved mentoring program required of educators within their first year of employment.

    C. Continuing License Renewal (valid 5 years; renewable)

      1. Fulfill 90-clock-hour requirement for professional growth

        a. At least 45 hours every 5 years must be in activities related to educator's work with students or staff.

        b. Professional development hours must take place during term of Continuing License.

        c. See Department of Education (Appendix 1) for detailed options.

        d. Disclose any criminal conviction history

III. Advanced Licensure (valid 5 years; renewable)

    A. Requirements

      1. Application by holder of National Board of Professional Teaching Standards Certification or equivalent program approved by Professional Standards Board

    B. Renewal

      1. Renewable for up to 10 years provided that educator maintains proficiency under program for which license was first issued

      2. If holder does not renew the Advanced License, a Continuing License will be issued upon expiration of the Advanced License.

Alternative Routes to Teacher Licensure and Certification Program

I. Candidates participating in an Alternative Routes to Teacher Licensure and Certification Program shall be issued an Initial License of no more than 4 years' duration. Emergency Certificates for content areas may be of no more than 3 years' duration. Certificates of Eligibility for special education areas may be of no more than 3 years' duration, and candidates must be actively participating in a state-approved Alternative Routes to Certification Certificate of Eligibility program.

II. Requirements:

    A. Hold a bachelor's degree from a regionally accredited college or university, with a major appropriate to the instructional field desired, which shall be no less than 24 credit hours appropriate to the instructional field

B. Pass an examination of content knowledge, such as Praxis II, in the instructional field desired, if applicable and available

C. Obtain and accept an offer of employment in a position that requires licensure and certification in the instructional field desired

III. Components of the Alternative Routes Program

A. Summer institute of approximately 120 instructional (clock) hours completed by candidates prior to the beginning of teaching assignments. A teacher candidate who will participate in the Alternative Routes for Teacher Licensure and Certification Program hired after July 1 of a school year will fulfill the 120-hour seminar/practicum requirement prior to the start of the following school year.

B. One-year, full-time practicum experience that includes a period of intensive on-the-job mentoring and supervision beginning the first day of classroom teaching and continuing for 30 weeks

C. Seminars on teaching that provide Alternative Routes to Teacher Licensure and Certification teachers with approximately 200 instructional (clock) hours or equivalent professional development during the first year of their teaching assignment and during an intensive seminar the following summer

Standard Certificate

I. Issued to an educator who holds a valid Delaware Initial, Continuing, or Advanced License; or a Standard or Professional Status Certificate issued prior to August 31, 2003, who has met the following requirements.

II. Preliminary Requirement
Satisfy at least 1 of the following:

A. Certification from the National Board for Professional Teaching Standards in area of certification

B. Meeting the requirements of the relevant Department or Standards Board regulation for obtaining a Standard Certificate in area of certification

C. Graduation from an educator preparation program approved by the National Council for Accreditation of Teacher Education (NCATE) or the Council for the Accreditation of Educator Preparation (CAEP), or from a Delaware-approved educator preparation program using National Association of State Directors of Teacher Education and Certification (NASDTEC) or NCATE (CAEP) standards, with a major or its equivalent in area of certification

D. Satisfactory completion of an Alternative Routes to Teacher Licensure and Certification Program, the Special Institute for Licensure and Certification, or other approved alternative educator preparation programs

E. Bachelor's degree from a regionally accredited college or university in non-content area—including 15 credit hours or their equivalent in professional development related to the area of certification, of which at least 6 credit hours must focus on pedagogy—selected by the applicant with the approval of the employing school district or charter school

III. Additional Requirements
   A. Meet or exceed Praxis II scores and/or required coursework or additional certificate requirements. Note: Some certifications require Praxis II only, and some certifications require Praxis II and coursework and/or degree, along with teaching experience.
   or
   B. Hold a valid and current license/certificate in certification area from another state

Early Childhood Teacher Standard Certificate (Birth–Grade 2)

I. Issued to an educator who holds a valid Delaware Initial, Continuing, or Advanced License; or a Standard or Professional Status Certificate issued by the Department prior to August 31, 2003
II. Requirements
   A. See Standard Certificate, I and II, above.

Elementary Teacher Standard Certificate (Grades K–6)

I. Issued to an educator who holds a valid Delaware Initial, Continuing, or Advanced License; or a Standard or Professional Status Certificate issued by the department prior to August 31, 2003
II. Requirements
   A. See Standard Certificate, I and II, above.

Administration

I. School Principal/Assistant Principal
   A. Educational Requirements
   Satisfy at least 1 of the following requirements:
      1. Master's or doctoral degree in educational leadership, offered by an NCATE (CAEP) specialty organization–recognized educator preparation program or state-approved educator preparation program where the state approval body employed the appropriate NASDTEC or NCATE (CAEP) specialty organization standards, at a regionally accredited college or university
      2. Master's or doctoral degree in any field from regionally accredited college or university and successful completion of 1 of the following:
         a. School Principal course of study, as defined in 14 DE Admin. Code 1595 Certification Programs for Leaders in Education
         b. School Principal certification program pursuant to 14 DE Admin. Code 1595 Certification Programs for Leaders in Education
   B. Experience Requirements
      1. Minimum of 5 years of teaching experience
II. Certified Central Office Personnel
   A. Education Requirements
      1. Master's or doctoral degree in educational leadership offered by an NCATE

(CAEP) specialty organization-recognized educator preparation program or state-approved educator preparation program where the state approval body employed the appropriate NASDTEC or NCATE (CAEP) specialty organization standards, at a regionally accredited college or university
or

2. Master's degree from a regionally accredited college or university in any field and 1 of the following:
   a. Successful completion of an approved Program pursuant to 14 DE Admin. Code 1595 Certification Programs for Leaders in Education
   b. Standard Certificate School Principal and successful completion of an additional 9 graduate-level credit hours from a regionally accredited college or university in educational leadership or the equivalent in professional development approved by the Department

B. Experience Requirements
   1. Minimum of 5 years of teaching experience

III. Superintendent or Assistant Superintendent
  A. Educational Requirements
     Satisfy at least 1 of the following additional education requirements:
     1. Doctoral degree in educational leadership offered by an NCATE (CAEP) specialty organization–recognized educator preparation program or state-approved educator preparation where the state approval body employed the appropriate NASDTEC or NCATE (CAEP) specialty organization standards, at a regionally accredited college or university
     2. Master's or doctoral degree from a regionally accredited college or university in any field and 1 of the following:
        a. Successful completion of an approved Superintendent Program pursuant to 14 DE Admin. Code 1595 Certification Programs for Leaders in Education
        b. Standard Certificate Certified Central Office Personnel or a Standard Certificate Special Education Director
           and
           Successful completion of an additional 9 graduate-level credit hours from a regionally accredited college or university in educational leadership or the equivalent in professional development approved by the Department
  B. Experience Requirements
     1. Minimum of 5 years of teaching experience
     2. Minimum of 2 years of full-time leadership experience working in any of the following areas:
        a. School Principal or Assistant School Principal
        b. Certified Central Office Personnel Educator
        c. Special Education Director
        d. Other leadership position

IV. Special Education Director
  A. Education Requirements
     Satisfy at least 1 of the following education requirements:
     1. Master's or doctoral degree in educational leadership offered by an NCATE

(CAEP) specialty organization–recognized educator preparation program or state-approved educator preparation program where the state approval body employed the appropriate NASDTEC or NCATE (CAEP) specialty organization standards, at a regionally accredited college or university

and

Thirty graduate-level semester hours from a regionally accredited college or university in Special Education taken either as part of a degree program or in addition to it, or the equivalent in professional development preapproved by the Department

2. Master's or doctoral degree in special education offered by an NCATE (CAEP) specialty organization–recognized educator preparation program or state-approved educator preparation program where the state approval body employed the appropriate NASDTEC or NCATE (CAEP) specialty organization standards, at a regionally accredited college or university

   and

   Successful completion of any approved Program pursuant to 14 DE Admin. Code 1595 Certification programs for Leaders in Education

3. Master's or doctoral degree from a regionally accredited college or university in any field

   and

   Successful completion of an approved Special Education Director Program pursuant to 14 DE Admin. Code 1595 Certification Programs for Leaders in Education

B. Experience Requirements

   Satisfy at least 1 of the following:

   1. Minimum of 5 years of teaching experience with exceptional children, special education students at the PreK–12 public school level or the equivalent as approved by the Department

   2. Minimum of 5 years of professional experience under a Delaware Standard Certificate or other Delaware professional license, including but not limited to school psychologist, speech pathologist, or audiologist, working with exceptional children special education students at the PreK to 12 level or the equivalent as approved by the Department

   3. Minimum of 5 years of administrative experience working with exceptional children special education students at the PreK to 12 level or the equivalent as approved by the Department

   4. Any combination of the types of experiences prescribed above that totals a minimum of 5 years

Guidance Counselor

I. Elementary School Counselor

   A. Requirements

      1. Holds a valid Delaware Initial, Continuing, or Advanced License or a Standard or Professional Status Certificate issued prior to August 31, 2003

2. Has met the requirements as set forth in 14 DE Admin. Code 1505 Standard Certificate

3. Has satisfied the following additional requirements:

    a. Graduated from an NCATE (CAEP) specialty organization–recognized educator preparation program, or from a state-approved educator preparation program where the state approval body employed the appropriate NASDTEC or NCATE (CAEP) specialty organization standards, offered by a regionally accredited college or university, with a master's degree in Elementary School Counseling

    or

    Holds a master's degree from a regionally accredited college in any field; and has satisfactorily completed 39 credits of graduate coursework or the equivalent in professional development as approved by the Department in the areas of: Introduction to School Counseling & Theories (3 credits); Human Behavior and Child Development (3 credits); Ethical Issues in School Counseling (3 credits); College & Career Readiness K–12 (3 credits); Testing, Measurements, and Research in School Counseling (3 credits); The Counselor as Consultant (3 credits); Special Education Law & the School Counselor's Role (3 credits); Group Counseling (3 credits); Individual Counseling Skills & Strategies (6 credits); Family Counseling (3 credits); and Principles and Practices of a School Counseling Program (6 credits)

    b. Has completed 700 hours of clinical experience in an elementary-school setting under the direct supervision of a State Department of Education– certified Elementary School Counselor

    c. Achieves a passing score on an examination of content knowledge, such as Praxis II, for Professional School Counselor

II. Secondary School Counselor

   A. Requirements

      1. Holds a valid Delaware Initial, Continuing, or Advanced License or a Limited Standard, Standard, or Professional Status Certificate issued prior to August 31, 2003

      2. Has met the requirements as set forth in 14 DE Admin. Code 1505 Standard Certificate

      3. Has satisfied the following additional requirements:

         a. Graduated from a NCATE (CAEP) specialty organization–recognized educator preparation program, or from a state-approved educator preparation program where the state approval body employed the appropriate NASDTEC or NCATE (CAEP) specialty organization standards, offered by a regionally accredited college or university, with a master's degree in Secondary School Counseling

         or

         Holds a master's degree from a regionally accredited college in any field; and has satisfactorily completed 39 credits of graduate coursework or the equivalent in professional development as approved by the Department in the areas of: Introduction to School Counseling & Theories (3 credits); Human Behavior and Child Development (3 credits); Ethical Issues in School Counseling (3 credits); College & Career Readiness K–12 (3 credits); Testing, Measurements, and Research in School Counseling (3 credits); The Counselor as Consultant (3 credits); Special Education Law & the School Counselor's Role (3 credits); Group Counseling (3 credits); Individual Counseling Skills & Strategies (6 credits); Family Counseling (3 credits); and Principles and Practices of a School Counseling Program (6 credits)

b. Has completed 700 hours of clinical experience in a secondary-school setting under the direct supervision of a State Department of Education–certified Secondary School Counselor

c. Achieves a passing score on an examination of content knowledge, such as Praxis II, for Professional School Counselor

School Psychologist

I. Licensure Requirements

A. The Department shall issue a Standard Certificate as a School Psychologist to an applicant who has met the following:

1. Holds a valid Delaware Initial, Continuing, or Advanced License or Standard or Professional Status Certificate issued by the Department prior to August 31, 2003

2. Has met the requirements as set forth in 14 DE Admin. Code 1505 Standard Certificate

3. Has satisfied at least 1 of the following additional education and internship requirements:

a. Graduate-level program of study, approved by the National Association of School Psychologists (NASP) or the American Psychological Association (APA), offered by a regionally accredited college or university, and titled "School Psychology," culminating in a master's degree with an additional Educational Specialist (ES) degree or doctoral degree in School Psychology *and*

Has successfully completed a supervised internship in an institution or agency approved by the Department or the applicant's graduate program

b. Holds a valid Nationally Certified School Psychologist (NCSP) Certificate from the National Association of School Psychologists (NASP)

c. Holds a valid and current license or certificate from another state in school psychology

School Social Worker

I. Requirements

A. The Department shall issue a Standard Certificate as a School Social Worker to an applicant who has met the following:

1. Holds a valid Delaware Initial, Continuing, or Advanced License or Standard or Professional Status Certificate issued by the Department prior to August 31, 2003
2. Has met the requirements as set forth in 14 DE Admin. Code 1505 Standard Certificate
3. Has satisfied the following additional education requirements:
    a. Master's degree in Social Work (MSW) from a regionally accredited college or university
    b. Two years of successful full-time work experience as a social worker
    c. One year of supervised experience in a school setting, or a 1-year internship of 1,000 hours approved by the Department and supervised by an appropriate school designee

School Library Media Specialist

I. Licensure Requirements
    A. The Department shall issue a Standard Certificate as a School Library Media Specialist to an applicant who has met the following:
        1. Holds a valid Delaware Initial, Continuing, or Advanced License or Standard or Professional Status Certificate issued by the Department prior to August 31, 2003
        2. Has met the requirements as set forth in 14 DE Admin. Code 1505 Standard Certificate
        3. Has satisfied at least 1 of the following additional education requirements:
            a. Holds a master's or doctoral degree from a regionally accredited college or university in an American Library Association–approved program in School Library Media
            b. Holds a master's or doctoral degree from a regionally accredited college or university in any area
                and
                Has completed a Department-approved School Library Media program that meets American Library Association standards

District of Columbia

Teaching Licenses/Credentials

For a list of documents required to apply for each credential, see https://osse.dc.gov/page/teacher-certification.

I. Initial Teacher Credential (valid 3 years; nonrenewable)
   A. Option 1, for those currently enrolled in an approved teacher preparation program—candidate:
      1. Holds a completed bachelor's degree;
      2. Has successfully passed the Praxis CORE, Pre-Professional Skills Test (PPST), or other accepted alternate basic skills exam;
      3. Has successfully passed the Praxis II subject content exam in the area of the credential;
      4. Is admitted into an Office of the State Superintendent of Education (OSSE)-approved teacher licensure program, or a teacher licensure program approved in another state accepted by OSSE, in the area of the credential;
         and
      5. Is employed or contracted as a teacher by a local education agency (LEA) operating in the District of Columbia.
   B. Option 2, for those who hold a valid license from another state and have demonstrated effective teaching performance experience—candidate:
      1. Holds a completed bachelor's degree;
      2. Has successfully passed the Praxis CORE, PPST, or other accepted alternate basic skills exam;
      3. Has successfully passed a corresponding subject content exam in another state or has passed the DC-required Praxis II exam;
      4. Has documentation satisfactory to OSSE to confirm that the candidate:
         a. Has completed at least 2 years of effective full-time teaching experience in another state as measured by a summative evaluation rating;
            or
         b. Has completed 2 years of effective or equivalent teaching experience as measured by the student growth component of an evaluation rating. The experience shall be completed within the previous 5 years, and the final year shall show a rating of Effective or higher;
         and
      5. Holds a valid teaching credential, in good standing, issued from another state accepted by OSSE.
   C. Option 3, for those currently employed or contracted as teachers by an LEA operating in the District of Columbia—candidate:

1. Holds a completed bachelor's degree;
2. Has successfully passed the Praxis CORE, PPST, or other accepted alternate basic skills exam;
3. Has successfully passed the Praxis II subject content exam in the area of the credential;
4. Is employed or contracted as a teacher by an LEA operating in the District of Columbia;
   and
5. Has a written request for issuance of an Initial Teacher Credential addressed to OSSE from the employing LEA.

II. Standard Teacher Credential (valid 4 years; renewable; may be used for interstate reciprocity with other US states, territories, and the Department of Defense Dependents Schools. For a list of documents required to apply, see https://osse.dc.gov/page/teacher-certification)

A. Option 1, for those who have completed an approved teacher licensure program—candidate:
1. Holds a completed bachelor's degree;
2. Has completed an approved teacher licensure program in the corresponding subject area;
3. Has successfully passed the Praxis CORE, PPST, or other accepted alternate basic skills exam;
4. Has successfully passed the Praxis II subject content exam in the area of the credential;
   and
5. Has successfully passed the Praxis II Principles of Learning & Teaching (PLT) exam for the grade level of the credential.

B. Option 2, for those who hold or have held a DC Initial Teacher Credential and demonstrate effective teaching performance experience within a DC LEA—candidate:
1. Holds or has held a DC Initial Teacher Credential;
2. Has completed at least 2 years of effective or equivalent full-time teaching experience while holding the initial credential at an LEA in the District of Columbia within the previous 5 years, as demonstrated by the applicant's summative evaluation rating from the employing LEA; the performance evaluation reviews must have been conducted by the same LEA and the evaluation system must have been accepted by OSSE;
   and
3. Has successfully passed the Praxis II PLT exam for the grade level of the credential.

C. Option 3, for those who hold a valid teaching license and demonstrate effective teaching performance experience in another state—candidate:
1. Holds a completed bachelor's degree;
2. Holds a valid full teaching credential from another reciprocal state;
3. Has successfully passed the Praxis CORE, PPST, or other accepted alternate basic skills exam;

4. Has successfully passed a corresponding subject content exam in another state or has passed the DC-required Praxis II exam;

5. Has successfully passed a corresponding pedagogy exam in another state or has passed the DC-required Praxis II exam;
   and

6. Has completed at least 2 years of effective or equivalent full-time teaching experience in another state, as measured by a summative evaluation rating of 2 years of effective or equivalent teaching based upon the student growth component of an evaluation rating. The experience shall be completed within the previous 5 years, and the final year shall show a rating of Effective or higher.

D. Option 4, for those who are currently employed as teachers within a DC LEA that does not require a license, but who demonstrate effective teaching performance experience—candidate:

1. Holds a completed bachelor's degree;

2. Has successfully passed the Praxis CORE, PPST, or other accepted alternate basic skills exam;

3. Has successfully passed the Praxis II subject content exam in the area of the credential;

4. Has successfully passed the Praxis II PLT exam for the grade level of the credential;

5. Has completed at least 2 years of effective or equivalent full-time teaching experience at an LEA in the District of Columbia within the previous 3 years, as demonstrated by the applicant's summative evaluation rating from the employing LEA. The performance evaluation reviews must have been conducted by the same LEA and the evaluation system must have been accepted by OSSE;
   and

6. Is currently employed as a "teacher of record" with a DC LEA.

Service Provider Credentials

For a list of documents required to apply for each credential, see https://osse.dc.gov/page/school-service-provider-certification#required.

I. School Counselor—candidate:

A. Holds a completed master's degree in school counseling education from an approved licensure program;
   or
   Holds a completed master's degree in counseling and has completed graduate level coursework in each area listed below. A letter grade of "C" or higher is required.

1. Counseling children and adolescents
2. Multicultural counseling
3. Counseling students with exceptionalities
4. Crisis and trauma counseling and interventions

       5. Career development and vocational education counseling

       6. Testing assessments and measurements

       7. Legal and ethical issues for school counselors

  B. Has successfully completed at least 300 hours of supervised school-based field, practicum, or internship experience as part of the degree program. Field experience may also be met by one of the following:

       1. A degree in school counseling from a program approved by the Council for Accreditation of Counseling and Related Educational Program (CACREP) or a valid National Certified Counselors (NCC) credential issued by the National Board for Certified Counselors (NBCC);

       or

       Appropriate documentation verifying at least 2 years of full-time teaching experience or 1 year of full-time experience as a school counselor.

       2. A passing score for the DC-required school counselor content exam or a comparable exam in another state where a school counselor license is held.

II. School Librarian — candidate:

  A. Holds a completed master's degree in school library media from an approved licensure program or a completed master's degree in library science and has completed graduate-level coursework in each area listed below. A letter grade of C or higher is required.

       1. Cataloging and classification

       2. Selection and use of media for children

       3. Instructional media design and development/production

       4. Information sources, services, and instruction

       5. School library organization

       6. Integration of technology into the curriculum

  B. Has completed directed field experience in a school library with an experienced library media specialist

    or

    Has completed 2 years of school-based teaching experience

    or

    Has completed 1 year of experience as a school librarian;

  C. Has achieved a passing score for the DC-required library media specialist content exam

    or

    Has passed a comparable exam in another state where a school library media specialist license is held.

III. Additional Service Provider Licenses: visit the Educator Licensure and Accreditation website at https://osse.dc.gov/page/school-service-provider-certification for full details on the following licenses:

  A. School Audiologist

  B. Reading Specialist

  C. School Psychologist

  D. School Social Worker

  E. School Speech Pathologist

Administrative Services Credentials

For a list of documents required to apply for administrative services credentials, see https://osse.dc.gov/page/principal-and-assistant-principal-certification.

I. Initial Administrator Credential (available to applicants who do not meet current requirements for a standard credential; valid 2 years; nonrenewable)—candidate:
  A. Holds a completed bachelor's degree;
  B. Has completed an approved program that leads to a state certification in school leadership and supervision;
      or
      Holds a valid full principal license in another state;
      or
      Holds a completed master's degree or higher;
  C. Has completed at least 2 years of school-based teaching, instructional leadership, or pupil services experience. Substitute teaching experience does not apply.
II. Standard Administrator Credential (valid 4 years; renewable)—candidate:
  A. Holds a completed bachelor's degree;
  B. Has completed an approved program that leads to a state certification in school leadership and supervision;
      or
      Holds a completed master's degree or higher;
  C. Has completed 4 years of school-based teaching, instructional leadership, or pupil services experience. Substitute teaching experience does not apply.
  D. Has passing scores for the DC-required school leadership licensure exam.

Teacher, Service Provider, and Administrator Licensure Renewal Requirements

I. Option A: Renewal by Performance Evaluation Rating (available to applicants currently employed by a DC LEA)
  A. Performance evaluation reviews must have been conducted while applicant was an employee of a DC LEA that administers an official educator performance evaluation system accepted by OSSE for the purposes of obtaining a state educator credential.
  B. Performance evaluation reviews must have been administered by the same DC LEA during the applicable renewal cycle of the credential being renewed.
  C. Applicant must have achieved at least an Effective or equivalent performance rating for at least 3 school years of the 4-year validity term of the credential. The ratings must be achieved based upon a summative or student growth component of the evaluation system.
  D. The assignment area of the performance evaluation review must have been conducted for the same assignment area of the credential being renewed.
II. Option B: Renewal by Completion of Professional Development Training Activity Hours
  A. Applicants must submit documentation verifying satisfactory completion of the

equivalent of 120 hours of professional development (PD) training activities completed within the 4-year term of the credential being renewed.

B.   The equivalent of 120 hours equals 120 actual clock hours of instruction/activity time completed, or 8 college credit hours, or a combination of both. One college credit hour equals 15 clock hours.

C.   A minimum of the equivalent of 60 hours must be directly related to the content area of the credential being renewed. The additional hours may align with any of the areas in the table on the website linked in letter E, below.

D.   The hours may be accrued by completion of college coursework or completion of training activities delivered by the employing local education agency, national education organizations, related industry organizations, and/or accredited PD provider organizations.

E.   For required content of PD training activities and required documentation, see https://osse.dc.gov/page/option-b-%E2%80%93-renewal-completion-professional -development-training-activity-hours.

Florida

The Bureau of Educator Certification at the Florida Department of Education determines individualized eligibility and testing requirements for certification. After an application for certification is on file, the Bureau will issue the applicant an Official Statement of Status of Eligibility. This statement will indicate individualized eligibility and testing requirements; these may include the Florida Teacher Certification Exams (FTCE) or, for candidates seeking certification in educational leadership, the Florida Educational Leadership Exam (FELE). Contact the Bureau (see Appendix 1) for complete information.

Types of Certificates

I. Professional Certificate Eligibility Requirements
   A renewable professional certificate, valid for 5 school years, may be issued to an applicant who meets all of the following:
   A. Files a completed application, including official degree transcripts and a complete fingerprint report that has been cleared by the Florida Department of Law Enforcement and the FBI;
   B. Holds a bachelor's or higher degree from an acceptable institution of higher learning;
   C. Has an acceptable major in a single subject in which Florida offers certification or meets specialization requirements in the subject, or, for subjects requiring only a bachelor's degree, has received a passing score on the Florida State–developed or Florida State–approved subject area examination for each subject or field to be shown on the certificate;
   D. Has obtained a 2.5 grade point average on a 4.0 scale in each subject shown on the certificate;
   E. Has received a passing score on the Florida General Knowledge Test;
   F. Has received a passing score on the Florida Professional Education Test;
   G. Has received a passing score on the Florida State–developed or Florida State–approved subject area examination for each subject or field to be shown on the certificate;
   H. Meets professional preparation requirements (see IV, below); *and*
   I. Successfully demonstrates professional education competencies identified by Florida statutes and administrative rules.
II. Temporary Certificate Eligibility Requirements
   A. A nonrenewable, temporary certificate, valid for 3 school years, may be issued to an applicant who satisfies I, A–D, of the above requirements for the professional certificate. Requirement I, E, must be satisfied within 1 calendar year from the date of employment under the Temporary Certificate.

III. Professional Certificate Renewal
   A. Completion of 6 semester hours of appropriate college credit, or 120 approved Florida in-service (staff-development) points specific to the subject(s) shown on the certificate, or training/course work related to the educational goals and performance standards outlined in Florida statutes during each 5-year validity period
      1. Beginning July 1, 2014, credit must include 1 semester hour or 20 approved Florida in-service (staff-development) points in teaching students with disabilities.

IV. Professional Preparation Requirements for Academic, Administrative, Degreed Vocational, and Specialty Class Coverages (PreK–12)
   A. Completes an undergraduate teacher education program at an institution approved by the Florida State Board of Education or another state
      or
   B. Possesses a valid full-time standard teaching certificate issued by another state or by the National Board for Professional Teaching Standards
      or
   C. Professional Preparation (for applications received beginning January 1, 2016)
      1. Completes a minimum of 15 semester hours in the following professional education areas:
         a. Classroom management with a focus on creating safe learning environments in which effective teaching and learning can take place by promoting a physically, emotionally, socially, and academically secure climate for students;
         b. Child and adolescent development, including theories and principles of learning;
         c. Educational assessment practices that include analysis and application of data from statewide standardized assessments and other multiple sources to improve instruction and learning;
         d. Effective instructional techniques, strategies, and materials to meet the needs of diverse learners, including students with disabilities;
         e. For certificate subject coverages classified by rule as academic or degreed vocational, applications of research-based instructional practices in reading; *and*
         f. Instructional strategies for teaching students of limited English proficiency, including instruction in the English language and development of the student's mastery of the 4 language skills of listening, speaking, reading, and writing.
      2. Completes practical experience in teaching, satisfied by 1 of the following methods:
         a. One year of full-time teaching experience in an approved elementary or secondary school,
            or
         b. Six semester hours earned in a college student teaching or supervised internship completed in an elementary or a secondary school in which the

candidate demonstrates ability to positively impact student learning growth with a diverse population of students.

    3. The requirements of professional preparation in C, 1, directly above, are not applicable and shall not be required for school social worker or speech-language impaired certification.

  D. For other options, see http://www.fldoe.org/teaching/certification/general-cert-requirements/professional-preparation-edu-competenc.stml.

Elementary School

  I. General Requirements
    A. General and professional preparation. See Professional Certificate Eligibility, above.
  II. Specific Requirements
    A. Bachelor's or higher degree with a major in elementary education that includes teaching reading at the K–6 level,
      or
      See https://www.flrules.org/gateway/RuleNo.asp?title=CERTIFICATION&ID=6A-4.0151.

Middle Grades (5–9)

  I. General Requirements
    A. General and professional preparation. See Professional Certificate Eligibility, above.
  II. Specific Requirements
    A. Middle Grades English: a bachelor's or higher degree major in middle grades English, or a bachelor's or higher degree in another subject or field and 18 semester hours above the freshman level in English, including specific courses in grammar and composition, speech, and 9 semester hours of literature
    B. Middle Grades Mathematics: a bachelor's or higher degree major in middle grades mathematics, or a bachelor's degree in another subject or field and 18 semester hours in mathematics, including specific courses in calculus (pre-calculus/trigonometry), geometry, probability, or statistics
    C. Middle Grades General Science: a bachelor's or higher degree major in middle grades general science, or a bachelor's or higher degree in another subject or field and 18 semester hours in science with associated lab experience, including specific courses in biology, earth-space science/earth science, and chemistry or physics
    D. Middle Grades Social Science: a bachelor's or higher degree major in middle grades social science, or a bachelor's or higher degree in another subject or field and 18 semester hours in social science, including specific courses in Western civilization (or European, Asian, African, Latin American, or Middle Eastern history), economics, United States government, geography, and 6 semester hours in United States history

Secondary School (6–12)

I.   General Requirements
  A.   General and professional preparation. See Professional Certificate Eligibility, above.
II. Special requirements for subject fields: agriculture, biology, business education, chemistry, drama, earth-space science, English, family and consumer science, marketing, mathematics, physics, social science (general), and engineering and technology education
  A.   Florida offers alternative plans for certification in the subject fields.
     1.   For all subject fields, applicants may qualify by having a bachelor's or higher degree with a major or 30 semester hours of specified courses in the field for which certification is being sought.
     2.   For English and social science, applicants may also qualify by having a bachelor's or higher degree with at least 30 semester hours in the field or in related fields for which certification is being sought. (See http://fldoe.org/teaching/certification/certificate-subjects/ for details on specific course distributions.)
     3.   For mathematics and the sciences, applicants may also qualify by 2 additional certification routes. In all cases, the applicant must have a bachelor's or higher degree with at least 30 semester hours of specified courses in the field or related fields for which certification is being sought. (See http://fldoe.org/teaching/certification/certificate-subjects/ for details on specific course distributions.)

All Grades (K–12)

I.   General Requirements
  A.   General and professional preparation. See Professional Certificate Eligibility, above.
II. Special requirements for subject fields: art, computer science, dance, English for speakers of other languages, exceptional student education, health, hearing impaired, humanities, music, physical education, reading, speech-language impaired, visually impaired, and world languages (See http://fldoe.org/teaching/certification/certificate-subjects/.)
  A.   Florida offers alternative plans for certification in the subject fields.
     1.   For all subject fields except reading and speech-language impaired, applicants may qualify by having a bachelor's or higher degree with a major of 30 semester hours of specified courses in the field for which certification is being sought.
     2.   For world language specializations in Arabic, Chinese, Farsi, French, German, Greek, Haitian Creole, Hebrew, Hindi, Italian, Japanese, Latin, Portuguese, Russian, Spanish, and Turkish, applicants may also qualify by 4 additional certification routes.
     3.   For reading, applicants may qualify by having a master's or higher degree with a major or 30 semester hours to include specified course work and a supervised reading practicum. (See http://fldoe.org/teaching/certification/certificate-subjects/ for details on specific distributions.)
     4.   For speech-language impaired, applicants may qualify by having a master's or higher degree major or 60 semester hours to include specified course work and a supervised clinical practice. (See http://fldoe.org/teaching/certification/certificate-subjects/ for details on specific distributions.)

Administration

I.   General Requirements
  A.   General and professional preparation. See Professional Certificate Eligibility, above.
II. Educational Leadership, Level One Certificate
  A.   Holds a master's or higher degree from an accredited institution
  B.   Documents successful completion of the Florida Educational Leadership Core Curriculum, through 1 of the following plans:
    1.   Successful completion of a Florida Department of Education–approved preservice program in educational leadership offered by an accredited institution;
    2.   A graduate degree major in educational administration, administration and supervision, or educational leadership awarded by an approved institution;
    3.   Successful completion of an Educational Leadership training program approved by the Florida Department of Education and offered by a Florida public school district;
    4.   A graduate degree with a major in a subject other than educational administration, administration and supervision, or educational leadership, and successful completion of a Department of Education–approved modified Florida program in educational leadership offered by an accredited institution; *or*
    5.   A graduate degree with a major in a subject other than educational administration, administration and supervision, or educational leadership awarded by an accredited institution, and 30 semester hours of graduate credit in each of the Florida-specified principal leadership standard areas and an internship or a course with associated field experience in educational leadership.
III. School Principal, Level Two Certificate
  A.   Holds a valid professional certificate covering educational leadership, school administration, or school administration/supervision,
       and
       Documents successful performance of the duties of school principalship,
       and
       Demonstrates successful performance of the competencies of the school principalship, which shall be verified by the Florida district school superintendent.

Educational Media Specialist (PreK–12)

I.   General Requirements
  A.   General and professional preparation. See Professional Certificate Eligibility, above.
II. Specialization Requirements
  A.   Bachelor's or higher degree with a major in educational media or library science, *or*
  B.   Bachelor's or higher degree with 30 semester hours in educational media or library science, including the following areas:

1. Management of library media programs
2. Collection development
3. Library media resources
4. Reference sources and services
5. Organization of collections
6. Design and production of educational media

School Counselor (Grades PreK–12)

I.   General Requirements
    A.   General and professional preparation. See Professional Certificate Eligibility, above.
II. Specialization Requirements
    A.   Master's or higher degree with a graduate major in guidance and counseling or in counselor education that includes 3 semester hours in a supervised counseling practicum in an elementary or secondary school,
        or
    B.   Master's or higher degree with 30 semester hours of graduate credit in guidance and counseling, including 3 semester hours in each of the following areas:
        1. Principles and administration of guidance
        2. Student appraisal
        3. Education and career development
        4. Learning, personality theory, and human development
        5. Counseling theories and individual counseling techniques
        6. Group counseling
        7. Consultation skills
        8. Legal and ethical issues
        9. Counseling techniques for special populations
        10. Supervised practicum in an elementary or secondary school

Note: Noncitizens, exchange teachers, and resident aliens and refugees may be issued a certificate on the same basis as citizens of the United States, provided they meet exact and specific qualifications established by the Florida State Board of Education. Proof of eligibility to work in the United States is required for noncitizens.

Georgia

Certification Classification

I. Categories
   A. Renewable (except for the Life certificate, valid 5 years, during which educator must satisfy standard renewal requirements)
      1. Performance-Based Professional
         a. Issued to teachers who are evaluated on the statewide evaluation system and leaders who have completed Georgia Professional Standards Commission (GaPSC)–approved performance-based Educational Leadership programs
         b. Not issued in service fields
         c. Indicates completion of all professional and Georgia-specific requirements for certification in the field
      2. Standard Professional
         a. Issued to those meeting professional requirements for certification who are not evaluated on the statewide evaluation system or do not meet the requirements for the Performance-Based Professional
         b. Indicates completion of all professional requirements for certification in the field
         c. May initially be issued without completion of all Georgia-specific requirements
      3. Advanced Professional
         a. Issued to teachers with expert classroom practice as evidenced by teachingexperience and 1 of the following: advanced degree in a teaching field beyond the initial preparation program; a valid professional certificate in Curriculum and Instruction or Instructional Technology; or a valid National Board for Professional Teaching Standards (NBPTS) Certification
         b. Not issued in service or leadership fields; indicates completion of all professional and Georgia-specific requirements for certification in the field
      4. Lead Professional
         a. Issued to qualified teachers who promote, support, and expand opportunities for teacher leadership in grades P–12, as evidenced by teaching experience, completion of related education/training, and successful completion of a Teacher Leadership assessment
         b. Not issued in service or leadership fields
         c. Indicates completion of all professional and Georgia-specific requirements for certification in the field
      5. Life: issued prior to July 1, 1974; remains valid for current holders
      6. Certificate of Eligibility
         a. Issued to individuals meeting all requirements for a particular certificate

with the sole exception of employment by a Georgia local unit of administration (LUA)

  b. Issued to individuals renewing their certificates who do not have at least 1 year of experience in Georgia.

  c. May be converted to the specified certificate upon employment

 7. Retired Educator Certificate

  a. Issued to individuals previously holding professional Georgia certification who have retired as verified by the Georgia Teacher's Retirement System

  b. Acceptable for substitute teaching only

B. Non-Renewable (valid for up to 5 years; except for the Pre-Service certificate, issuance must be requested by an employing Georgia LUA)

 1. Pre-Service (valid 5 years, issued at the request of an educator preparation provider, may be extended)

  a. Issued to candidates enrolled in state-approved educator preparation programs and participating in field and clinical experiences in Georgia schools

  b. Requires exposure to the Georgia Code of Ethics for Educators and successful state background check

  c. Authorizes the holder to participate in supervised field experience, clinical practice, student teaching, or residency work in Georgia schools

 2. Induction (valid 3 years, may be extended in some circumstances): includes 4 pathways with distinct requirements

  a. Induction Pathway 1: issued to those who have completed educator preparation programs in Georgia; indicates that all professional requirements for certification in the field have been met; outstanding Georgia-specific requirements for Professional certification include 3 years of teaching experience

  b. Induction Pathway 2: issued to those who have completed educator preparation programs based outside of Georgia but completed field and clinical experiences in a Georgia school; indicates that all professional requirements for certification in the field have been met; outstanding Georgia-specific requirements for Professional certification include 3 years of teaching experience

  c. Induction Pathway 3: issued to those who have completed all parts of an educator preparation program outside of Georgia and to those holding professional out-of-state educator certificates that do not qualify for a Georgia Professional certificate; indicates that all professional requirements for certification in the field have been met; outstanding Georgia-specific requirements for Professional certification may include up to 3 years of teaching experience

  d. Induction Pathway 4: issued at the request of an employing Georgia LUA to those meeting minimum education and testing requirements who have not met professional requirements for certification; with the exception of certain career and technical fields, the maximum usable validity of this certificate is 3 years

3. Supplemental Induction (valid for up to 3 years)
   a. Issued to Induction educators teaching outside of their base certificate field
   b. For most teaching fields, issuance requires passing a content assessment in the field
   c. For endorsements, issuance only requires LUA request
4. Non-Renewable Professional (validity period depends on the field; non-renewable)
   a. Non-Renewable Professional teaching fields are issued for 3 years to those professionally certified educators teaching out-of-field; outstanding requirements for renewable professional certification may include content assessment or approved program completion.
   b. Non-Renewable Professional endorsements are issued for 2 years to professionally certified educators; outstanding requirements for renewable professional certification include approved program completion.
   c. Non-Renewable Performance-Based Professional leadership certificates are issued for 5 years to those employed in a leadership position who hold at least a master's degree; outstanding requirements for renewable professional certification may include content assessment or approved program completion.
   d. Non-Renewable Professional leadership certificates are issued for 1 year to Educators holding professional out-of-state leadership certificates applying for initial certification that are missing the required content assessment.
   e. Non-Renewable Professional service certificates are issued for 3 to 5 years to individuals who have not met certain requirements for renewable professional certification in a service field; outstanding requirements for renewable professional certification may include content assessment, approved program completion, or completion of a higher degree.
   f. Non-Renewable Professional certificates may also be issued for 1 year to educators lacking standard renewal requirements.
5. International Exchange (valid for 3 years; may be extended in some circumstances): issued at the request of an employing Georgia LUA to educators certified in other nations who wish to teach in Georgia schools
6. Waiver (valid for up to 1 year; may be extended in some circumstances): issued at the discretion of the GaPSC to educators who have not satisfied all certification requirements
7. Military Support Certificate (valid for 5 years)
   a. Standard Professional Military Support Certificate
      i. Issued to military service members and spouses of service members applying for Georgia certification based on reciprocity
      ii. Valid for 5 years in order to meet any outstanding special Georgia requirements (content assessment, ethics exit assessment, and course in identifying exceptional children)
      iii. Converted to a renewable Standard Professional certificate upon meeting special Georgia requirements

       b. Military Support Induction Certificates (issued to military service members and military spouses):

          i. Military Support Induction Pathway 1 (valid 3 years): issued to those who have completed educator preparation programs in Georgia; outstanding Georgia-specific requirements for Professional certification may include 3 years of teaching experience.

          ii. Military Support Induction Pathway 2 (valid 3 years): issued to those who have completed educator preparation programs outside of Georgia but have completed field and clinical experiences in a Georgia school; indicates that all professional requirements for certification in the field have been met; outstanding Georgia-specific requirements for Professional certification may include 3 years of teaching experience.

          iii. Military Support Induction Pathway 3 (valid 3 years): issued to those who have completed all parts of an educator preparation program outside of Georgia and to those holding professional out-of-state educator certificates who do not qualify for a Georgia Professional certificate; indicates that all professional requirements for certification in the field have been met; outstanding Georgia-specific requirements for Professional certification may include up to 3 years of teaching experience.

          iv. Military Support Induction Pathway 4 (maximum usable validity 3 years in 1-year increments, with the exception of certain career and technical fields): issued at the request of an employing Georgia LUA to those meeting minimum education and testing requirements who have not met professional requirements for certification.

II. Types

    A. Adjunct (valid for 1 year, renewable)

       1. Issued at the request of an employing Georgia LUA to individuals with specific knowledge, skills and experience in various professions

       2. Authorizes the holder to provide instruction for up to 50 percent of the school day in specific subjects in grades 6–12 only

    B. Clearance (valid for 5 years, renewable): issued at the request of the employing Georgia LUA to educators who satisfactorily complete fingerprint and criminal background check requirements and do not have a certificate that is currently revoked or suspended in Georgia or any other state

    C. Educational Interpreter: issued to individuals who serve as sign language interpreters in schools

    D. Leadership: issued in fields that prepare an educator to administer or supervise a Georgia LUA, school, or school program

    E. Non-Instructional Aide: issued to eligible individuals hired to perform routine non-instructional tasks; has no assigned level

    F. Paraprofessional (valid for 5 years, renewable): issued to eligible individuals hired as paraprofessionals; requires passing an assessment or meeting a minimum education level of an associate's degree or completion of 60 semester hours of college course work; has no assigned level

G. Permit (valid for 3 years, renewable): issued at the request of an employing Georgia LUA to retired teachers and individuals with specific experience in the teaching fields of performing arts (art, music, dance, and drama), foreign language, JROTC, Career, Technical, and Agricultural Education (CTAE) specializations, and the position of superintendent

H. Service: issued in fields that prepare an individual to provide support services to students, school personnel, and school operations

I. Support Personnel: issued at the request of an employing Georgia LUA to individuals who serve in positions of leadership over support functions in the LUA; has no assigned level

J. Teaching: issued in fields that prepare an educator to teach subject matter offered as part of school curriculum

III. Certificate Fields

A. Teaching Fields

1. Early Childhood: Birth through Kindergarten; Early Childhood Education (P–5); Special Education General Curriculum / Early Childhood Education (P–5)

2. Middle Grades (Grades 4 – 8): Language Arts; Math; Reading; Science; Social Science

3. Secondary (Grades 6 – 12): Behavioral Science; Biology; Chemistry; Earth / Space Science; Economics; English; Geography; History; Mathematics; Physics; Political Science; Science; Speech

4. Career, Technical, and Agricultural Education (Grades 6 – 12): Agriculture; Business; Family and Consumer Sciences; Healthcare Science; Marketing; Career and Technical Specializations

5. P–12 Fields: Art; Dance; Drama; English for Speakers of Other Languages (ESOL); Engineering and Technology; Gifted P–12; Health; Health and Physical Education; Music; Reading Specialist

6. Special Education (Grades P–12): Special Education Adapted Curriculum; Behavior Disorders; Deaf Education; Special Education General Curriculum; Learning Disabilities; Physical and Health Disabilities; Special Education Preschool (Ages 3–5); Visual Impairment

7. Foreign Languages (Grades P–12): American Sign Language; Arabic; Chinese (Mandarin); Farsi; French; German; Greek (Classical); Hebrew; Hindi; Italian; Japanese; Korean; Latin; Portuguese; Russian; Spanish; Swahili; Turkish; Urdu

B. Service Fields: Audiology; Curriculum and Instruction; Instructional Technology; Media Specialist; School Counseling; School Nutrition Director; School Psychology; School Social Work; Speech and Language Pathology; Teacher Leadership

C. Leadership Fields: Educational Leadership; Superintendent

D. Endorsements: Birth through Age 5; Career Exploration; Career Technical Instruction; Coaching; Computer Science; Coordinated Career Academic Education; Culinary Arts; ESOL; Gifted In-Field; Intervention Specialist; K–5 Mathematics; K–5 Science; Middle Grades; Online Teaching; Reading; Safety and Driver Education; Special Education Deaf Education; Special Education Physical and Health Disabilities; Special Education Preschool Ages 3–5; Special Education Transition Specialist; Special Education Visual Impairment; Student Support Team

Coordinator; Teacher Leader; Teacher Support and Coaching; Work-Based Learning; Dual Immersion Early Childhood Education; Autism; STEM education. Each endorsement requires a prerequisite certificate and may be added by completing course work within an approved college or staff development endorsement program.

IV. Certificate Levels

A. Indicate the highest degree level recognized by the GaPSC that has been awarded to the certificate holder, according to the following guidelines:

1. Level 1 (Selected Career, Technical, and Agricultural Education fields only): completion of a high school diploma or the GED equivalent

2. Level 2 (Selected Career, Technical, and Agricultural Education fields only): completion of an associate's degree or GaPSC-determined equivalent

3. Level 4: completion of a bachelor's degree or GaPSC-determined equivalent; a bachelor's degree is the minimum degree requirement for teaching certification except for selected Career, Technical, and Agricultural Education fields

4. Level 5: completion of a master's degree or GaPSC-determined equivalent

5. Level 6: completion of an education specialist degree or GaPSC-determined equivalent or completion of a minimum of 36 semester hours of course work and comprehensive examinations required for a level 7 doctoral degree

6. Level 7: completion of a Ph.D., Ed.D. or GaPSC-determined equivalent

B. An educator who earns an advanced degree in Educational Leadership may be assigned Leader Level in addition to a general certificate level; a leader level is used for placement on the state salary schedule only if the holder is employed in a designated leadership position

V. Renewal Requirements

A. Standard renewal requirements for employed Georgia educators may be fulfilled by successful completion of a Professional Learning Plan (PLP) or Professional Learning Goals (PLG) established by the educator with oversight by his/her supervisor during the validity period of the certificate.

B. Standard renewal requirements for non-employed Georgia educators may be fulfilled by completion of 1 of the following options within 5 years of the date of renewal:

1. Six semester hours of college course work

2. Ten Georgia Professional Learning Units earned through an approved provider

3. Ten approved Continuing Education Units

4. One full year of acceptable educator experience earned in another state

5. Retaking and passing the Georgia Assessments for the Certification of Educators (GACE) content assessment in the field(s) of certification

C. Educators with less than 1 year of acceptable teaching experience in the state of Georgia while holding a professional certificate will receive a Certificate of Eligibility. The certificate will be issued at the request of an employing LUA.

D. Educators employed by a Georgia LUA at the time of renewal must undergo a criminal record check.

E. Renewal Cycle

1. Georgia certificates usually have a beginning date of July 1 and an ending date of June 30.

2. Valid certificates may be renewed from December 1 of the year preceding

the ending validity date to September 30 of the calendar year in which the certificate expires.

Routes to Teaching Certification

I. Traditional Route to Induction Certification
    A. Requirements:
        1. Hold at least a bachelor's degree, except for certain career, technical, and agricultural education fields
        2. Complete all requirements of state-approved certification program, including field experience or clinical practice
        3. Complete applicable Special Georgia Requirements, including content assessment
    B. Certification program may lead to a degree (bachelor's or advanced) or may be a certification-only postbaccalaureate program
    C. Induction Pathway 1, 2, or 3 certificate will be issued upon employment depending on the location of the certification program and field experience
    D. Requirements to convert from Induction to Professional certification will include 3 years of successful teaching experience
II. Interstate reciprocity
    A. Requirements:
        1. Hold a renewable, professional teaching certificate in another US state
        2. Complete applicable Special Georgia Requirements, including content assessment; some Special Georgia Requirements may be deferred until renewal of the initial certificate
    B. Induction Pathway 3 or Standard Professional certificate will be issued depending on the years of acceptable experience
III. Alternative Route to Certification: Georgia offers a nontraditional certification preparation program known as Georgia Teacher Academy for Preparation and Pedagogy (GaTAPP).
    A. Admission Requirements:
        1. Content assessment or degree major in the teaching field
        2. Employment by a Georgia LUA
        3. Minimum of a bachelor's degree
        4. Basic skills assessment
        5. Ethics Entry assessment
    B. Program Framework:
        1. Candidate Support Team trained in Coaching Standards and GaTAPP Assessments
        2. School-based Administrator
        3. School-based Mentor
        4. Provider Supervisor
        5. Content Specialist (May be dual role for existing member)
        6. Individualized based on Candidate Performance Assessment Data
        7. Job-embedded Clinical Practice
    C. Induction Pathway 4 certificate is issued upon employment.

Special Georgia Requirements

I. Content Knowledge
   A. The Georgia Assessments for the Certification of Educators (GACE) are the accepted content assessments for most certification fields.
      1. GACE content assessments have 2 passing levels: Induction and Professional; until further notice, all passing scores earned on GACE assessments will be treated as Professional level scores even if the official score report reflects an Induction level score.
      2. The Praxis exam is the state-approved content assessment for the field of Speech and Language Pathology, and the proficiency exams offered by the American Council on the Teaching of Foreign Languages (ACTFL) are the state-approved content assessments for foreign language fields in which there is no GACE exam available.
      3. Georgia does not have a content assessment for the fields of Audiology, Dance, Drama, School Nutrition Director, School Social Work, Speech, Physical and Health Disabilities, Special Education Preschool, Visual Impairment, and some foreign language fields. In fields for which there is no state-approved or state-accepted content assessment, passing a content assessment for certification is not required.
   B. The following individuals are required to pass the GACE content assessment for the desired certification field at the Induction level or higher, unless meeting exemption criteria:
      1. Applicants seeking an Induction certificate through any of the 4 pathways, with the following exceptions:
         a. Applicants for Induction Pathway 4 certification in Special Education Consultative fields are not required to pass the content assessment; however, they will need to satisfy this requirement before the certificate can be converted.
         b. Applicants for Induction Pathway 4 certification who are enrolled in a GaTAPP program may not be required to pass the content assessment if content knowledge has been verified in another way, such as a degree major in the field.
      2. Induction certificate holders applying to add a supplemental Induction field
         a. Applicants for the Supplemental in Special Education are not required to pass the content test; however, they will need to satisfy this requirement before the certificate can be converted.
      3. Applicants seeking an initial permit in a foreign language field
   C. The following applicants may be exempt from passing the GACE content knowledge assessment(s):
      1. Out-of-state certificate holders applying for initial Georgia certification who have worked in the same certificate field for all of the most recent 5 years or have passed the out-of-state content assessment required for issuance of the out-of-state certificate field
      2. Individuals holding valid National Board for Professional Teaching Standards

(NBPTS) Certification in the specific field, with the exception of the Middle Grades Generalist Field

3. Individuals seeking certification in a field for which the GaPSC has not adopted a content assessment

II. Standards of Conduct

A. An applicant for certification in Georgia must comply with the ethical standards of the profession.

B. An FBI background check (fingerprint) is required for employment in Georgia public schools and a Georgia criminal history check is required every 5 years for certificate renewal.

C. Applicants for certification must respond to background check questions on the application form.

III. Special Education

A. Certification in a teaching field, leadership field, or the service fields of Media Specialist and School Counseling requires completion of an approved course in the identification and education of children who have special educational needs

B. May be satisfied by NBPTS Certification

C. May be issued prior to completion of this requirement; the course must be completed as part of requirements to renew or convert the certificate

D. Out-of-state certificate holders applying for initial Georgia certification who have worked in the same certificate field for all of the most recent 5 years may exempt this requirement.

IV. Ethics Assessment: required as of January 1, 2015, for the following:

A. Issuance of an Induction Pathway 1, 2, or 4 certificate

B. Reissuance or conversion of an Induction Pathway 3 certificate

V. Content Pedagogy Assessment

A. The GaPSC-approved content pedagogy assessment is currently the Education Teacher Performance Assessment (edTPA).

B. A passing score is required for the following:

1. Issuance of an Induction Pathway 1 or 2 certificate on or after September 1, 2015

2. Conversion of an Induction Pathway 4 certificate on or after September 1, 2015

3. Reissuance or Conversion of an Induction Pathway 3 certificate attained on or after September 1, 2015; the following applicants may exempt this requirement:

   a. Applicants with at least 1 year of acceptable out-of-state educator experience

   b. Applicants who were required to pass another acceptable pedagogy assessment for completion of a state-approved educator preparation program or out-of-state certification

   c. Applicants who were not required to complete a content pedagogy assessment during their educator preparation program and pass the Praxis Performance Assessment for Teachers

Leadership Certificate Requirements

I. Tier II Performance-Based Educational Leadership
   A. Issued to Georgia educators who completed the previously approved Building Level of System Level Educational Leadership program
   B. Issued to Georgia educators who complete a state-approved Tier II Performance-Based Educational Leadership program
   C. Qualifications
      1. Complete a GaPSC-approved program at the education specialist level or higher
      2. Meet applicable Special Georgia Requirements, including GACE content assessment
   D. Non-Renewable Professional issued at the request of an employing Georgia LUA to the following individuals:
      1. Those holding an expired Georgia Performance-Based Educational Leadership certificate but not meeting renewal requirements (valid 1 year)
      2. Those holding a master's degree or higher and employed in a leadership position that supervises other leaders (valid 3 years)
II. Tier II Standard Professional Educational Leadership
   A. Issued to Georgia educators who completed a state-approved Educational Leadership program by September 30, 2009, and have fulfilled Special Georgia Requirements, including content assessment
   B. Issued to out-of-state educators holding professional leadership certification that meet 1 of the following requirements along with fulfilling Special Georgia Requirements, including content assessment:
      1. Have completed a leadership preparation program at the education specialist level or higher
      2. Have completed a leadership preparation program at the master's degree level and have at least 3 years of acceptable leadership experience
   C. Non-Renewable Professional (valid 1 year): Issued at the request of an employing Georgia LUA to those holding an expired Georgia Tier II Standard Professional Educational Leadership certificate but not meeting renewal requirements
III. Tier I Standard Professional Educational Leadership
   A. Issued to Georgia educators who complete a state-approved Tier I Educational Leadership program and have fulfilled Special Georgia Requirements, including content assessment
   B. Issued to educators applying to Georgia by reciprocity who completed a state-approved Educational Leadership program at the master's degree level and have fewer than 3 years of educational leadership experience while holding a professional certificate in another state
   C. Non-Renewable Tier I Professional issued at the request of an employing Georgia LUA to the following individuals:
      1. Those holding an expired Georgia Tier I Standard Educational Leadership certificate but not meeting renewal requirements (valid 1 year)
      2. Those holding a bachelor's degree or higher and employed in a leadership position that does not supervise other leaders (valid 3 years)

Certificate Level Upgrade Requirements

I. Accreditation Requirements: colleges/universities offering advanced degrees leading to upgrades must meet at least 1 of the following criteria at the time of admittance:
    A. Approved by the GaPSC
    B. Accredited by the National Council for Accreditation of Teacher Education (NCATE), the Teacher Education Accreditation Council (TEAC) or the Council for the Accreditation of Educator Preparation (CAEP)
    C. Hold a Carnegie Classification of Research University-Very High Research Activity (RU/VH) or Research University-High Research Activity (RU/H)
II. Certificate and Degree Requirements
    A. The following certificates may be upgraded:
        1. Renewable, professional certificates; includes Standard Professional, Performance-Based Professional, Advanced Professional, and Lead Professional
        2. Induction Pathway 1, 2, or 3 certificates
    B. The field or degree major of the advanced degree program must be closely related to a field in which the educator is certified.
        1. The certificate field must be one that is currently offered by the GaPSC.
        2. If the certificate field in which the educator completes an advanced degree is not a leadership field, the resulting level upgrade will apply to all fields held.
        3. An educator who earns an advanced degree in Educational Leadership may be assigned a Leader Level in addition to a general certificate level; a leader level is used for placement on the state salary schedule only if the holder is employed in a designated leadership position.
    C. The certificate level may not be upgraded by completing an initial certification program in a field in which the educator has already completed such a program.
    D. An educator may upgrade and add a new field simultaneously by completing an advanced degree that leads to certification in a new field and fulfilling any applicable Special Georgia Requirements.
III. Grandfathering Timelines: Advanced degrees started as late as January 2013 may fall under less rigorous requirements; please visit www.gapsc.com for more information.

Hawaii

Licenses

I. Standard License
   A. This is a National Association of State Directors of Teacher Education and Certification (NASDTEC) Stage 3 License whose requirements include that the individual:
      1. Hold a minimum of a bachelor's degree,
      2. Complete a State-approved Teacher Education Program,
         and
      3. Meet all jurisdiction-specific requirements of the issuing Member Jurisdiction.
   B. Routes to Obtain the Standard License
      Note: All routes require completion of the Standard License application online at hawaiiteacherstandardsboard.org.
      1. Applicants who will complete an Educator Preparation Program (EPP) prior to licensure but do not hold a teaching license in any state must submit:
         a. Verification of completion of preparation program,
         b. Verification of meeting basic skills and content knowledge expertise,
            and
         c. Verification of at least 3 out of the past 5 years of satisfactory full-time teaching in Hawaii or another state.
      2. Applicants who hold a current, valid National Board for Professional Teaching Standards (NBPTS) Certificate and a current, valid out-of-state teaching license must submit:
         a. Copy of current, valid NBPTS Certificate,
         b. Copy of current valid out-of-state license,
            and
         c. Verification of at least 3 out of the past 5 years of satisfactory full-time teaching in Hawaii or another state.
      3. Applicants who hold a current, valid out-of-state teaching license with the Meritorious New Teacher Candidate (MNTC) designation must submit:
         a. Copy of current, valid out-of-state license with the MNTC designation,
            and
         b. Verification of at least 3 out of the past 5 years of satisfactory full-time teaching in Hawaii or another state.
      4. Applicants who hold a teaching license issued for the first time in another state since July 1, 2006, must submit:
         a. Hawaii Teacher Standards Board (HTSB) Form OS3009 or a copy of the out-of-state license, if that state's licensing agency does not have a public license look-up,
            and

b.   Verification of at least 3 out of the past 5 years of satisfactory full-time teaching in Hawaii or another state.

5.   Applicants who have held a valid, unrevoked teaching license from another state for at least 3 out of the past 5 years must submit:

a.   HTSB Form OS3009 or a copy of the out-of-state license, if that state's licensing agency does not have a public license look-up,

b.   Verification of basic skills and content knowledge expertise using Hawaii or options from state that issued license,
and

c.   Verification of at least 3 out of the past 5 years of satisfactory full-time teaching in Hawaii or another state.

6.   For applicants who are recommended by a Hawaii preparation program under an alternative method for preparation, the Hawaii EPP will submit to the HTSB verification of the preparation program completion, basic skills and content knowledge.

a.   Applicants must submit verification of at least 3 out of the past 5 years of satisfactory full-time teaching in Hawaii or another state.

7.   Applicants who completed a non-US teacher education program must submit:

a.   National Association of Credential Evaluation Services (NACES) evaluation of foreign transcript providing evidence of completion of a teacher preparation program,

b.   Verification of basic skills and content knowledge expertise,
and

c.   Verification of at least 3 out of the past 5 years of satisfactory full-time teaching in Hawaii or another state.

II.   Provisional License (valid 3 years; nonrenewable)

A.   This is a NASDTEC Stage 2 License for applicants who have not yet met the jurisdiction-specific requirements for a Stage 3 license. Requirements include that the individual:

1.   Hold a minimum of a bachelor's degree,

2.   Complete a State-approved EPP,
and

3.   Submit verification of meeting basic skills and content knowledge.

III.   Career and Technical Education (CTE) Limited Standard License: teachers holding this license may only be assigned to the content field on their license and may not add any additional fields to the license.

A.   Applicants must apply online at http://www.hawaiiteacherstandardsboard.org and submit:

1.   An official transcript showing completion of an associate's degree from a regionally accredited college;

2.   Documentation of a minimum of 3 years of industry experience in the content field;

3.   Evidence of 1 of the following ways to meet content knowledge:

a.   Content test in the field,
or

    b. Current valid national industry certification in the content field,
     or
    c. Current valid industry license in the content field,
     or
    d. Thirty hours of course work in the content field;
    and
   4. Evidence of 1 of the following:
    a. Fifteen hours of pedagogy course work from a state-approved EPP in the grade level of the license,
     or
    b. Twelve hours of pedagogy course work from a state-approved EPP in the grade level of the license and a passing score on the Principles of Learning and Teaching (PLT) exam in the appropriate grade level of the license.

IV. Advanced License
  A. This is a NASDTEC Stage 4 License whose requirements include that the individual:
   1. Hold a minimum of a master's degree or the equivalent,
   2. Has completed an approved EPP,
   and
   3. Has met any jurisdiction-specific requirements beyond those required for the Stage 3 License of the issuing Member Jurisdiction.
  B. Routes to obtain the Advanced License
   1. For teachers who have held a Standard License in Hawaii or another state and have at least 5 years of experience within the past 8 years in Hawaii or another state:
    a. Submit the Advanced License application;
    b. Submit 1 of the following with application:
     i. An official transcript verifying a master's, specialist, or doctoral degree from a regionally accredited institution in an area relevant to the teaching field for which license is sought or a field that improves the practice of teaching (examples of which include but are not limited to curriculum and instruction, technology, reading, and teacher leadership), and this degree must be different from the one used to obtain a Standard License;
      or
     ii. Verification of a valid NBPTS Certificate and a current, valid out-of-state teaching license (Hawaii-licensed teachers do not need to submit a copy of the Standard License or NBPTS Certificate if it was earned while a Hawaii-licensed teacher);
      or
     iii. Verification of being designated a teacher leader by the Hawaii Department of Education, a Hawaii Charter School, or a member school of the Hawaii Association of Independent Schools;
     and
    c. Submit the Verification of Qualifying Experience for Advanced License to document satisfactory full-time teaching experience in the state which issued the Standard License for 5 out of past 8 years.

V. Documentation and Verification Procedures for Basic Skills and Content Knowledge
    Note: For a list of tests and scores, consult http://hawaiiteacherstandardsboard.org/
    content/licensure-test-categories/.
    A. Basic Skills
        1. Basic skills licensure tests in reading, writing, mathematics (applicants licensed
            out of state may use those tests to meet this requirement);
            or
        2. Bachelor's degree from a regionally accredited institution;
            or
        3. SAT in reading and mathematics and writing (for tests taken after March 2016;
            for tests taken before March 2016, Praxis score for writing can be used in lieu of
            SAT writing score);
            or
        4. ACT in reading and mathematics and writing.
    B. Content Knowledge
        1. Licensure test in the content field (applicants licensed out of state may use those
            tests to meet this requirement);
            or
        2. Content major in the content field from a bachelor's degree from a regionally
            accredited institution;
            or
        3. Thirty credit hours of course work in the content field, 15 of which must be
            upper-division courses, from a regionally accredited institution;
            or
        4. Advanced degree (master's, specialist, doctorate) in the content field from a
            regionally accredited institution;
            or
        5. NBPTS Certification in the content field.
        6. Elementary education (K–6) only: A total of 36 semester hours, including
            9 semester hours in each of the following core content areas: language arts,
            mathematics, science, social studies. At least 3 semester hours in each of the
            core content areas must be upper-division level.

Idaho

For the most current information, visit the "Rules Governing Uniformity" section of the "Rules of the Board Governing Education" at https://adminrules.idaho.gov/rules/current/08/080202.pdf. Additional details are available at the Certification website: http://www.sde.idaho.gov/cert-psc/.

General Requirements for All Teachers and Administrators

I. Standard Instructional Certificate (valid 5 years; 6 semester credit hours required every 5 years for renewal)
   A. Hold a baccalaureate degree from an accredited college or university
   B. Meet or exceed qualifying score(s) for appropriate Praxis II test(s). See http://www.ets.org/praxis/idaho/requirements.
      1. Applicants for certificates in Administration or Pupil Personnel Services are exempt from this requirement.
   C. Have a minimum of 20 semester credit hours, or 30 quarter credit hours, in the philosophical, psychological, and methodological foundations; in instructional technology; and in the professional subject matter, including at least 3 semester credit hours, or 4 quarter credit hours, in reading and its application to the content area
      1. Credit hours must include at least 6 semester credit hours, or 9 quarter credit hours, of student teaching in the grade range and subject areas as applicable to the endorsement
   D. Complete an approved teacher preparation program
   E. Receive an institutional recommendation from an accredited college or university specifying the grade ranges and subjects for which applicant is eligible to receive an endorsement
      1. Those seeking endorsement in a secondary grade range must complete preparation in at least 2 fields of teaching: 1 consisting of at least 30 semester credit hours or 45 quarter credit hours; and a second consisting of at least 20 semester credit hours or 30 quarter credit hours.
         a. Preparation of not less than 45 semester credit hours or 67 quarter credit hours in a single subject area may be used in lieu of the 2 teaching field requirements.
   F. Meet or exceed the qualifying score on the state board–approved content area and pedagogy assessments
II. Out-of-State Applications
   A. The State Department of Education or the Division of Career Technical Education, as applicable, is authorized to issue a 3-year interim certificate to applicants who hold a valid certificate or license from another state or other entity that participates in the National Association of State Directors of Teacher Education and Certification (NASDTEC) Interstate Agreement.

B. An educator who has graduated from a foreign institution may be issued a non-renewable, 3-year interim certificate.
1. Determination of eligibility for certification will be made by the State Department of Education.
2. All other procedures in effect at the time must be followed at the time of application.

III. Alternative Authorizations and Provisional Certificate Details and Requirements
A. Alternative Authorization—Teacher to New Certification (valid 1 year; may be renewed for 2 additional years with evidence of satisfactory progress toward completion of an approved alternative route preparation program). This option allows school districts to request additional certification when a professional position cannot be filled by someone with the correct certification.
1. Candidate must hold a baccalaureate degree and a valid Idaho instructional certificate before applying.
2. School district must provide supporting information attesting to the ability of the candidate to fill the position.
3. Candidate must participate in an approved alternative route preparation program through a participating college or university and the employing school district.
    a. Candidate must complete a minimum of 9 semester credit hours annually to maintain eligibility for renewal.
    b. Participating college or university shall provide procedures to assess and credit equivalent knowledge, dispositions, and relevant life/work experiences.
B. Alternative Authorization to Endorsement (candidates must meet all requirements of the chosen option)
1. Option I: An official statement from the college of education of competency in a teaching area or field is acceptable in lieu of courses for a teaching field if the statement is:
    a. Created in consultation with the department or division of the accredited college or university in which the competency is established, and
    b. Approved by the director of teacher education of the recommending college or university.
2. Option II: By earning national board certification in content-specific areas, teachers may gain endorsement in a corresponding subject area.
3. Option III: By earning a graduate degree in a content-specific area, candidates may add an endorsement in that area to a valid instructional certificate.
4. Option IV: Testing and/or Assessment. Two pathways are available to some teachers, depending upon endorsement(s) already held.
    a. Pathway 1: Endorsements may be added through state-approved testing and mentoring. The test must be successfully completed within the first year of authorization in an area closely compatible with an endorsement for which the candidate already qualifies. This pathway also requires the successful completion of a 1-year state-approved mentoring component.
    b. Pathway 2: Endorsements may be added through state-approved testing in an area less closely compatible with an endorsement for which the

candidate already qualifies; the test must be successfully completed within the first year of the authorization. This pathway also requires successful completion of a 1-year state-approved mentoring component and passing a final pedagogy assessment.

C. Alternative Authorization—Content Specialist (valid 1 year; may be renewed for 2 additional years). This option is an expedited route to certification for those who are highly qualified in a subject area to teach in a district with an identified need for teachers in that area.

1. Candidate must hold a baccalaureate degree or have completed all the requirements of a baccalaureate degree except the student teaching or practicum portion.

2. Hiring district shall ensure the candidate is qualified to teach in the area of identified need through demonstrated content knowledge via a combination of employment experience and education.

3. A consortium (comprised of a designee from the college/university to be attended or other state board–approved certification program, a representative from the school district, and the candidate) shall determine the preparation needed to meet the Standards for Initial Certification. This plan must include mentoring, a minimum of 1 classroom observation by the mentor per month, and annual progress goals.

4. The candidate must complete a minimum of 9 semester credit hours (or its equivalent of accelerated study) in education pedagogy prior to the end of the first year of authorization, with the number of required credits specified in the consortium-developed plan.

5. The candidate must enroll in and work toward completion of the alternative route preparation program through a participating college or university (or other state board-approved certification program) and the employing school district. Program attendance, participation, and completion are conditions of annual renewal.

D. Non-Traditional Routes to Certification (e.g., American Board for Certification of Teacher Excellence; Teach for America). To complete this non-traditional route, the candidate must earn interim certification (valid 3 years; available to candidates only once) by:

1. Holding a baccalaureate degree or higher from an accredited institution of higher education

2. Completing a state board–approved program

3. Passing state board–approved pedagogy and content knowledge exams

4. Completing the Idaho Department of Education background check

5. Completing a 2-year teacher mentoring program during the term of the interim certificate

6. Adhering to all laws and rules governing conduct, discipline, and professional standards under any Idaho certificate

7. Obtaining a valid renewable Idaho Educator Credential during the 3-year interim certification term

E. Emergency Provisional Certificate (valid 1 year; cannot be renewed)

       1.   In declared emergencies, the state board may authorize the issuance of provisional certificates based on not less than 2 years of college training.

IV. Career and Technical Education

    A. The Idaho State Division of Career and Technical Education is authorized to determine whether applicants meet requirements for instructing or administering professional-technical programs at the secondary and postsecondary levels. For additional information on CTE certification and endorsements, please see https://cte.idaho.gov/educators/ and https://adminrules.idaho.gov/rules/current/08/080202.pdf.

V. Renewal of Certification

    A. All 5-year clear credentials may be renewed upon completion of at least 6 semester credit hours of college courses within the 5-year period of validity. For administrators, 3 of the credits must be in the Framework for Teacher Evaluation.

VI. Criminal History and Background Check

    A. All individuals who work in Idaho public schools and have unsupervised contact with children, whether or not they hold certificates or are applying for certification, are required to have results of a criminal history check on file with the State Department of Education. Please see the Professional Standards Commission website at http://www.sde.idaho.gov/cert-psc/psc/ for details and current information.

VII. Administrator Certificates (valid 5 years; 6 semester credit hours required every 5 years to renew)

    A. Every person who serves as a superintendent, a director of special education, a secondary school principal, or principal of an elementary school with 8 or more teachers (including the principal), or is assigned to conduct the summative evaluation of certified staff, is required to hold an Administrator Certificate.

        1.   Certificate may be endorsed for service as a school principal, a superintendent, or a director of special education.

        2.   Assistant superintendents are required to hold the Superintendent endorsement.

        3.   Assistant principals or vice principals are required to hold the School Principal endorsement.

        4.   Directors of special education are required to hold the Director of Special Education endorsement.

        5.   Possession of an Administrator Certificate does not entitle the holder to serve as a teacher at a grade level for which the educator is not qualified or certificated.

        6.   All Administrator Certificates require candidates to meet the Idaho Standards for School Principals.

    B. School Principal Endorsement

        1.   Hold a master's degree from an accredited college or university

        2.   Have 4 years of full-time certificated experience working with PreK–12 students while under contract in an accredited school setting

        3.   Have completed an administrative internship in a state-approved program, or have 1 year of experience as an administrator in grades PreK–12

        4.   Provide verification of completion of a state-approved program of at least 30 semester credit hours or 45 quarter credit hours of graduate study in school administration for the preparation of school principals at an accredited college

or university. This program shall include the competencies of the Idaho Standards for School Principals.

    5.   Obtain an institutional recommendation

C. Superintendent Endorsement

    1.   Hold an education specialist or doctorate degree or complete a comparable post-master's sixth-year program at an accredited college or university

    2.   Have 4 years of full-time certificated/licensed experience working with PreK–12 students while under contract in an accredited school setting

    3.   Have completed an administrative internship in a state-approved program for the superintendent endorsement or have 1 year of out-of-state experience as an assistant superintendent or superintendent in grades PreK–12

    4.   Provide verification of completion of an approved program of at least 30 semester credit hours or 45 quarter credit hours of post-master's degree graduate study for the preparation of school superintendents at an accredited college or university. This program in school administration and interdisciplinary supporting areas shall include the competencies in Superintendent Leadership in addition to the competencies in the Idaho Standards for School Principals

    5.   Obtain an institutional recommendation

D. Director of Special Education Endorsement (K–12)

    1.   Hold a master's degree from an accredited college or university

    2.   Complete 4 years of full-time certificated/licensed experience working with PreK–12 students while under contract in a school setting

    3.   Obtain college or university verification of demonstrated the competencies of the Director of Special Education in Idaho Standards for Initial Certification of Professional School Personnel

    4.   Obtain college or university verification of demonstrated competencies in the following areas, in addition to the competencies in the Idaho Standards for School Principals: Concepts of Least Restrictive Environment; Post-School Outcomes and Services for Students with Disabilities Ages 3 to 21; Collaboration Skills for General Education Intervention; Instructional and Behavioral Strategies; Individual Education Programs (IEPs); Assistive and Adaptive Technology; Community-Based Instruction and Experiences; Data Analysis for Instructional Needs and Professional Training; Strategies to Increase Program Accessibility; Federal and State Laws and Regulations and School District Policies; Resource Advocacy; and Technology Skills for Referral Processes and Record Keeping

    5.   Complete an administrative internship/practicum in the area of administration of special education

    6.   Obtain an institutional recommendation

VIII. Pupil Service Staff Certificate

A. School counselors, school psychologists, speech-language pathologists, school social workers, school nurses, and school audiologists are required to hold the Pupil Service Staff Certificate, with the following endorsement(s) for which they qualify.

Occupational therapists and physical therapists may be required, as determined by the local educational agency, to hold the certificate, with the endorsements for which they qualify.

1. Standard Counselor Endorsement (K–12)
    a. Have a master's degree in school counseling
    b. Have completed 700 clock hours of supervised field experience, 75 percent of which must be in a K–12 school setting
    c. Obtain an institutional recommendation
2. Speech-Language Pathologist Endorsement
    a. Have a master's degree in speech-language pathology
    b. Have completed a state-approved program in speech-language pathology
    c. Obtain an institutional recommendation
3. Audiology Endorsement
    a. Have a master's degree in speech-language pathology
    b. Have completed a state-approved program in audiology
    c. Obtain an institutional recommendation
4. School Social Worker Endorsement
    a. Have a master's degree in social work (MSW)
    b. Have completed a school social work practicum in a K–12 setting (post-MSW extensive experience working with children and families may be substituted)
    c. Obtain an institutional recommendation
5. School Nurse Endorsement (valid 5 years; renewable)
    a. Hold a valid nursing (RN) license issued by the Idaho State Board of Nursing, and a baccalaureate degree in nursing, education, or a health-related field from an accredited institution
    b. Have completed 9 semester credit hours from a university or college in at least 3 of the following areas: health program management; child and adolescent development; counseling, psychology, or social work; or methods of instruction
    c. Two years of full-time (or part-time equivalent) school nursing, community health nursing, or any area of pediatric, adolescent, or family nursing experience

IX. Postsecondary Specialist Certificate (valid 5 years; renewable by application accompanied by a new written recommendation from a representative of the postsecondary institution at the level of college dean or higher)
A. Granted to a current academic faculty member whose primary employment is with any accredited Idaho postsecondary institution
B. Used primarily for distance education, virtual classroom programs, and public and postsecondary partnerships
C. Candidates must:
    1. Hold a master's degree or higher in the content area being taught
    2. Be currently employed by the postsecondary institution in the content area to be taught
    3. Supply a recommendation from the employing institution (i.e., the college dean)

X.   American Indian Language Certificate
    A.   Each Indian tribe shall provide to the State Department of Education the names of highly and uniquely qualified individuals who have been designated to teach the tribe's native language; these individuals may apply for this certificate.
    B.   The Office of Indian Education at the State Department of Education will process applications. Approved applications will be forwarded to the Office of Certification.
    C.   The Office of Certification will review the application and verify eligibility.
    D.   The State Department of Education will authorize eligible applicants to be American Indian Language teachers.

XI. Junior Reserve Officer Training Corps (ROTC) Instructors
    A.   Each school district with a Junior ROTC program shall provide the State Department of Education with a list of names of those who have completed an official armed forces training program to qualify as high school Junior ROTC instructors.
    B.   Each school district with a Junior ROTC program shall provide the State Department of Education with a notarized copy of instructors' certificate(s) of completion.

Illinois

Requirements for Illinois Licenses with Endorsements

I. Licensure requirements for applicants completing Illinois-approved programs for teaching
    A. Passing score on a test of basic skills, defined as:
        1. Test of Academic Proficiency (TAP 400);
            or
        2. ACT:
            a. Prior to September 1, 2015—Composite score of 22 or higher and a minimum score of 19 on the Combined English/Writing portion
            b. September 1, 2015, to September 9, 2016—Composite score of 22 or higher and a minimum score of 16 on the Writing portion
            c. September 10, 2016, and later—Composite score of 22 or higher and a minimum score of 6 on the Writing portion
            or
        3. SAT:
            a. Prior to March 5, 2016—Composite score of 1030 (critical reading + mathematics = 1030 or higher) and a minimum score of 450 on writing
            b. March 5, 2016, and later—Composite score of 1110 (evidence-based reading and writing + mathematics = 1110 or higher) *and* a minimum score of 26 on writing and language
            or
        4. Out-of-state test of basic skills that led to licensure in another state
        5. Test of basic skills scores are valid indefinitely.
        6. Passing score of the test of basic skills is required for student teaching or before the last semester or term of the internship.
        7. Those who seek to add a subsequent endorsement and have already passed an Illinois or other state's test of basic skills are not required to pass the test again.
        8. Those who seek to add a subsequent endorsement that requires a content-area test must pass the applicable Illinois content-area test. Out-of-state testing is not accepted.
    B. Passing score on the applicable content area test(s) prior to student teaching (or the last semester or term of internship if completing an approved program leading to an administrative or school service personnel endorsement)
        1. Content tests are valid indefinitely.
    C. Passing score on the Assessment of Professional Teaching (APT 188) test for program completion (teaching endorsements only) if student teaching was completed prior to August 31, 2015
        1. Individuals completing student teaching September 1, 2015, or after will be

required to pass the Education Teacher Performance Assessment (edTPA) instead of the Assessment of Professional Teaching (APT 188).

    2.   APT 188/edTPA scores are valid indefinitely.

D.   Completion of an approved Illinois educator preparation program for the type of endorsement sought that includes course work addressing:

    1.   Cross-categorical special education methods
       and

    2.   Methods of reading and reading in the content area.

    3.   Upon completion of the program, the Illinois institution will notify the Illinois State Board of Education (ISBE) via the Educator Licensure Information System (ELIS) that applicant qualifies for a license and/or endorsement. For details, consult http://www.isbe.net/licensure/requirements/endsmt_struct.pdf.

E.   Educators Completing an Alternative Preparation Program

    1.   Requirements for the alternative provisional educator and alternative provisional superintendent endorsement on an educator license with stipulations may be found at https://www.isbe.net/Pages/Educator-License-with-Stipulations.aspx.

II. Professional Educator License (PEL) Requirements for Applicants Trained Out-of-State or Out-of-Country for Teaching (valid 5 fiscal years; renewable upon completion of professional development requirements)

Note: PEL Checklist is available at https://www.isbe.net/Documents/PEL-Checklist-0817.pdf.

A.   Option 1

    1.   Bachelor's degree or higher from a regionally accredited institution of higher education

    2.   A valid out-of-state license

B.   Option 2

    1.   Bachelor's degree or higher from a regionally accredited institution of higher education

    2.   Illinois State Board of Education form 80-02 submitted to ISBE. Note: Form is available at http://www.isbe.net/Documents/80-02-standards-verification.pdf.

    3.   Student teaching or 1 year experience on a valid license

    4.   Completion of course work addressing methods of teaching exceptional children, reading methods, content area reading, and methods of teaching English-language learners. For details, consult http://www.isbe.net/Documents/pre-app-pel-coursework.pdf.

    5.   Licensure Tests: APT/edTPA, content tests, and tests of basic skills are all valid indefinitely. See I, A–C, directly above, for details. Note: The APT 188 test is an option only for applicants who have completed student teaching before Fall 2015; for applicants relying on 1 year of valid teaching experience, the teaching experience must have been completed before Fall 2015. Those who seek to add a subsequent endorsement that requires a content-area test must pass the applicable Illinois content-area test. Out-of-state testing is not accepted.

    6.   If edTPA has not been passed at time of application, 1 of the below options may be utilized:

a. Educator can enroll in student teaching portion of an educator preparation program and complete the edTPA during this time.

b. Educator can provide evidence with application of having at least 1 year of full-time teaching experience and having achieved a "proficient" or higher (or equivalent) rating on most recent performance evaluation. Use form 80-01: Out-of-State Applicant Request to Waive edTPA.

C. Endorsements available are listed below; for more information on specific requirements for each, consult http://www.isbe.net/Pages/Subsequent-Teaching-Endorsements.aspx.

1. Teaching
   a. Early Childhood Education (Birth–grade 3)
   b. Elementary Education (K–9)
      i. Middle Grades teaching endorsement applications submitted after February 1, 2018, will be subject to new requirements. For more information, refer to http://www.isbe.net/Pages/MiddleGradesTeachingEndorsements.aspx.
   c. Secondary Education (6–12)
   d. Special Teaching (K–12)
   e. Special Education (PreK–age 21). A specific content area endorsement should be selected if applicant applies for the Special Teaching (K–12) license.

2. Administrative
   a. Teacher Leader (PreK–12) (Note: at this time, through the entitlement process only from an Illinois institution upon completion)
   b. General Administrative (K–12)
   c. Principal (PreK–12)
   d. Superintendent (PreK–12)
   e. Chief School Business Official (PreK–12)
   f. Director of Special Education (PreK–age 21)

3. School Support Personnel
   a. School Social Worker (PreK–age 21)
   b. School Counselor (PreK–age 21)
   c. School Psychologist (PreK–age 21)
   d. School Nurse (PreK–age 21)
   e. Speech-Language Pathologist—nonteaching (PreK–age 21)

III. Requirements for Educator License with Stipulations Endorsements can be viewed in full at http://www.isbe.net/Pages/Educator-License-with-Stipulations.aspx and include:

A. Alternative Provisional Educator
B. Alternative Provisional Superintendent
C. Resident Teacher
D. Career and Technical Educator
E. Provisional Career and Technical Educator
F. Part-Time Provisional Career and Technical Educator
G. Chief School Business Official

    H. Transitional Bilingual Educator

    I. Paraprofessional Endorsement

IV. Substitute Teaching License (valid 5 years; renewable without evidence of passing a test of basic skills or the ACT WorkKeys)

    A. Hold a bachelor's degree from a regionally accredited institution of higher education

V. Content Area Endorsement Structure (teaching endorsements)

    A. Primary Endorsements

        1. Primary content endorsements are no longer available, with the exception of Learning Behavior Specialist I. This endorsement is only available for an evaluation if an educator holds the following:

            a. Early childhood education (K–3). Note: To earn an endorsement at the PreK level, applicants must seek Early Childhood Special Education Approval. Requirements are available at http://www.isbe.net/Pages/educator-licensure-approvals.aspx.

        2. To add an additional grade-range endorsement outside the grade range of the original certificate or license, applicant must complete a state-approved educator preparation program and submit Form 80-02, available at http://www.isbe.net/Pages/Licensure-Forms.aspx.

        3. For detailed endorsements available with requirements, please refer to the Subsequent Teaching Endorsements page at http://www.isbe.net/Pages/Subsequent-Teaching-Endorsements.aspx.

    B. Middle School Endorsements. For applications submitted February 1, 2018, and after, please refer to the requirements at http://www.isbe.net/Pages/MiddleGradesTeachingEndorsements.aspx.

    C. Senior High School Endorsements

        1. To add a senior high school content endorsement, you must already hold 1 of the following endorsements on your license:

            a. Elementary education (K–9)

                i. If you hold only an elementary education (K–9) endorsement, the senior high school content endorsement will be valid for 9th grade only.

            b. Secondary education (6–12; endorsements will be for grades 9–12)

            c. Special (K–12 or PreK–age 21; endorsements will be for grades 9–12)

        2. To add an additional grade-range endorsement outside the grade range of the original certificate or license, applicant must complete a state-approved educator preparation program and submit Form 80-02, available at https://www.isbe.net/Pages/Licensure-Forms.aspx.

        3. Applicants receiving a second designation in the senior high school sciences or social sciences must either complete 12 semester hours of course work in the designation and pass the test required for the designation

            or

            Complete a major, or construct a major by completing 32 semester hours, in the content area of the designation; no upper division course work is required.

4.   For a detailed list of endorsements and their requirements, refer to the Subsequent Teaching Endorsements page at http://www.isbe.net/Pages/Subsequent-Teaching-Endorsements.aspx. For detailed requirements for Learning Behavior Specialist I (LBS I) and Learning Behavior Specialist II (LBS II), refer to the Special Education Requirements page at http://www.isbe.net/Pages/Special-Education-Requirements.aspx.

Indiana

Rules for Educator Preparation and Accountability 3 (REPA 3) went into effect on January 16, 2015. Certain components of the previous Rules for Educator Preparation and Accountability will remain in place until the transition to REPA 3 is complete on August 31, 2019. For full and current details, consult http://www.doe.in.gov/licensing.

Licensure Overview

For all license-specific details, consult REPA 3 Rule at http://www.in.gov/legislative/iac/20141217 -IR-511130399FRA.xml.pdf.

I. Levels of Licensure
   A. Initial Practitioner (valid 2 years; renewable under conditions). The first-level license for teaching, school services, and school administration
      1. Residency is the 2-year internship requirement which accompanies all Initial licenses and may include a school corporation-sponsored mentoring program.
      2. All license additions require successful completion of the required Pearson Core (CORE) content test if there is an approved test for the content area, as well as any course work requirements.
      3. A CORE content licensure test for candidates for initial licensure as school counselors is required.
      4. Out-of-state applicants with less than 3 years of teaching experience in an accredited institution (note: substitute teaching experience does not count) are eligible for this license if they:
         a. Have obtained an instructional license in another state by completing a state-approved educator preparation program or a state-approved alternative preparation program;
         b. Have passed a licensure test in their content area(s) and provide official documentation of passing scores;
         c. Possess a valid license from another state, which must be a full license (i.e., not temporary, emergency, substitute, or other);
            and
         d. Have completed an approved preparation program and passed a content test if they wish to receive license reciprocity in the 7 content areas listed in B3. directly below.
   B. Practitioner (valid 5 years; renewable for 5 years)
      1. For renewal, the second-level license requires 1 of the following:
         a. Completion of a Professional Growth Plan (PGP)
            or

        b.   Six semester hours of specified course work
            or
        c.   National Board Certification.

2. All license additions require successful completion of the required Pearson Core (CORE) content test if there is an approved test for the content area, as well as any course work requirements.

3. The 7 content areas that require both an approved program of course work and testing in order to be added to an existing license include:
   a. Communication Disorders
   b. Teachers of English Learners
   c. Early Childhood Education
   d. Elementary Generalists
   e. Exceptional Needs (Mild Intervention, Intense Intervention, Blind and Low Vision, Deaf and Hard of Hearing)
   f. Fine Arts content areas (Visual Arts, Vocal and General Music, Instrumental and General Music, and Theater Arts)
   g. High Ability

4. Out-of-state applicants with more than 3 years of teaching experience in an accredited institution are eligible for this license if they:
   a. Have obtained an instructional license in another state by completing a state-approved educator preparation program or a state-approved alternative preparation program;
   b. Have passed a licensure test in their content area(s) and provide official documentation of passing scores;
   c. Possess a valid license from another state, which must be a full license (i.e., not temporary, emergency, substitute, or other);
      and
   d. Have completed an approved preparation program and passed a content test if they wish to receive license reciprocity in the 7 content areas listed in B3. directly above.

C. Accomplished Practitioner (Valid 10 years; renewable for 10 years)

1. National Board Certification (NBTPS) can be used to obtain a 10-year Accomplished Practitioner license.

2. For renewal, the third-level license requires 1 of the following:
   a. Completion of a PGP
      or
   b. Six semester hours of specified course work
      or
   c. National Board Certification.

3. Certain licenses have additional renewal requirements; for these and other license-specific details, consult REPA 3 Rule at http://www.in.gov/legislative/iac/20141217-IR-511130399FRA.xml.pdf.

D. Reciprocal Permit

1. All persons who completed educator preparation in another US state, who have

a valid license from that state, and who have satisfied the testing and degree requirements, are eligible for the Initial Practitioner License.

2. All persons who completed educator preparation in another US state, who have a valid license from that state, who have satisfied the testing and degree requirements, and who have 3 years of teaching in accredited schools from that state, are eligible for the Practitioner License.

E. Emergency Permit (renewable upon documentation of progress toward full licensure)

1. Reserved for use by a school employer when it cannot locate a properly licensed educator for an assignment.

2. The "continuing education" Emergency Permit is available under REPA, but it is not renewable.

F. Transition to Teaching (T2T) Permit (valid for 3 years; nonrenewable)

1. All Indiana educator preparation institutions must offer the Transition to Teaching option for the Initial teaching license for all of their approved programs.

   a. Applicants enrolled in the T2T program must already hold a bachelor's degree.

   b. The course of study of a Transition to Teaching program may be a part of a degree program, but a participant is not required to earn a degree to successfully complete the T2T program.

   c. Permit is available to a school corporation when it cannot locate a properly licensed person for a teaching assignment and hires a person who is not properly licensed who has been admitted into a T2T program.

G. Advanced Degree License

1. Applicant must have a master's degree or higher in the content area for which licensure is sought; must satisfy the test requirements for an Initial-level license in a content teaching area; and must have completed 1 year of teaching experience as defined by the statute.

Licensure Curriculum Requirements

I. Initial license for Elementary Generalist and Early Childhood Education: 3 routes available

A. Completion of bachelor's degree from an institution of higher learning that includes a minor in a REPA content area, and a major with general education, professional education, and student teaching requirements;
   or

B. Completion of a bachelor's degree from an institution of higher learning in a noneducation area, *and either*:

1. A minor in education that includes the essential pedagogy as described in the REPA,
   or

2. A T2T program for career changers;
   or

C.   Completion of bachelor's degree from an institution of higher learning and a Master of Arts in Teaching (MAT) program approved by the Advisory Board.

D.   All Indiana teacher preparation institutions must offer Option A (above) and must offer both the minor in education and the T2T program from Option B above.

II.   Initial license for Secondary Education, Middle School Education, and P–12 Education: 3 routes available

A.   Completion of an approved program for a REPA content area where the content area or major meets or exceeds the curriculum requirements of any other major offered by the institution for higher learning for that content area;
or

B.   Completion of a bachelor's degree from an institution of higher learning that includes an appropriate major or content area, *and either*:

1.   An education minor that includes the essential pedagogy as defined by the REPA,
or

2.   Completion of a T2T program;
or

C.   Completion of a bachelor's degree from an institution of higher learning and a Master of Arts in Teaching degree approved by the Advisory Board.

D.   All Indiana teacher preparation institutions must offer Option A (above) and must offer both the minor in education and the T2T program from Option B above.

School Settings and License Content Areas

I.   School Settings
   A.   Elementary (K–6)
   B.   Secondary (5–12)
   C.   Preschool through Grade 12 (P–12)
   D.   Early Childhood (P–3)
   E.   Middle School (5–9)

II.   License Content Areas
   A.   Career and Technical Education: agriculture, business information and technology, marketing, family and consumer sciences, health science education, trade and industrial education
   B.   Business, computer education, early childhood education, elementary generalist, engineering and technology, exceptional needs, fine arts, high ability education, health, journalism, language arts, mathematics, physical education, reading, school librarian, science, social studies, teachers of English learners, virtual instruction, world languages
   C.   School Administration
      1.   Building-level administrator
      2.   District level: superintendent, director of career and technical education, director of curriculum and instruction, director of exceptional needs
      3.   Temporary superintendent
   D.   School services: communication disorders, school psychologist, school counselor, school nurse, school social worker

Iowa

Types of Licenses

I. Initial License (valid 2 years: renewable under prescribed conditions)
   A. Baccalaureate degree from a regionally accredited institution;
   B. Completion of an approved teacher preparation program;
   C. Completion of an approved human relations component;
   D. Completion of requirements for a teaching endorsement;
   E. Completion of the Iowa mandated tests (for applicants who graduated after January 1, 2013 and have less than 3 years' experience)
   F. Completion of the recency requirement of either 6 college credits or teaching experience within the last 5 years.
   G. These requirements must be completed for college semester-hour credit through a regionally accredited institution. Applicants who have completed a nontraditional program may or may not be eligible for Iowa licensure.

II. Standard License (valid 5 years; renewable under prescribed conditions)
   A. Completion of requirements for the initial license—see I, A–F, directly above; and
   B. Evidence of 2 years of successful teaching experience in a public school in Iowa, or of 3 years in any combination of public, private, or out-of-state schools.

III. Master Educator License (valid 5 years; renewable under prescribed conditions)
   A. Completion of requirements for the initial license—see I, A–F, directly above;
   B. Five years of teaching experience; and
   C. Master's degree in a recognized endorsement area or in curriculum, effective teaching, or a similar degree program which has a focus on school curriculum or instruction.

IV. Initial Administrator License (valid 1 year; renewable under prescribed conditions)
   A. Hold or be eligible for a standard license—see II, A and B, directly above;
   B. Three years of teaching experience;
   C. Does not have administrative experience;
   D. Completion of the requirements for an administrative endorsement; and
   E. Completion of a master's degree.

V. Professional Administrator License (valid 5 years; renewable under prescribed conditions)
   A. Standard license or eligibility for one (see II, A and B, directly above);
   B. Three years of teaching experience;
   C. Completion of the requirements for an administrative endorsement;
   D. Completion of the recency requirement listed under the 1-year conditional license; and
   E. Evidence of 1 year of successful administrative experience in a public school in Iowa, or of 2 years in any combination of public, private, or out-of-state schools.

VI. Exchange License (valid 2 years; nonrenewable)
   A. Must complete a teacher preparation program from a state-approved and regionally accredited institution, then submit transcripts to verify;
   B. Hold a baccalaureate degree from a regionally accredited institution;
   C. Hold a valid or expired teaching license from another state;
   D. Have no disciplinary action pending;
   E. Have completed the Iowa mandated tests (for applicants who graduated after January 1, 2013 and have less than 3 years' experience); and
   F. Have not completed all Iowa requirements for a teaching endorsement.
VII. Initial Professional Service License (valid 2 years; renewable under prescribed conditions). May be issued to an applicant for licensure to serve as a school audiologist, school psychologist, school social worker, speech-language pathologist, supervisor of special education (support), director of special education of an area education agency, or school counselor who:
   A. Has a master's degree in a recognized professional educational service area from a regionally accredited institution;
   B. Has completed a state-approved program which meets the requirements for an endorsement in a professional educational service area;
   C. Has completed the requirements for 1 of the professional educational service area endorsements; and
   D. Meets the recency requirement.
      1. For details, see 282—subrule 13.10(3) at http://www.boee.iowa.gov/agency _282.pdf.
VIII. Standard Professional Service License (valid 5 years; renewable under prescribed conditions)
   A. Completes requirements listed for the initial professional service license; see VII, A–D directly above; and
   B. Shows evidence of successful completion of a state-approved mentoring and induction program by
      1. Meeting the Iowa standards as determined by a comprehensive evaluation; and
      2. Completing two years of successful service experience in an Iowa public school.
      3. In lieu of completion of a state-approved mentoring and induction program, the applicant must provide evidence of 3 years of successful service area experience in an Iowa nonpublic school or 3 years of successful service area experience in an out-of-state K–12 educational setting.

Teaching Endorsements

I. General requirements for the issuance of a license with an endorsement
   A. Baccalaureate degree from a regionally accredited institution;
   B. Completion of an approved human relations component;
   C. Completion of the exceptional learner program, which must include preparation that contributes to the education of individuals with disabilities and the gifted and talented; and

D. Professional education core, with completed course work or evidence of competency in:

1. Student learning: the practitioner understands how students learn and develop, and provides learning opportunities that support intellectual, career, social, and personal development;

2. Diverse learners: the practitioner understands how students differ in their approaches to learning and creates instructional opportunities that are equitable and are adaptable to diverse learners;

3. Instructional planning: the practitioner plans instruction based upon knowledge of subject matter, students, the community, curriculum goals, and state curriculum models;

4. Instructional strategies: the practitioner understands and uses a variety of instructional strategies to encourage students' development of critical thinking, problem solving, and performance skills;

5. Learning environment/classroom management: the practitioner uses an understanding of individual and group motivation and behavior to create a learning environment that encourages positive social interaction, active engagement in learning, and self-motivation;

6. Communication: the practitioner uses knowledge of effective verbal, nonverbal, and media communication techniques, and other forms of symbolic representation, to foster active inquiry, collaboration, and support interaction in the classroom;

7. Assessment: the practitioner understands and uses formal and informal assessment strategies to evaluate the continuous intellectual, social, and physical development of the learner;

8. Foundations, reflection and professional development: the practitioner continually evaluates the effects of the practitioner's choices and actions on students, parents, and other professionals in the learning community, and actively seeks out opportunities to grow professionally;

9. Collaboration, ethics and relationships: the practitioner fosters relationships with parents, school colleagues, and organizations in the larger community to support students' learning and development;

10. Computer technology related to instruction;

11. Completion of pre–student teaching field-based experiences;

12. Methods of teaching, with an emphasis on the subject and grade level endorsement desired;

13. Student teaching in the subject area and grade level endorsement desired;

14. Preparation in reading programs, including reading recovery, and integration of reading strategies into content area methods course work; and

15. Content/subject matter specialization: the practitioner understands the central concepts, tools of inquiry, and structure of the discipline(s) the practitioner teaches and creates learning experiences that make these aspects of subject matter meaningful for students.

    a. This is evidenced by completion of a 30-semester-hour teaching major that must minimally include the requirements for at least 1 of the basic endorsement areas, special education teaching endorsements, or secondary level occupational endorsements.

b. For specific endorsement requirements, consult www.boee.iowa .gov—endorsements.

Administrator Licenses

Applicants for the administrator license must first comply with the requirements for all Iowa practitioners set out in 282—Chapter 13 (for details, consult https://www.legis.iowa.gov/docs/aco/ agency/282.pdf). Additionally, the requirements of rules 282—13.2(272) and 282—13.3(272) and the license-specific requirements set forth under each license must be met before an applicant is eligible for an administrator license.

I. Initial Administrator License (valid 1 year) may be issued to an applicant who:
   A. Is the holder of or is eligible for a standard license;
   B. Has 3 years of teaching experience;
   C. Has completed a state-approved PK–12 principal and PK–12 supervisor of special education program;
      1. For details, see subrule 18.9(1) at https://www.legis.iowa.gov/docs/aco/agency/ 282.pdf.
   D. Is assuming a position as a PK–12 principal and PK–12 supervisor of special education for the first time or has 1 year of out-of-state or nonpublic administrative experience;
      1. For details, see subrule 18.9(1) at https://www.legis.iowa.gov/docs/aco/agency/ 282.pdf.
   E. Has completed an approved human relations component;
   F. Has completed an exceptional learner component; and
   G. Has completed an evaluator approval program.
II. Superintendent/AEA Administrator. The holder of this endorsement is authorized to serve as a superintendent for PK–12 or as an Area Education Agency (AEA) administrator.
   A. Program requirements
      1. Specialist degree (or its equivalent: a master's degree plus at least 30 semester hours of planned graduate study in administration beyond the master's degree);
      2. Content: through completion of a sequence of courses and experiences which may have been part of, or in addition to, the degree requirements, the administrator has knowledge and understanding of:
         a. Models, theories, and practices that provide the basis for leading educational systems toward improving student performance;
         b. Federal, state and local fiscal policies related to education;
         c. Human resources management, including recruitment, personnel assistance and development, evaluation and negotiations;
         d. Current legal issues in general and special education;
         e. Non-instructional support services management including but not limited to transportation, nutrition and facilities; and

     f.   Practicum in PK–12 school administration in which, or in related course work, the administrator facilitates processes and engages in activities for:
- i. Developing a shared vision of learning through articulation, implementation, and stewardship;
- ii. Advocating, nurturing, and sustaining a school culture and instructional program conducive to student learning and staff professional growth;
- iii. Ensuring management of the organization, operations, and resources for a safe, efficient, and effective learning environment;
- iv. Collaborating with school staff, families, community members and boards of directors; responding to diverse community interests and needs; and mobilizing community resources;
- v. Acting with integrity, fairness, and in an ethical manner; and
- vi. Understanding, responding to, and influencing the larger political, social, economic, legal, and cultural context.

B. Administrative experience
1. The applicant must have had 3 years of experience as a building principal.
   a. PK–12 or area education agency administrative experience is acceptable if the applicant acquires the 3 years of experience while holding a valid administrator license.

Kansas

Regardless of the type of license requested, any applicant for a first Kansas license must submit a fingerprint card and fee for the purpose of a Kansas Bureau of Investigation/Federal Bureau of Investigation background clearance.

License Types and Requirements

I. Initial Teaching License (valid 2 years; renewable)
 A. In-state applicants
  1. Bachelor's degree from a regionally accredited college or university
  2. Completion of a state-approved teacher preparation program
  3. Recency: have at least 8 credit hours or 1 year of accredited teaching experience completed within the last 6 years
  4. Passing scores on the content assessment in each of the endorsement areas on license
  5. Passing scores on the pedagogy assessment: Principles of Learning and Teaching (PLT)
 B. Out-of-state applicants
  1. See I, A, 1–3, directly above;
   and
  2. Passing scores on content and pedagogy tests: tests completed to achieve the out-of-state license may be acceptable;
   or
  3. May be issued a 2-year exchange license, if applicable;
   or
  4. May be issued a 1-year nonrenewable license;
   or
  5. May be issued a substitute license;
   or
  6. Meet experience requirements to come in at the professional license level.
II. Professional Teaching License (valid 5 years; renewable)
 A. In-state applicants
  1. Hold a currently valid Initial teaching license
  2. During its validity period, successfully complete the prescribed performance assessment
 B. Out-of-state applicants
  1. Bachelor's degree
  2. Completion of a state-approved preparation program in subject or field for which licensure is sought

3. Recency: at least 1 year of accredited teaching experience or 8 semester hours of college credit within the 6 year period immediately prior to application
4. Out-of-state professional license
5. Three years of recent accredited experience under a standard teaching license

   or

   Meet recency and verify at least 5 years of accredited experience under an initial or professional license

   or

   Passing scores on assessments in content and pedagogy, with an already completed performance assessment

III. Accomplished Teaching License (valid 10 years; renewable)
   A. Available only to teachers who have achieved National Board Certification from the National Board for Professional Teaching Standards (NBPTS) through completion of their advanced-level performance assessment process.
      1. Kansas-licensed teachers must also hold a currently valid Kansas professional level teaching license as well as achieving National Board Certification.
      2. National Board–certified teachers coming from out-of-state may apply for this license as their initial Kansas license, as long as they also hold a currently valid professional-level teaching license in another state.
         a. Accomplished license will be valid for the validity length of National Board Certification.

IV. One-Year Nonrenewable Teaching License (valid only for current school year)
   A. Meet all requirements for an Initial license (see I, A, 1–5, directly above) except for all or part of the prelicensure tests
   B. Tests in which individual is deficient must be completed during the school year in order to upgrade to the Initial license.

V. Two-Year Exchange (Teaching or School Specialist) License (valid 2 years)
   A. Exchange Teaching
      1. Complete a state-approved teacher education program through college in home state
      2. Hold a standard valid license in that state
      3. Rectify all deficiencies in initial Kansas requirements during 2-year period
   B. Exchange School Specialist (school counselor, library media, reading specialist)
      1. Complete a state-approved school specialist program in home state
      2. Hold a standard valid school specialist license in that state
      3. Rectify all deficiencies in initial Kansas requirements during 2-year period
         a. Deficiencies may include completion of the content licensure examination; a 3.25 cumulative GPA in graduate course work; and/or recency credit.
      4. Hold a Kansas professional-level teaching license
      5. Neither leadership licenses nor alternative routes to licensure are eligible for exchange licensure.

VI. Substitute Licenses
   A. Standard Substitute License (valid 5 years; renewable)
      1. Hold a bachelor's degree

2. Complete a teacher preparation program
3. Submit 1 fingerprint card for an FBI and Kansas Bureau of Investigation (KBI) background clearance report

B. Emergency Substitute License (valid for current school year)
1. Complete a minimum of 60 semester credit hours from regionally accredited college or university
2. Submit 1 fingerprint card for an FBI and KBI background clearance report

VII. Provisional License (valid 2 years; renewable)
A. Provisional Teaching Endorsement License
1. Hold a valid Kansas license and have a plan of study for completing an approved program for a new teaching subject
2. Fifty percent of the program for the new teaching area is complete
3. A Kansas district must verify assignment of teacher in the provisional subject area at the appropriate level.
4. To qualify for a second provisional, complete half the remaining course work deficiencies (have 75 percent of approved program completed).
5. For Provisional Teaching Endorsement License in Special Education, see VII, A, 2, directly above.
   a. A valid license for general education is required.
   b. Course work in areas of methodology, characteristics, and a practicum is already completed.
   c. Kansas district must verify assignment of teacher in provisional special education area at the appropriate level.

B. Provisional School Specialist License for school counselor, library media, or reading specialist
1. Hold a valid 5-year professional teaching license
2. Fifty percent of the school specialist program is completed
3. Kansas district must verify assignment of applicant as a school specialist.

C. Provisional license is not available for school leadership licenses.

VIII. Restricted Teaching License Alternative Pathway (valid 3 years while employed in school system)
A. Meet all eligibility requirements:
1. Hold a bachelor's degree or higher from a regionally accredited university
2. Degree must be in a regular education content area in which applicant desires to teach or equivalent content course work must be completed.
3. Most recent 60 semester credit hours of college course work show a cumulative GPA of 2.75.
4. Passing score on the appropriate content assessment

B. Request that the university hosting the alternative route program evaluate transcript to ensure that content requirements for subject matter teaching area are adequate
1. Develop a plan of study with the alternative certification program staff; program length may vary depending on situation.

C. Locate and apply for a teaching position, verifying that a restricted license is appropriate for it

   D. Apply for restricted license, coordinating application among individual, employing school district, and higher education institution providing the course work.
   E. Once license is issued, applicant will teach full time while completing required professional education course work towards full licensure.
   F. Submit a progress report every year verifying appropriate progress towards a full license; otherwise, restricted license will be cancelled
   G. Apply for a full Kansas license with institutional recommendation once applicant successfully completes all course work and testing requirements on plan of study
   H. Complete the PLT assessment
IX. School Specialist License
   A. Initial School Specialist License
      1. Graduate degree from a regionally accredited college
      2. Complete graduate-level state-approved program
      3. Cumulative GPA of 3.25 in graduate course work
      4. Recency: have at least 8 credit hours or 1 year of accredited experience completed within the last 6 years
      5. Currently valid Kansas professional teaching license (if applying for library media, reading specialist)
      6. Successfully complete a school specialist content assessment
         a. School counselor content test: complete Praxis II test number 0420—School Guidance and Counseling—with score of 600 or above
         b. Library media specialist content test: complete Praxis II test number 0311—Library Media Specialist—with score of 630 or above
         c. Reading specialist content test: complete Praxis II test number 0300—Reading Specialist—with score of 560 or above
   B. Professional School Specialist License
      1. In-state applicants
         a. Hold a currently valid Initial School Specialist License (see IX, A, 1–6, directly above)
         b. Complete the performance assessment while employed as a school specialist
      2. Out-of-state applicants
         a. See IX, A, 1–5, directly above;
            and
         b. Successfully complete a school specialist content and performance assessment,
            or
            Three years of recent accredited experience in a school specialist position while holding a valid standard school specialist license,
            or
            Meet recency and at least 5 years of accredited school specialist experience under a standard school specialist license.
X. School Leadership Licenses: includes Program Leadership (supervisor/coordinator); Building Leadership (principal); District Leadership (superintendent)
   A. Initial School Leadership License (valid 2 years)

       1. Graduate degree from a regionally accredited college

       2. Complete graduate-level state-approved program in school leadership

       3. If applying for a district leadership license, completion of an approved building leadership program

       4. Cumulative GPA of 3.25 in graduate course work

       5. Recency: at least 8 credit hours or 1 year of accredited experience completed within the last 6 years

       6. Minimum of 5 years of accredited experience under a valid standard license/certificate and having achieved the professional level license

       7. School leadership licensure assessment

   B. Professional School Leadership license (valid 5 years)

       1. Hold a currently valid Initial School Leadership License

       2. Complete performance assessment while employed as an administrator

   C. Out-of-state applicants

       1. See X, A, 1–7, directly above;
          and

       2. Successfully complete a school leadership content and performance assessment,
          or

          Three years of recent accredited experience in a school leadership position while holding a standard school leadership license,
          or

          Meet recency and at least 5 years of accredited school leadership experience under a standard school leadership license.

XI. New Licenses: Contact the Kansas State Department of Education (see Appendix 1) for full details

   A. Transitional License (valid 1 year)

       1. Provides immediate access to practice for:

          a. Out-of-state applicant without recent credit or experience

          b. Kansas educator with expired full license who is retired or out of practice

   B. Interim Alternative License (valid 1 year; renewable for another year)

       1. Guarantees license for immediate access to practice to out-of-state applicant whose preparation was through an alternative pathway

   C. Restricted School Specialist License (for school counselor or library media)

       1. Requires graduate degree and 3 years of professional experience in the counseling or library field

       2. Must complete professional education during 3-year restricted license period while employed in school system

   D. STEM License (valid for 1 school year; renewable for additional years)

       1. Degree in life science, physical science, earth and space science, mathematics, engineering, computer technology, finance, or accounting

       2. Five years of professional work experience in the subject matter for which the degree is held

       3. District hire to teach only that subject matter based on the degree and experience

Endorsements by Levels

I. Early Childhood: Birth–Grade 3 or Birth–K
   A. Requires combined general education and special education curriculum: Early Childhood Unified
   B. Must be done with a general education license: Deaf or Hard of Hearing; Visually Impaired; School Psychologist
II. Early Childhood–Late Childhood: K–6
   A. Elementary
   B. Provisional is available for the following: Adaptive; Functional; Gifted; English for Speakers of Other Languages (ESOL).
III. Late Childhood–Early Adolescence: Grades 5–8
   A. Provisional is available for the following: History Comprehensive; Science; English Language Arts; Mathematics
IV. Early Adolescence–Late Adolescence/Adulthood: Grades 6–12
   A. Provisional is available for the following: English Language Arts; Mathematics; Agriculture; Biology; Business; Chemistry; Earth and Space Science; Family & Consumer Science; History and Government; Journalism; Physics; Psychology; Speech/Theatre; Technology Education; Communication Technology; Power, Energy, Transportation Technology; Production Technology; Adaptive; ESOL; Functional; Gifted
V. Early Childhood–Late Adolescence/Adulthood: PreK–12
   A. School Psychologist; Building Leadership; District Leadership; Program Leadership
   B. Provisional is available for the following: Deaf or Hard of Hearing; Visually Impaired; Adaptive, Functional; Gifted; ESOL; Library Media Specialist; Music; Instrumental Music; Vocal Music; Physical Education; Reading Specialist; School Counselor
VI. Grades 8–12
   A. STEM license

Kentucky

General Requirements

I. Recency of preparation
   A. Completed program of preparation within 5 years preceding date of receipt of certification application form
      or
      Completed 6 semester hours of additional graduate credit within preceding 5 years
      1. Applicants who have completed a 5th-year program and have 2 years of successful teaching experience within the last 10 years are exempt from the 6-hour requirement.
   B. Initial 1-year certification for special circumstances
      1. Those not meeting recency requirements in I, A, directly above, who have not previously held a regular Kentucky teaching certificate, but who otherwise qualify for certification shall be issued a 1-year initial certificate that
         a. Ends June 30 of next calendar year
         b. Is conditional on 6 semester hours of graduate credit applicable toward the usual renewal requirements being completed by September 1 of year of expiration
II. Duration of teaching certificates
   A. Issued for 5 years, with provisions for subsequent 5-year renewals, provided that by September 1 of the year of expiration, the applicant has completed
      1. Three years of successful teaching experience
         or
         At least 6 semester hours of graduate credit or the equivalent
   B. One-year certificates shall be issued for
      1. Beginning teacher internship*
         a. Upon successful completion of such internship as judged by majority vote of beginning teacher committee, 1-year certificate will be extended for remainder of the 5-year period.
      2. Initial certification for applicants not meeting recency requirements in I, A, directly above
      *This requirement is waived for the 2018–19 and 2019–20 school years.
III. Renewal of teaching certificates
   A. Requirements for subsequent 5-year renewals
      1. Completion by September 1 of the year of expiration of
         a. Three years of successful teaching experience
            or
            Six semester hours of graduate credit or the equivalent
      2. Credits for certificate renewal shall be earned after the issuance of the certificate.

3. Applicants holding a lapsed regular Kentucky teaching certificate shall not be required to take the written tests or to participate in the beginning teacher internship program.

IV. Out-of-State Applicants
A. Those who have completed 2 or more years of acceptable teaching experience outside of the Commonwealth of Kentucky and who otherwise qualify for certification shall not be required to take the written tests or to participate in the beginning teacher internship program.

V. Requirements for 1-year certificate for beginning teacher internship*
A. Completion of an approved program of preparation that corresponds to the certificate desired
B. Passing scores on the Praxis II Subject Assessment appropriate for each content area in which certification is requested, in addition to the appropriate Principles of Learning and Teaching (PLT) test
1. All new teachers are required to take the PLT test in addition to the specialty(ies) test appropriate for the certification they are seeking. Contact the Education Professional Standards Board (see Appendix 1) for detailed information.
C. Evidence of full-time employment in a Kentucky school as attested by the prospective employer
*This requirement is waived for the 2018–19 and 2019–20 school years.

VI. Upon successful completion of the approved program of preparation and upon completion of the designated tests with acceptable scores, the Education Professional Standards Board shall issue a statement of eligibility for employment that shall serve as evidence of eligibility for the 1-year certificate once a teaching position is secured. The statement of eligibility shall be valid for a 5-year period.

Approved Programs

The Commonwealth of Kentucky follows the "approved program" approach to certification. An individual should follow the program in effect at the college or university with the guidance of the college advisor and meet the General Requirements (see above). Applicants interested in certification should contact the Division of Certification (see Appendix 1) for the latest information.

I. Interdisciplinary Early Childhood Education (Birth to Primary)
II. Elementary School (Primary through Grade 5)
III. Middle School (Grades 5 through 9)
A. Preparation in 1 major or equivalent
or
B. Preparation in 2 teaching fields selected from the following: English and communications, mathematics, science, and social studies
1. Candidates who choose to prepare simultaneously for teaching in the middle school and for teaching exceptional children are required to complete only 1 middle school teaching field.
IV. Secondary School (Grades 8 through 12)

A. Preparation includes 1 or more of the following specializations: English, mathematics, social studies, biological science, physics, chemistry, or earth science.

V. Middle/Secondary School (Grades 5 through 12)

A. Preparation includes 1 or more of the following specializations: agriculture, business and marketing, family and consumer science, industrial education, technology education.

VI. Elementary/Middle/Secondary School (Primary through Grade 12)

A. Preparation includes 1 or more of the following specializations: art, foreign language (Arabic, Chinese, French, German, Japanese, Latin, Russian, or Spanish), health, physical education, integrated music, vocal music, instrumental music, school media librarian.

VII. Exceptional Children (Primary through Grade 12, and for collaborating with teachers to design and deliver programs for pre-primary children)

A. Preparation includes 1 or more of the following specializations: learning and behavior disorders; moderate and severe disabilities; hearing impaired or hearing impaired/sign proficiency; visually impaired; communication disorders (master's level); speech-language pathology assistant (bachelor's level).

VIII. Endorsements to Certificates (Primary through Grade 12)

A. Computer science (8–12), English as a second language (P–12), gifted education (P–12), driver education (8–12), reading and writing (P–12), instructional computer technology (P–12), learning and behavior disorders (8–12), school nutrition (P–12), and school safety (P–12)

B. Restricted Base Certificates: psychology (8–12), sociology (8–12), journalism (8–12), speech/media communications (8–12), theater (P–12), dance (P–12), computer information systems (P–12), English as a second language (P–12), school nurse (P–12), school social worker (P–12), Junior Reserve Officer Training Corps (8–12)

IX. Professional Certificate for Instructional Leadership

A. Certification is offered for the following positions: Supervisor of Instruction, Level 1; Supervisor of Instruction, Level 2; Principal, All Grades, Level 1; Principal, All Grades, Level 2; Director of Special Education; Director of Pupil Personnel; School Psychologist; Guidance Counselor; and School Superintendent.

Principal, All Grades

I. Requirements for Principal, All Grades, Level 1

A. As prerequisites for the Level 1 program of preparation for the initial Professional Certificate for Instructional Leadership, the candidate shall

1. Have been admitted to the preparation program on the basis of criteria, developed by the teacher-education institution,
2. Have completed 3 years of full-time teaching experience,
3. Have completed a 30-hour post-master's degree program in school administration,
4. Qualify for a Kentucky teaching certificate, and
5. Successfully complete the School Leaders Licensure Assessment (SLLA) and the Kentucky specialty test of instructional and administrative practices.

       a.   Applicants with out-of-state principal certification and 2 years of verified full-time principal experience are exempt from the SLLA.

    6.   All applicants without 2 years of verified full-time principal experience must successfully complete a 1-year Kentucky principal internship program.

B.   The initial Professional Certificate for Instructional Leadership shall be issued for a period of 1 year upon successful completion of Level 1 preparation and the tests prescribed and upon obtaining employment for an internship position as principal or assistant principal. Upon proof of employment as a principal/assistant principal, the certificate shall be extended for 4 years.

C.   The certificate shall be renewed subsequently for 5-year periods. The first renewal shall require the completion of the curriculum identified as the Level 2 program in the curriculum standards. Each 5-year renewal thereafter shall require the completion of 2 years of experience as a principal, or 3 semester hours of additional graduate credit related to the position of school principal, or 42 hours of approved training selected from programs approved for the Kentucky Effective Leadership Training Program.

D.   If a lapse in certification occurs because of lack of completion of the Level 2 preparation, the certificate may be reissued for a 5-year period upon successful completion of the Level 2 preparation. If a certificate lapses with Level 2 preparation, but because of lack of the renewal requirements, the certificate may be reissued after the completion of an additional 6 semester hours of graduate study appropriate to the program.

E.   Persons applying for the Professional Certificate for Instructional Leadership who satisfy the curriculum requirements and all other prerequisites and who have completed at least 2 years of successful full-time experience, including at least 140 days per year, as a school principal, within a 10-year period prior to making application will be exempt from the internship requirements for school principals but shall be required to pass the written examinations.

II.   Standards for School Principal

    A.   Individuals must meet the standards for principals taken from the Standards for School Leaders developed by the Interstate School Leaders Licensure Consortium (ISLLC). Please contact the Kentucky Division of Certification (see Appendix 1) for additional information.

Guidance Counselor

I.   Provisional Certificate Requirements, Primary–Grade 12 (valid 5 years)

    A.   Complete an approved master's level program in guidance counseling

    B.   Renewable with proof of completion of at least 9 semester hours of graduate credit in areas of counseling or guidance counseling

II.   Standard Certificate Requirements, Primary–Grade 12 (valid 5 years)

    A.   Option 1

        1.   Successfully complete an approved master's level program in guidance counseling

        2.   Successfully complete additional 3–6 credit hours from an approved graduate-level counseling or guidance counseling program

      3.   One year of full-time employment as a provisionally certified guidance counselor in an accredited public or private school

      4.   Hold a valid Kentucky Professional teaching certificate

      5.   Complete at least 1 year of full-time classroom teaching experience

B. Option 2

      1.   See II, A, 1 and 2, directly above.

      2.   Complete at least 2 years of successful employment as a provisional full-time certified guidance counselor

C. Renewable upon completion of Effective Instructional Leadership Act (EILA) hours as specified by the Kentucky Department of Education by September 1 of the year of expiration

Library Media Specialist

I. This standards- and performance-based credential is awarded for work with all grade levels after the following requirements have been met:

  A. Transcript reflecting appropriate grades and courses,

  B. Recommendation of the college or university,

  C. Praxis II: Library Media Specialist test with satisfactory score, *and*

  D. Internship.

II. For applicants with 2 years of experience as a Library Media Specialist, C and D, directly above, may be waived. Contact the Education Professional Standards Board (see Appendix 1) for more detailed information.

School Psychologist

I. Provisional Certificate for School Psychologist

  A. Requirements

      1.   Recommendation of the applicant's preparing institution

      2.   Successful completion of the institution's approved program of preparation

      3.   Passing score on the required assessment

  B. Issued for a duration period of 1 year; may be renewed for an additional year if the individual is serving in the position of the school psychologist on at least a half-time basis.

  C. Individual serves under the supervision of the preparing institution. During this first year of service, the employer of the Provisional Certificate shall permit the individual to engage in the preparing institution's internship component.

  D. Internship may be served full-time during 1 school year or half-time during 2 consecutive years.

II. Standard Certificate for School Psychologist

  A. Option 1

      1.   Completion of an approved program of preparation that corresponds to the certificate at a teacher-education institution that adheres to the National Association of School Psychologists Standards for Training Programs

    2.   Completion of the appropriate assessment and a passing score as established in state regulations

B.   Option 2

    1.   Possession of a valid certificate as a nationally certified school psychologist issued by the National School Psychology Certification System

C.   The Standard Certificate for School Psychologist shall be issued for a period of 5 years and may be renewed for subsequent 5-year periods with completion of 1 of the following:

    1.   At least 3 years of experience as a school psychologist within each certification period and 72 hours of continuing professional development activities, *or*

    2.   Six semester hours of graduate training related to school psychology.

Teacher for Gifted Education

I.   Standards for Certificate Endorsement

A.   Classroom teaching certificate

B.   One year of teaching experience

C.   The completion of an approved graduate-level curriculum

    1.   At least 9 semester hours of credit giving emphasis to the following content:

        a.   Nature and needs of gifted education

        b.   Assessment and/or counseling of the gifted

        c.   Curriculum development for the gifted

        d.   Strategies and materials for teaching the gifted

        e.   Creative studies

    2.   At least 3 semester hours of credit in a supervised practicum for gifted education; however, with 2 years of experience as a teacher for gifted, the practicum requirement may be waived.

Louisiana

I. Level 1 Professional Certificate (valid for 3 years)
   A. Eligibility requirements for Louisiana graduate
      1. Successfully complete state-approved traditional or alternate teacher preparation program;
      2. Hold minimum 2.50 grade point average (GPA) on a 4.00 scale;
      3. Present appropriate scores on the National Teacher Examination (NTE) core battery (common exams) or the corresponding Praxis exams (core academic skills for educators in reading, writing, and mathematics); the Principles of Learning and Teaching (PLT) or other pedagogy exam required for the area(s) of certification; and the specialty area exam in the certification area in which the teacher preparation program was completed or in which the initial certificate was issued;
      and
      4. Be recommended by a state-approved university or private program provider for certification.
   B. Eligibility requirements for out-of-state graduate
      1. Possess a minimum of a bachelor's degree from a regionally accredited college or university;
      2. Successfully complete a teacher preparation program in another state;
      3. Hold a standard out-of-state teaching certificate; or if no certificate was issued, a letter from the State Department of Education in the state of origin verifying eligibility in that state for a certificate in the certification area(s);
      4. Pass all parts of Praxis exam(s) required for Louisiana certification:
         a. Present appropriate scores on the NTE core battery (common exams) or the corresponding Praxis exams (core academic skills for educators in reading, writing, and mathematics); the PLT or other pedagogy exam required for the area(s) of certification; and the specialty area exam in the certification area in which the teacher preparation program was completed or in which the initial certificate was issued;
         and
         b. If applicant has obtained National Board Certification (NBC) in corresponding areas for which certification is being sought as well as certification/licensure in the state of origin, the examination required for NBC will be accepted to fulfill the testing requirements for certification;
      5. Successfully complete student teaching, an internship, or 3 years of teaching experience in the candidate's area of certification;
      and
      6. Has not been out of teaching in the 5 years immediately preceding first employment or application for a Louisiana certificate.

    a.   A candidate who has not taught in 5 years may be issued a 1-year nonrenewable out-of-state (OS1) certificate while completing the 6 semester hours required for issuance of a 3-year nonrenewable (OS) certificate.

    b.   A candidate who is certified in another state can qualify for exclusion from the Praxis exam(s) required for Louisiana certification under the following criteria:

        i.   Meet all requirements for Louisiana certification except the Praxis exam requirements; has at least 3 years of successful teaching experience in another state, as determined by the Board; and teaches on an out-of-state certificate for 1 year in a Louisiana-approved public or an approved private school system.

        ii.   The teacher's employing authority must verify that he/she has completed 1 year of successful teaching experience in a Louisiana-approved public or an approved private school and that he/she has been recommended for further employment.

        iii.   The employing authority must request that the teacher be granted a valid Louisiana teaching certificate.

C.   Eligibility requirements for Foreign Applicant—(OS) Certificate

    1.   Possess a bachelor's or higher degree verified by a regionally accredited institution in the United States

        a.   If the institution is located in Louisiana, the dean of the College of Education must recommend the applicant for certification based upon Louisiana requirements.

        b.   If the institution is located in another state/country, the guidelines prescribed for out-of-state applicants must be followed.

        or

        c.   Credentials may be submitted for evaluation to a credentialing agency that follows the standards of the American Association of Collegiate Registrars and Admissions Officers (AACRAO). The original course-by-course evaluation must be submitted directly from the agency on "safe script" paper and must include a statement verifying the comparability of the baccalaureate degree in the field of education.

D.   Eligibility requirements for Foreign Applicant—Level 1 Certificate

    1.   Possess a bachelor's degree or higher verified by a regionally accredited institution in the United States;

        a.   If the institution is located in Louisiana, the dean of the College of Education must recommend the applicant for certification based upon Louisiana requirements.

        b.   If the institution is located in another state/country, the guidelines prescribed for out-of-state applicants must be followed.

        or

        c.   Credentials may be submitted for evaluation to a credentialing agency that follows the standards of the AACRAO. The original course-by-course evaluation must be submitted directly from the agency on "safe script" paper and must include a statement verifying the comparability of the baccalaureate degree in the field of education.

2. Present appropriate scores on the NTE core battery (common exams) or the corresponding Praxis exams (core academic skills for educators in reading, writing, and mathematics); the PLT or other pedagogy exam required for the area(s) of certification; and the specialty area exam(s) in the certification area(s) in which the teacher preparation program was completed or in which the initial certificate was issued.

II. Level 2 Professional Certificate (valid 5 years)
   A. Eligibility requirements
      1. Hold or meet eligibility requirements for a Level 1 certificate; see Level 1 Professional Certificate, directly above;
      2. Either successfully meet the standards of effectiveness for 3 years pursuant to Bulletin 130 and mandated by Act 54 of the Louisiana 2010 Legislative Session
         or
         Receive a waiver of this provision from the Louisiana Department of Education, at the request of the employing local education agency (LEA), if the teacher was unable to meet the standards of effectiveness due to administrative error in the local implementation of the evaluation system any year prior to the 2015–2016 school year;
         and
      3. Accrue 3 years of experience in area(s) of certification in an approved educational setting.
   B. If the Level 2 certificate is the applicant's first certificate, a state-approved teacher preparation program provider must submit the request.
   C. If the Level 1–certificated teacher qualifies for advancement to a Level 2 certificate, the request for the higher certificate must be submitted directly to the Louisiana Department of Education by the employing authority.

III. Level 3 Professional Certificate (valid 5 years)
   A. Eligibility requirements:
      1. Hold or meet eligibility requirements for Level 2 certificate; see Level 2 Professional Certificate, directly above;
      2. Hold a master's degree from a regionally accredited college or university;
         and
      3. Have 5 years of experience in area(s) of certification in an approved educational setting.
   B. If the Level 3 certificate is applicant's first certificate, a state-approved teacher preparation program provider must submit the request.
   C. If the Level 2–certificated teacher qualifies for advancement to a Level 3 certificate, the request for the higher certificate must be submitted directly to the Louisiana Department of Education by the employing authority.

IV. Renewal/Extension Guidelines for Level 1, Level 2, and Level 3 certificates
   A. Valid for 5 years initially and may be renewed thereafter for a period of 5 years at the request of a Louisiana employing authority. For renewal of level 2 and level 3 certificates, candidates must successfully meet the standards of effectiveness

for at least 3 years during the 5-year initial or renewal period pursuant to state law and Bulletin 130.

   B. LEAs may request a one-time, 5-year renewal of the certificate if a teacher was unable to successfully meet the standards of effectiveness due to administrative error in the local implementation of the evaluation system in any year before the 2015–2016 school year.

V. Out-of-State (OS) Certificate (valid 3 years; nonrenewable)

   A. Issued to a teacher who has completed an out-of-state teacher preparation program and either holds or is eligible for a certificate in the state in which the program was completed. The teacher is not initially eligible for a Level 1, 2, or 3 Louisiana certificate but meets Louisiana certification requirements with the exception of the Praxis/National Teacher Exam requirements. It provides a transition period that permits the holder to be employed in Louisiana K–12 schools while he/she complies with Louisiana Praxis/NTE requirements or meets Praxis exclusion eligibility requirements. For continued employment as a teacher in a Louisiana school system after the 3-year period has elapsed, the OS certificate holder must fulfill guidelines for a Level 1 or higher certificate.

   B. Eligibility requirements:
      1. Hold a bachelor's degree from a regionally accredited college or university;
      2. Successfully complete a teacher preparation program in another state;
      3. Hold a standard out-of-state teaching certificate, or if no certificate was issued, a letter from the state department of education or college of education dean verifying eligibility in that state for a certificate in the certification area(s);
      4. Successfully complete student teaching or internship in a certification area, or in lieu of student teaching or internship, have 3 years of successful teaching experience in a certification area;
      and
      5. If applicant earned a degree 5 or more years prior to date of application, he/she must have been a regularly employed teacher for at least 1 semester, or 90 consecutive days, within the 5-year period immediately preceding first employment in Louisiana or application for a Louisiana certificate. Lacking this experience, he/she must earn 6 semester hours of credit in state-approved courses (see Chapter 12 of Bulletin 746 on website) during the 5-year period immediately preceding application. A candidate who has not taught in 5 years may be issued a 1-year nonrenewable (OS1) certificate while he/she completes 6 semester hours required for the issuance of a 3-year nonrenewable (OS) certificate.

VI. Advancing from OS to Professional Level 1, 2, or 3 Certificate

   A. Pass all parts of Praxis exam(s) required for Louisiana certification:
      1. Present appropriate scores on the NTE core battery (common exams) or the corresponding Praxis exams (core academic skills for educators in reading, writing, and mathematics); the PLT or other pedagogy exam required for the area(s) of certification; and the specialty area exam in the certification area in which the teacher preparation program was completed or in which the initial certificate was issued.

2.   If applicant has obtained NBC in corresponding areas for which certification is being sought as well as certification/licensure in the state of origin, the examination required for NBC will be accepted to fulfill the testing requirements for certification.

3.   A candidate who is certified in another state can qualify for exclusion from the Praxis exam(s) required for Louisiana certification under these criteria:

    a.   He/she meets all requirements for Louisiana certification except the Praxis exam requirements; has at least 3 years of successful teaching experience in another state, as determined by the Board; and teaches on an OS certificate for 1 year in a Louisiana-approved public or an approved private school system;

    b.   The teacher's Louisiana employing authority verifies that he/she has completed 1 year of successful teaching experience in a Louisiana-approved public or an approved private school and that he/she has been recommended for further employment;
and

    c.   The employing authority requests that the teacher be granted a valid Louisiana teaching certificate.

VII.   Other Licenses and Certificates
Consult https://www.teachlouisiana.net/ for more details on the following credentials.

A.   World Language Certificate (WLC) PK–12 (valid 6 years). May be issued to a foreign associate teacher who participates in the Department of Education (LDE) Foreign Associate Teacher Program, and who teaches world language and/or immersion in grades PK–12.

B.   Practitioner Licenses

1.   Practitioner Licenses 1 and 2 (issued for 1 school year, renewed annually, held a maximum of 3 years while the holder completes an alternate program). Upon completion of 3 years of employment on this certificate, the holder must fulfill guidelines for a Level 1 or higher certificate for continued employment in a Louisiana school system.

2.   Practitioner License 3 (issued for 1 school year, renewed annually, held a maximum of 4 years while the holder completes an alternate program). Upon completion of 4 years of employment on this certificate, the holder must fulfill guidelines for a Level 1 or higher certificate for continued employment in a Louisiana school system.

C.   Extended Endorsement License (EEL) (issued for 1 school year, renewable annually, held a maximum of 3 years while the holder pursues certification in the content area of the license)

D.   Standard Certificates for Teachers in Nonpublic Schools

1.   A standard certificate with an asterisk (*) following the certificate type is issued to a teacher in a nonpublic school. The asterisk (*) refers to a statement printed at the bottom of the certificate: "If this teacher enters a public/charter school system in Louisiana, he/she will be required to meet the standards of effectiveness pursuant to Bulletin 130 and mandated by Act 54 of the

Louisiana 2010 Legislative Session for issuance of a Level 2 or Level 3 teaching certificate."

Educational Leadership Certificates

An individual who serves as an administrator and/or supervisor in Louisiana schools is required to obtain the appropriate credential for the area of assignment. A teacher already certified in Louisiana can have an educational leader certificate issued to provide administrative or supervisory services in a Louisiana school system.

I. Educational Leader Certificate Level 1 (EDL 1) (valid 3 years initially; may be extended 1 year at request of an LEA; limited to 2 such extensions). For those who fill school and district educational leadership positions (e.g., assistant principal, principal, parish or city supervisor of instruction, supervisor of child welfare and attendance, special education supervisor, or comparable school/district leader positions).
    A. Master's Degree Pathway
        1. Hold or be eligible to hold a valid Louisiana Type B or Level 2 teaching certificate, or have a comparable level out-of-state teaching certificate;
        2. Have 3 years of teaching experience in area of certification;
        3. Completion of a competency-based graduate degree preparation program in the area of educational leadership from a regionally accredited institution of higher education;
            and
        4. Have a passing score on the School Leaders Licensure Assessment (SLLA) in accordance with state requirements.
    B. Alternate Pathway 1—For persons who already hold a master's degree:
        1. Hold or be eligible to hold a valid Louisiana Type B or Level 2 teaching certificate, or have a comparable level out-of-state teaching certificate;
        2. Have 3 years of teaching experience in area of certification;
        3. Have earned a graduate degree from a regionally accredited institution of higher education;
        4. Meet competency-based requirements, as demonstrated by completion of an individualized program of educational leadership from a regionally accredited institution of higher education. (An individualized program will be developed based on a screening of each candidate's competencies upon entering into the graduate alternative certification program);
            and
        5. Have a passing score on the SLLA in accordance with state requirements.
    C. Alternate Pathway 2—For persons who already hold a master's degree in education:
        1. Hold or be eligible to hold a valid Louisiana Type B or Level 2 teaching certificate, or have a comparable level out-of-state teaching certificate;
        2. Have 3 years of teaching experience in area of certification;
        3. Have previously completed a graduate degree program in education from a regionally accredited institution of higher education;

4. Provide documented evidence of leadership experiences (240 clock hours or more) at the school and/or district level;
and

5. Earn a passing score on the SLLA in accordance with state requirements.

D. Alternate Pathway 3—For persons who already hold a bachelor's degree from a regionally accredited institution of higher education and are seeking to add Educational Leader certification to a valid teaching certificate through a competency-based educational leader practitioner (residency) program:

1. Hold or be eligible to hold a valid Louisiana Type B or Level 2 teaching certificate, or have a comparable level out-of-state teaching certificate;

2. Have 3 years of teaching experience in area of certification;

3. Demonstrate strong knowledge of instruction through a rigorous screening process by an approved program provider;

4. Complete a competency-based educational leader practitioner/residency preparation program in the area of educational leadership from a state-approved private provider or a regionally accredited institution of higher education;
and

5. Have a passing score on the SLLA in accordance with state requirements.

II. Educational Leader Certificate Level 2 (EDL 2) (valid 5 years initially; may be extended for 5 years at request of an LEA)

A. Hold a valid EDL 1 certificate, Louisiana provisional principal certification, or comparable level out-of-state educational leader certificate;

B. Have 3 years of teaching experience in area(s) of certification;

C. Participate in an education leader induction administered, if required by the LEA;
and

D. Either meet standards of effectiveness as an educational leader for 3 years pursuant to Bulletin 130 and R.S. 17:3902
or
Receive a waiver of this provision from the local department of education, at the request of the employing LEA, if the educational leader was unable to meet the standards of effectiveness any year prior to the 2015–2016 school year due to administrative error in the local implementation of the evaluation system.

III. Educational Leader Certificate Level 3 (EDL 3) (valid 5 years initially; may be extended for 5 years at the request of an LEA). This certificate is required in order to serve as a school system superintendent or assistant superintendent.

A. Valid EDL 2 or 1 of the Louisiana administrative/supervisory certifications that preceded the educational leadership certification structure;

B. Five years of teaching experience in area of certification;

C. Five years of successful administrative or management experience in education at the level of assistant principal or above. The assistant principal experience would be limited to a maximum of 2 years of experience in that position;
and

D. Passing score on the School Superintendent Assessment (SSA), in keeping with state requirements.

Counselor K–12

I. Counselor K–12 (Counselor in a School Setting)
   A. Valid Louisiana teaching certificate (see I, E, below)
   B. Complete a standards-based master's degree program in school counseling from a regionally accredited college or university approved by the Council for Accreditation of Counseling and Related Educational Program (CACREP)
   C. Complete a practicum/internship:
      1. Practicum in school counseling to include 100 contacts hours in a school setting
        or
      2. Internship in school counseling to include 600 contact hours in a school setting
   D. Complete the PRAXIS examination in school guidance and counseling (0421 or 5421)
   E. An Ancillary Counselor K–12 certificate can be issued if applicant is not a certified teacher but fulfills all other requirements listed above.

School Librarian

I. School Librarian
   A. Valid Louisiana elementary or secondary teaching certificate;
   B. Eighteen semester hours in library science, as follows:
      1. Elementary and/or secondary school library materials: 9 semester hours;
      2. Organization, administration, and interpretation of elementary and/or secondary school library service: 6 semester hours;
        and
      3. Elementary and/or secondary school library practice: 3 semester hours;
        or
      Three years of successful experience as a school librarian.
II. Ancillary School Librarian
   A. Master's degree in library science from a regionally accredited institution;
      and
   B. Passing score on Praxis Library Media Specialist examination (0311 or 5311).

Maine

At press time, Maine was in the process of making significant revisions to its certification requirements for educators. For the most up-to-date information, please visit http://www.maine.gov/doe/cert#.

Teacher and Educational Specialist Certificates

I. Conditional Certificate (valid 3 years, nonrenewable)
   A. Bachelor's degree from a regionally accredited college
   B. Completion of all content area (24 semester hours) course requirements (or, in the case of special education, 9 semester hours)
   C. Applicants who hold another professional certificate must have 6 semester hours in the content area for which they are applying. If the content area is designated a targeted need, the candidate must have 9 semester hours.
   D. Once a candidate qualifies, they must request issuance of the Conditional Certificate in writing.
II. Professional Certificate (valid 5 years; renewable)
   A. Meets all requirements for professional license as detailed in Chapter 115 in the Code of Maine Rules, available for download at https://www.maine.gov/sos/cec/rules/05/chaps05.htm.

Endorsements and Credentialing

PDFs detailing the most current requirements for each endorsement are available for download at http://www.maine.gov/doe/cert#.

I. Teacher Endorsements
   A. General Elementary Endorsement (K–8)
   B. Early Elementary Endorsement (K–3)
   C. Early Childhood Teacher (0 to age 5)
   D. English (5–8)
   E. English (7–12)
   F. Social Studies (5–8)
   G. Social Studies (7–12)
   H. Teacher of Students with Disabilities (0 to age 5)
   I. Teacher of Students with Disabilities (K–8)
   J. Teacher of Students with Disabilities (7–12)
   K. Teacher of Severely Impaired Students (K–12)
   L. Teacher of Blind or Visually Impaired (K–12)
   M. Teacher of Deaf or Hearing Impaired (K–12)

    N.   Mathematics (5–8)
    O.   Mathematics (7–12)
    P.   Science (5–8)
    Q.   Physical Science (7–12)
    R.   Life Science (7–12)
    S.   Physical Education (K–12)
    T.   Adapted Physical Education (K–12)
    U.   Dance (K–12)
    V.   Health Education (K–12)
    W.   Driver Education (7–12)
    X.   Music (K–12)
    Y.   Art (K–12)
    Z.   Theater (K–12)
    AA. Business Education
    BB. English as a Second Language (K–12)
    CC. Family and Consumer Science (K–12)
    DD. Computer Technology (K–12)
    EE. Gifted and Talented (K–12)
    FF. Industrial Arts/Technology (K–12)
    GG. Special Needs Teacher (9–12) Vocational Education
    HH. Adult Education
    II.   Career and Technical Education (9–12)
    JJ. World Language (K–12)

II. Administrator Endorsements
    A.   Superintendent
    B.   Assistant Superintendent
    C.   Administrator of Special Education
    D.   Assistant Administrator of Special Education
    E.   Building Administrator
    F.   Assistant Building Administrator
    G. Teaching Principal
    H.   Adult and Community Education Director
    I.   Assistant Adult and Community Education Director
    J.   Curriculum Coordinator

III. Educational Specialist Endorsements
    A.   Library/Media Specialist
    B.   School Counselor
    C.   Special Education Consultant
    D.   Literacy Specialist
    E.   Vocational Education Evaluator
    F.   Athletic Director
    G. Speech and Hearing Clinician
    H.   School Nurse (K–12)
    I.   Cooperative Education Coordinator (9–12) CTE

IV. School Psychologist Endorsement

Maryland

Types of Certificates

I. Professional Eligibility Certificate (PEC). Valid for 5 years.
    A. Issued to an applicant who meets all certification requirements and is not currently employed in a Maryland local school system.
II. Standard Professional Certificate I (SPC I). Valid for 5 years.
    A. Issued to an applicant who meets all certification requirements and is employed by a Maryland local school system, state institution, or publicly funded nonpublic school.
III. Standard Professional Certificate II (SPC II). Valid for 5 years.
    A. Issued to an applicant who completes the SPC I, is employed by a Maryland local school system, state institution, or publicly funded nonpublic school, has a professional development plan designed by the employee and employer, and submits the following:
        1. Verification of 3 years of satisfactory professional experience;
            and
        2. Six semester hours of acceptable credit.
IV. Advanced Professional Certificate (APC). Valid for 5 years.
    A. Issued to an applicant who submits the following:
        1. Verification of 3 years of full-time professional school-related experience;
        2. Six semester hours of acceptable credit;
            and
        3. A master's degree
            or
            A minimum of 36 semester hours of post-baccalaureate course work, which must include at least 21 semester hours of graduate credit (the remaining 15 semester hours may include graduate or undergraduate course work and/or Maryland State Department of Education Continuing Professional Development [CPD] credits)
            or
            National Board Certification and a minimum of 12 semester hours of approved graduate course work after the conferral of the bachelor's or higher degree.
V. Resident Teacher Certificate (RTC). Valid for 2 years.
    A. Issued to an applicant who has been selected by a local school system to participate in an alternative teacher preparation program.
VI. Conditional Certificate (COND). Valid for 2 years.
    A. Issued only at the request of a local school system superintendent to an applicant employed in a local school system who does not meet all professional certification requirements.

Teacher Areas Overview

I. Maryland issues certificates in the following teaching areas:
    A. Early Childhood Education (PreK–3)
    B. Elementary Education, grades 1–6
    C. Mathematics Instructional Leader (PreK–6) (4–9) (endorsement only)
    D. Instructional Leader: STEM, PreK–6 (endorsement only)
    E. Middle School Areas: (4–9)
        1. English Language Arts; Mathematics; Science; Social Studies; Mathematics Instructional Leader 4–9 (endorsement only)
    F. Secondary Academic Areas: (7–12)
        1. Agriculture/Agribusiness and Renewable Natural Resources; Biology; Business Education; Chemistry; Computer Science; Earth/Space Science; English; Environmental Science; Family and Consumer Sciences; Geography; History; Marketing; Mathematics; Physical Science; Physics; Political Science, Professional and Technical Education; Social Studies; Specialized Professional Areas; Speech Communication; Technology Education, Theater; Work-Based Learning Coordinator (endorsement only)
    G. Special Education
        1. Infant/primary (birth–grade 3); Elementary/middle (grades 1–8); Secondary/adult (grades 6–adult); Deaf and Hard of Hearing; Severely and Profoundly Disabled; Blind/Visually Impaired
    H. Specialty Areas (PreK–12)
        1. American Sign Language; Art; Dance; English for Speakers of Other Languages; Environmental Education; Health; Music; Physical Education; World Languages

Testing

I. All candidates applying for an initial teacher certificate are required to present qualifying scores on the Praxis CORE, ACT, SAT, or GRE, and the appropriate content and pedagogy assessments where required (Praxis II or ACTFL).
    A. The tests may be taken at any valid test site in the nation.
    B. Applicants must meet testing requirements current at the time of application.
II. Out-of-state candidates who do not hold a professional certificate from their respective state must meet Maryland's qualifying scores. Some out-of-state candidates may be eligible for a test exemption.
III. Applicants who have taken the teacher certification tests must submit their scores when applying for a Maryland certificate. Test scores must be sent to the Maryland State Department of Education in 1 of the following ways:
    A. Notation on an official college transcript;
    B. Photocopy of examinee's score report;
        or
    C. Verification from a state department of education.

Administrative or Supervisory Areas

Consult http://www.dsd.state.md.us/COMAR/SubtitleSearch.aspx?search=13A.12.04 for full regulations and for references to regulations, chapter, COMAR, and §B below.

I. Superintendent. For certification as a superintendent, deputy superintendent, associate superintendent, assistant superintendent or equivalent position, candidates should:

   A. Have a master's degree from an institution of higher education (IHE);

   B. Have 3 years of satisfactory teaching experience and 2 years of satisfactory administrative or supervisory experience in a PreK–12 school setting; *and*

   C. Submit a minimum of 24 credits of post-master's, graduate course work in educational administration and supervision to include a balance of course work in the following:

      1. Developing and Articulating Shared Vision;

      2. Organizational Management;

      3. Promoting and Maintaining a Positive School Culture and Instructional Program for Learning;

      4. Demonstrating Values and Ethics of Leadership; *and*

      5. Collaboration with Diverse Stakeholders.

   D. A superintendent who enters Maryland from another state may obtain superintendent certification if that superintendent held a valid professional state certificate and presents verification of at least 27 months of satisfactory performance as a superintendent during the past 7 years on the basis of which application is being made for a like or comparable Maryland certificate.

II. Supervisors of Instruction, Assistant Principals, and Principals. For certification as an Administrator I or Administrator II:

   A. Administrator I. To be assigned as a supervisor of instruction or assistant principal, candidates should

      1. Have a master's degree from an IHE;

      2. Have 27 months of satisfactory teaching performance or satisfactory performance on a professional certificate or satisfactory performance as a certified specialist; *and*

      3. Complete 1 of the following:

         a. Department-approved program which leads to certification as a supervisor of instruction, assistant principal, or principal that includes the outcomes in the Maryland instructional leadership framework;

         b. Approved program that leads to certification as a supervisor of instruction, assistant principal, or principal in accordance with the interstate agreement; *or*

         c. Eighteen semester hours of graduate course work taken at an IHE at the post-baccalaureate level to include a balance of content in the following categories: curriculum, instruction, and assessment; development, observation, and evaluation of staff; legal issues and ethical decision-making; school leadership, management and administration; special education (3 semester hours); and practicum, internship, or a collaboratively designed and supervised experience by the local school system and IHE to include department-approved instructional leadership outcomes with verification of this experience submitted by the applicant.

B. Administrator II. For an individual to be assigned as a school principal
1. The applicant, before initial appointment as principal, shall:
   a. Complete the requirements for Administrator I; *and*
   b. Present evidence of a qualifying score as established by the state board on a department-approved principal certification assessment.
2. A principal who enters Maryland from another state may obtain an Administrator II certificate if that principal held a valid professional state certificate and verifies at least 27 months of satisfactory performance as a principal during the past 7 years on the basis of which application is being made for a like or comparable Maryland certificate.

C. Special Provisions
1. An applicant who successfully completes the requirements under Regulation .05D of the chapter cited in the link above for the resident principal certificate may obtain an Administrator II certificate; consult the link above for full details.
2. A Standard Professional certificate or Advanced Professional certificate shall be considered valid for service as principal of an elementary school of not more than 6 teachers if the principal teaches at least 50 percent of the school day.
3. A person who holds the position of assistant principal on the date this regulation becomes effective shall meet the requirements of §B of the regulation cited in the link above not later than the end of the first full validity period after the renewal of the currently held certificate.

III. Library Media Administrator
A. The person designated by the local superintendent of schools as having respon'sibility for:
1. Administration and supervision of the library media program, including the supervision of the library media program in the individual schools; *and*
2. Development of policies, programs, budgets, and procedures for the library media services of the school system and its schools.

B. Education and Experience. To be certified as library media administrator, the applicant shall meet the requirements for certification as a library media specialist:
1. Have a master's degree from an IHE;
2. Have 3 years of satisfactory library media program experience; however, at the recommendation of the local school superintendent, 2 years of related satisfactory experience may be substituted for 2 years of library media program experience; *and*

3.   Complete 1 of the options listed under Regulation .04B(3) of the chapter cited in the link above that would lead to certification as Administrator I.

C.   Certificate Renewal. In addition to meeting the requirements of COMAR 13A.12.01.11B (see the link above), a library media administrator or a holder of a valid certificate for an education media administrator (Level III) shall satisfy the required reading course work contained in COMAR 13A.12.01.11A(5)(c) to renew the certificate.

IV.   Supervisor of Guidance. For certification, the applicant shall:

A.   Meet the requirements for certification as a guidance counselor;

B.   Have 3 years of satisfactory performance as a guidance counselor; *and*

C.   Have 12 semester hours of graduate credit from an IHE in any of the following areas, with at least 6 of those semester hours in school supervision or school administration: management; school supervision; school administration; program development; and program evaluation.

V.   Supervisor of School Psychological Services. For certification, the applicant shall:

A.   Meet the requirements for certification as a school psychologist under COMAR 13A.12.03.07 (see the link above);

B.   Have a doctoral degree:

1.   From a state or regionally credited school psychology program or National Association of School Psychologists (NCATE), or American Psychological Association–accredited school psychology program, *or*

2.   In psychology or education or human development;

C.   As part of or in addition to §B of the regulation cited in the link above, have 9 semester hours of graduate credits, including 3 semester hours in school law and 6 semester hours in supervision, management, or administration of schools; *and*

D.   Have 3 years of experience as a school psychologist under COMAR 13A.12.03.07 (see the link above).

VI.   Supervisor of Pupil Personnel. For certification, the applicant shall:

A.   Meet the requirements for certification as a pupil personnel worker;

B.   Have a master's degree from an IHE;

C.   As part of or in addition to §B of the regulation cited in the link above, have a graduate course in the area of administration and supervision; *and*

D.   Have 3 years of successful teaching experience. At the recommendation of the local superintendent of schools, 2 years of related experience may be counted for 2 years of teaching experience.

VII.   Supervisor of Special Education

A.   Principal (Handicapped Facility). For certification, the applicant shall:

1.   Meet the requirements for certification in special education; *and*

2.   Meet the requirements for certification as an Administrator II.

B. Supervisor of Special Education (Sole Assignment). For certification, the applicant shall:
   1. Mcct thc requirements for certification in special education;
      and
   2. Meet the requirements for certification as an Administrator I.
C. Special Provision. Supervisors with multiple area assignments shall meet the requirements set forth in Regulation .04 of the chapter cited in the link above.

VIII. Supervisor of Teachers of Hearing Impaired. The applicant shall:
   A. Meet the requirements for certification as a teacher of the hearing impaired;
   B. Have a master's degree from an IHE with at least 1 course in administrative and supervisory techniques and 1 course in curriculum development;
      and
   C. Have experience which includes:
      1. Three years of successful teaching experience with the hearing impaired,
         or
      2. Four years of paid experience or its equivalent in a school setting, with 2 years of successful teaching experience with the hearing impaired.

Specialist Areas

For full requirements, consult http://www.dsd.state.md.us/COMAR/SubtitleSearch.aspx?search=13A.12.03.

   I. Gifted & Talented Specialist
  II. School Counselor
 III. Library Media Specialist
  IV. Pupil Personnel Worker
   V. Reading Specialist
  VI. Reading Teacher
 VII. Psychometrist
VIII. School Psychologist
  IX. School Social Worker

Massachusetts

The following outlines general requirements. To identify specific requirements of the license you seek, please use the online Licensure Requirements Tool at https://gateway.edu.state.ma.us/elar/licensurehelp/LicenseRequirementsCriteriaPageControl.ser.

Academic (PreK–12) Licenses

I. Provisional License (valid for 5 years of employment; nonrenewable; beginning July 1, 2019, an educator who holds 1 or more provisional licenses may be employed under said license[s] for no more than 5 years in total). Appropriate for an applicant who:
   A. Seeks a license as a core academic teacher and does not hold the Sheltered English Immersion Endorsements (SEI)
   B. Has passed all required Massachusetts Tests for Educator Licensure (MTEL)
      1. For licenses that do not have a subject matter knowledge MTEL (e.g., moderate special needs, instructional technology), applicants must complete a Competency Review (downloadable at http://www.doe.mass.edu/licensure/academic-prek12/teacher/license-types.html).

II. Initial License (valid for 5 years of employment; may be extended once for an additional 5 years). Appropriate for an applicant who:
   A. Has a bachelor's degree
   B. Has passed all required MTEL tests
   C. Holds the SEI endorsement (core academic teacher, principal/assistant principal, or supervisor/director only)
   D. Fulfills one of the following:
      1. Has completed an approved educator preparation program in Massachusetts
      or
      Has completed a state-approved educator preparation program in a state with which Massachusetts has signed the National Association of State Directors of Teacher Education and Certification (NASDTEC) Interstate Agreement or other agreement accepted by the Commissioner
      or
      Has completed an educator preparation program sponsored by a college or university outside Massachusetts that has been accredited by a national organization accepted by the Commissioner
      or
      Possesses the equivalent of at least an Initial license/certificate issued by a state with which Massachusetts has signed the NASDTEC Interstate Agreement or other agreement accepted by the Commissioner
      or

Has prepared outside of the United States and completed a Panel Review in accordance with Department guidelines.

III. Professional License (valid for 5 calendar years; renewable every 5 years thereafter). Appropriate for an applicant who:

    A. Holds an Initial license in the same field as the Professional license sought

    B. Has been employed under the Initial license for at least 3 years and has completed a 1-year induction program with a mentor and at least 50 hours of a mentored experience beyond the induction year

    C. Has completed 1 of the following:

        1. An approved licensure program for the Professional license sought as set forth in the Guidelines for Program Approval

          or

          A program leading to eligibility for master teacher status, such as those sponsored by the National Board for Professional Teaching Standards and others accepted by the Commissioner

          or

          A master's or higher degree or other advanced graduate program in an accredited college or university, including at least 12 credits of graduate-level courses in subject matter knowledge or pedagogy based on the subject matter knowledge of the professional license sought. These may include credits earned prior to application for the license.

IV. Temporary (valid for 1 year of employment; nonrenewable). Appropriate for an applicant who:

    A. Has a bachelor's degree

    B. Has been employed in another state under a valid license or certificate comparable to a Massachusetts initial license for at least 3 years

    C. Has not passed all of, or has not failed any of, the required MTEL tests

Administrator Licenses

I. Provisional License (Superintendent/Assistant Superintendent only; valid for 5 years of employment; cannot be extended or renewed; beginning July 1, 2019, an educator who holds one or more provisional licenses may be employed under said license[s] for no more than 5 years in total). Appropriate for an applicant who:

    A. Has a bachelor's degree

    B. Has passed the Communication and Literacy Skills MTEL

    C. Has completed at least 3 full years of employment in an executive management/leadership role or in a supervisory, teaching, or administrative role in a public/charter school, private school, higher education, or other educational setting accepted by the Department

II. Initial License (valid for 5 years; cannot be extended). Appropriate for an applicant who:

    A. Has passed the Communication and Literacy Skills MTEL

    B. Has completed 1 of the following pathways:

        1. A state-approved educator preparation program

2. An apprenticeship
3. Panel Review

III. Professional License (valid for 5 calendar years; renewable every 5 years)
   A. Requirements for each administrator license at the Professional level are unique to each license field. Please use the online Licensure Requirements Tool to identify the appropriate pathway/requirement set.

IV. Temporary (valid for 1 year of employment; nonrenewable). Appropriate for an applicant who:
   A. Is an experienced teacher from out of state
   B. Has a bachelor's degree
   C. Has been employed in another state under a valid license or certificate comparable to a Massachusetts Initial license for at least 3 years
   D. Has not passed or failed the Communication and Literacy Skills MTEL

Professional Support Personnel Licenses

I. The Department issues the following professional support personnel licenses: School Counselor (PreK–8 and 5–12); School Nurse (all levels); School Psychologist (all levels); School Social Worker/School Adjustment Counselor (all levels). Requirements for each license are unique to each field; please use the online Licensure Requirements Tool to identify the appropriate pathway/requirement set.
   A. Initial License (valid for 5 years of employment; can be extended once for an additional 5 years of employment)
   B. Professional License (valid for 5 calendar years; renewable every 5 years)
   C. Temporary License (valid for 1 year of employment; nonrenewable). Appropriate for an applicant who:
      1. Is an experienced teacher from out of state
      2. Has a bachelor's degree
      3. Has been employed in another state under a valid license or certificate comparable to a Massachusetts Initial license for at least 3 years
      4. Has not passed or failed the Communication and Literacy Skills MTEL

Michigan

Teaching Certificate Validity Levels

I. Elementary: An elementary certificate issued after September 1, 1988, is valid for teaching all subjects grades K–5, all subjects grades K–8 in a self-contained classroom, and subject area endorsements, as listed on the certificate.

II. Secondary: A secondary certificate issued after September 1, 1988, is valid for teaching in designated discipline areas in any grade or grade range from grades 6 to 12.

Types of Certificates

I. Standard Teaching Certificate (initial teaching license/credential; valid for 5 years)
   A. Issued upon successful completion of a state-approved teacher preparation program and a passing score on the appropriate Michigan Test for Teacher Certification (MTTC) exams.
      1. For information on Michigan-approved Educator Preparation Institutions (EPI) and programs, consult https://mdoe.state.mi.us/proprep/.
   B. Programs completed through colleges/universities outside of Michigan must be approved for the certification of teachers by another state; contact that state's education department for information. Upon completion of the out-of-state program, candidates must apply for a Michigan teacher certification, and their credentials must be evaluated by the Office of Educator Excellence (OEE).
   C. An applicant who has completed an alternative route teacher certification program in another state and holds a valid, Standard Teaching Certificate issued based on completion of that program can submit an application to be evaluated for certification. This option is not available to applicants who have temporary, preliminary, or interim teaching certificates from other states.
   D. Standard Teaching Certificate Renewal (each renewal valid for 5 years)
      1. Completion of 1 of the following since the issuance of the Standard Teaching Certificate:
         a. Six semester credit hours in an education-related professional learning program at an approved regionally accredited college or university;
            or
         b. A total of 150 State Continuing Education Clock Hours (SCECHs) appropriate to the grade level and content endorsement(s) of the certificate held;
            or
         c. A total of 150 annual District Provided Professional Development (DPPD) hours, in accordance with Michigan School Code Section 380.1527, through professional development programs that are appropriate to the grade level and content endorsement(s) of the certificate;

or

    d.   A combination of semester credit hours and SCECHs (25 SCECHs = 1 semester credit hour) totaling 150 hours.

  2.   A teacher who holds a Standard Teaching Certificate may be granted a one-time 5-year renewal of the certificate based upon submission of evidence of having earned at any time an education-related master's degree or higher.

  3.   A teacher who holds an expired Standard Teaching Certificate and holds a valid teaching certificate from another state is eligible for a one-time 5-year renewal of the Standard Teaching Certificate.

II.   Standard Temporary Teacher Employment Authorization (T2EA) (valid for 1 year; nonrenewable)

   A.   The T2EA allows out-of-state candidates 1 year to pass the appropriate MTTC exam(s) after OEE evaluation determining that they meet the following criteria:

     1.   Hold a valid, acceptable teaching certificate from another state;

     2.   Have never held a Michigan teaching certificate;

     3.   Have applied for initial Standard Teaching certification;
        and

     4.   Meet all the requirements for the Standard Teaching Certificate, except for passing the MTTC examinations.

   B.   Candidates do not apply for the T2EA; it is issued upon evaluation for initial certification.

   C.   Once a T2EA has been issued, the candidate must complete MTTC requirements in order to be issued any Michigan teaching certificate.

III. Professional Teaching Certificate (initial advanced teaching credential; valid for 5 years)

   A.   Three years of successful teaching experience since the issue date and within the validity and grade level of the Standard Certificate

   B.   In-state applicants who have completed a teacher preparation program through a Michigan EPI must meet the reading methods requirements:

     1.   Completion of 6 semester credit hours of reading methods for elementary or 3 semester credit hours for secondary;

     2.   Completion of 6 semester credit hours of reading diagnostics and remediation, including a field experience, in accordance with Michigan Revised School Code MCL 380.1531(4). For approved Michigan courses that meet this requirement, consult http://www.michigan.gov/teachercert.

   C.   Any combination of the following since the issue date of the Standard Certificate or Standard Renewal, totaling 150 hours:

     1.   Completion of 6 semester credit hours in an education-related professional learning program at an approved EPI, or 6 semester credit hours of academic credit appropriate to the grade level and content endorsement(s) of the certificate at any regionally accredited college or university;
        and/or

     2.   Completion of 150 SCECHs appropriate to the grade level and content endorsement(s) of the certificate held;
        and/or

     3.   Completion of 150 annual DPPD hours, in accordance with Michigan

School Code Section 380.1527, through professional development programs appropriate to the grade level and content endorsement(s) of the certificate.

    a.   SCECHs and/or DPPD hours must be earned after the issue date of the Standard Certificate.

    b.   25 SCECHs = 1 semester credit hour = 25 DPPD hours.

D.   Out-of-state applicants for the initial Professional Teaching Certificate who have completed an approved out-of-state teacher preparation program must meet the reading methods requirements in III, B, above.

E.   Candidates who hold a valid Standard Teaching Certificate from another state and meet all requirements for the Professional Teaching Certificate at the time of application are not required to meet MTTC testing requirements.

IV. Professional Temporary Teacher Employment Authorization (Professional T2EA) (valid for 1 year; nonrenewable)

A.   Issued to out-of-state candidates who hold a valid, acceptable certificate from another state and

    1.   Have never held a Michigan teaching certificate;
       and

    2.   Meet all the requirements for the Professional Teaching Certificate, except for the reading methods course work.

B.   Candidates do not apply for this authorization; it is issued upon evaluation for initial certification.

    1.   Once the Professional T2EA has been issued, the candidate must complete the reading methods requirement within 1 year of issuance in order to be issued a Michigan Professional Teaching Certificate.

    2.   If the reading methods requirement is not met within 1 year after Professional T2EA issuance, the candidate must be evaluated for the Standard Teaching Certificate and pass the appropriate testing requirements.

V. Interim Teaching Certificate (valid for 5 years; nonrenewable). Candidates are eligible for enrollment in an alternative route program if they meet the following criteria:

A.   Hold at least a bachelor's degree from a regionally accredited college or university, with a grade point average of at least 3.0 on a 4.0 scale (or equivalent);

B.   Pass the appropriate MTTC discipline area exam(s);

C.   Fulfill CPR/First Aid certification in accordance with the Michigan Department of Education Approved Provider List.

D.   To progress to the Standard Teaching Certificate while working under the Interim Certificate, the individual must:

    1.   Submit to and pass a criminal history check, including FBI fingerprinting, in accordance with Michigan School Safety law, prior to employment by a local district or school;

    2.   Receive intensive observation and coaching;

    3.   Complete 3 years of satisfactory teaching experience under the Interim Teaching Certificate;

    4.   Be recommended by the approved alternative route provider for the Standard Teaching Certificate once all requirements have been met.

E.   Additional endorsements shall not be added to an Interim Teaching Certificate.

VI. Standard Career and Technical Education (CTE) Certificate (initial certificate; valid for 5 years)

    A. To qualify for a Standard CTE Certificate based on completion of an in-state CTE program, applicant must be recommended by the CTE educator preparation program and meet the following requirements:

       1. Has a bachelor's degree;

       2. Has a major or minor in the field of specialization in which CTE certification is being requested;

       3. Has a minimum of 2 years (4,000 hours) of recent and relevant experience, as defined by the superintendent of public instruction, in the CTE area; *and*

       4. Has successfully completed a minimum of 6 satisfactory semester credit hours of professional or CTE education credit.

    B. Applicants who have completed an approved out-of-state CTE program must follow the guidelines provided on the Michigan Department of Education website at https://www.michigan.gov/documents/mde/Out_Of_State_Applicants_534635_7.pdf.

    C. A Standard CTE Certificate is valid for teaching courses in which instruction is limited to the occupation specified on the certificate in approved CTE programs.

VII. Professional CTE Certificate (valid for 5 years)

    A. Three years of successful teaching experience within the validity of the Standard CTE Certificate;

    B. The reading methods and reading diagnostic requirements outlined in Section 1531(4) at http://legislature.mi.gov/doc.aspx?mcl-380-1531.

    C. To progress to the Professional CTE Certificate from the Standard CTE, an applicant must fulfill at least 1 of the following criteria:

       1. Earn a master's degree or higher in an education-related area since the issue date of the most recent Standard CTE Certificate or renewal;

       2. Any combination of the following, totaling 150 hours (1 semester credit hour = 25 SCECHs or 25 DPPD hours) appropriate to the grade level and endorsement(s) of the certificate:

          a. Completion of 6 satisfactory semester credit hours earned at a regionally accredited college or university;

          b. Completion of 150 SCECHs via approved professional development activities;

          c. Completion of 150 DPPD hours via district-approved professional development programs.

    D. The Professional CTE Certificate has the same validity and renewal conditions as the Professional Teaching Certificate.

VIII. Preliminary School Psychologist Certificate (initial certificate; valid for 3 years; renewable one time upon completion of 6 additional semester credit hours in an approved school psychologist preparation program after issuance of the Preliminary School Psychologist Certificate)

    A. Completion of a minimum of 45 graduate semester credit hours in an approved school psychologist program;

B. Completion of a supervised practicum of not less than 600 hours under the supervision of a certified school psychologist.

C. If the school psychologist program was completed out of state, the candidate must have a valid out-of-state school psychologist certificate or license.

IX. Preliminary School Psychologist Renewal (valid for 3 years; a one-time, 3-year renewal may be granted upon application and verification of one of the following):

A. Six semester credit hours in an approved school psychologist program from an approved EPI, completed since the issue date of the Preliminary School Psychologist Certificate;

or

B. A valid out-of-state school psychologist certificate.

X. School Psychologist Certificate (valid for 5 years; renewable)

A. In-state applicants must:

1. Hold a current or expired Michigan Preliminary School Psychologist Certificate;

2. Complete a state-approved specialist-level degree or the equivalent (no fewer than 60 semester credit hours) in school psychology via an EPI with an approved school psychology program;

3. Complete an internship of no fewer than 1,200 clock hours.

B. Out-of-state applicants must:

1. Complete a specialist-level degree or the equivalent (no fewer than 60 semester credit hours) in school psychology with a 1,200 clock-hour internship from an out-of-state EPI;

2. Hold a valid Nationally Certified School Psychologist (NCSP) credential issued by the National Association of School Psychologists (NASP), or a valid, standard school psychologist certificate from the state where the program was completed.

XI. School Psychologist Certificate Renewal (valid for 5 years). Applicants must:

A. Hold a valid Michigan School Psychologist Certificate;

B. Hold a valid NCSP credential or a valid out-of-state school psychologist certificate (may be renewed once);

C. Any combination of the following, totaling 150 hours:

1. Completion of 6 semester credit hours appropriate for performing the role of a school psychologist, or sufficient semester credit hours at a regionally accredited college or university applicable to a school psychologist position (1 semester credit hour = 25 SCECHs);

or

2. Completion of 150 SCECHs appropriate for performing the role of a school psychologist;

or

3. Completion of 150 DPPD hours appropriate for performing the role of a school psychologist.

a. SCECHs and/or DPPD hours must be earned after the issue date of the School Psychologist Certificate.

XII. Preliminary Authorization to Work as a School Counselor (valid for 3 years; nonrenewable). Applicants must:
   A. Be enrolled in and have completed a minimum of 30 semester credit hours of course work in a school counselor education program;
   B. Have passed the school counselor subject area MTTC exam;
   C. Complete any outstanding courses/practicum during the 3-year validity period to be recommended by the in-state school counselor preparation institution for:
      1. The school counselor endorsement (NT) on a Michigan Teaching Certificate; *or*
      2. The School Guidance Counselor License (SCL).
XIII. Temporary School Counselor Authorization (valid for 1 year; issued to applicants who have completed an out-of-state approved school counselor education program; nonrenewable)
   A. Candidates do not apply for this authorization; it is issued upon evaluation of initial application for a School Guidance Counselor License.
   B. Once a Temporary School Counselor Authorization has been issued, the candidate must meet Michigan testing requirements on the MTTC School Counselor (NT) exam within 1 year.
   C. Can also be issued to applicants who have:
      1. At least a bachelor's degree;
      2. Successfully served for at least 5 of the immediately preceding 7 years in the role of a school counselor;
      3. A valid out-of-state school counselor credential.
XIV. School Guidance Counselor License (valid for 5 years; effective February 6, 2020, renewable upon completion of requirements of MCL 380.1233[7–9]; see D, below, for renewal instructions prior to that date)
   A. Available to in-state and out-of-state applicants who have completed an advanced degree or the equivalent in an approved school counselor education program.
   B. In-state applicants must have:
      1. Completed a program through a Michigan-approved school counselor preparation institution;
      2. Completed a minimum of 30 graduate-level semester credit hours in an approved school counselor preparation program, including an internship;
      3. Completed a 600-clock-hour internship (with at least 300 of the clock hours in a school setting), based on an approved school counselor program with school-aged pupils, under the supervision of a credentialed school counselor or a school counselor educator;
      4. Passed the MTTC School Counselor (NT) exam.
   C. Out-of-state applicants must have:
      1. Completed an out-of-state approved school counselor education program;
      2. Successfully served for at least 5 of the immediately preceding 7 years in the role of a school counselor in another state;
      3. A bachelor's degree;
      4. Authorization/certification to work as a school counselor in another state; *or*

        Completed all requirements of an approved school counselor preparation program at an out-of-state institution and earned an advanced degree in school counseling or its equivalent;

    5.   Passed the MTTC School Counselor (NT) exam.

XV.   School Guidance Counselor Renewals

    A.   Before February 6, 2020, the School Guidance Counselor License may be renewed for one 5-year period when a candidate has:

        1.   An education-related master's degree or higher from a regionally accredited college or university;

        2.   A valid out-of-state certificate/license (may be renewed once);
           or

        3.   Any combination of the following:

           a.   Completion of 6 semester credit hours in an education-related professional learning program at an approved school counselor educator preparation institution;
               or

           b.   Completion of 150 SCECHs, earned since the issuance of the most recent school counselor license or renewal;
               or

           c.   Completion of 150 DPPD hours, in accordance with Michigan School Code Section 380.1527, completed through a district professional development program appropriate to the School Guidance Counselor License.

    B.   After February 5, 2020, all counselors who hold a current Michigan teaching certificate plus the school counselor endorsement (NT) and the School Guidance Counselor License must meet new professional development standards, as follows:

        1.   Per MCL 380.1233(7–9), counselors must complete 50 school counselor–specific professional development clock hours that align with MCL 380.1233(7–9).

           a.   These 50 hours count toward the 150 hours required for renewal.

           b.   Counselors must also complete 25 hours related to college preparation and selection, and 25 hours related to career consultation (5 of which must include the exploration of military career options).

XVI.   School Administrator Certificate (initial license; valid for 5 years)

    A.   Two basic endorsements available: Elementary/Secondary Administrator K–12 (Building) or Central Office (District).

    B.   Certification requires completion of master's degree or higher from an approved program in educational leadership or administration offered by a regionally accredited college or university.

    C.   A superintendent, principal, assistant principal, or other person whose primary responsibility is administering instructional programs:

        1.   If employed as a school administrator after January 4, 2010, must hold a valid Administrator Certificate in accordance with SB 981.

        2.   If employed as a school administrator on or before January 4, 2010, does not need to hold the Administrator Certificate for their current position, but must hold the Experience-Based School Administrator Certificate.

       3.   A noncertified school administrator may be employed by a school district if enrolled in a program leading to certification as a school administrator not later than 6 months after date of employment.

          a.   The school administrator has 3 years to meet the certification requirements.

          b.   Districts that employ noncertified school administrators must obtain an annual School Administrator Permit and document the noncertified school administrator's progress toward obtaining a School Administrator Certificate. Failure to meet ongoing requirements eliminate a school administrator's eligibility for the Permit.

XVII.   School Administrator Certificate Renewal (valid for 5 years)

    A.   A valid out-of-state certificate, appropriate for K–12 administration, may be used one time to renew a School Administrator Certificate.

    B.   A school administrator who holds a valid Michigan Professional Teaching Certificate meets the requirement for renewal of the School Administrator Certificate.

    C.   Without a valid out-of-state certificate or Michigan Professional Teaching Certificate, certificate renewal requires any combination of the following, totaling 150 clock hours, completed since the issue date of the most recent School Administrator Certificate renewal:

       1.   Completion of 6 semester credit hours in an education-related professional learning program appropriate to the School Administrator Certificate;
          or

       2.   Completion of 150 SCECHs appropriate to the content and grade level of the certificate and endorsement;
          or

       3.   Completion of 150 DPPD hours, in accordance with Michigan School Code Section 380.1527.

XVIII.   Previously Issued Certificates

    A.   Michigan no longer issues the following certificates; however, they are still valid for those who hold them:

       1.   Eighteen-Hour and 30-Hour Continuing Certificate

       2.   Permanent Certificate

       3.   Full Vocational Authorization

Minnesota

Minnesota's 2017 Omnibus Education bill created a new system for the Professional Educator Licensing and Standards Board (PELSB) to issue educator licenses. Teaching licenses are now granted in one of four licensure tiers depending on the teacher's qualifications. Administrative licensure did not change.

Tiered Licensure for Teachers

I. Requirements for all tiered licensure applicants:
   A. A bachelor's degree from a regionally accredited institution. The only exception is for those seeking a Career and Technical Education (CTE) license, who must hold credentials in the relevant content area through one of the following:
      1. Associate's degree
      2. Professional certification
      3. Five years of work experience
   B. A criminal background check, including a fingerprint check. Fingerprint card information is available from PELSB (see Appendix 1).
II. Tier 1 (valid for up to 1 school year). Requirements include:
   A. Meet requirements for all tiered licensure applicants.
   B. A job offer with a Minnesota public school district or charter school. The district or charter school must attest that it could not find any qualified Tier 2, 3, or 4 candidates.
   C. For first renewal, Tier 1 teachers must attempt the Minnesota Teacher Licensure Examinations (MTLE) content tests aligned to their licensure area and participate in cultural competency training.
   D. License is renewable up to 3 times, unless the school district or charter school can verify good cause for additional renewals.
III. Tier 2 (valid for up to 2 school years). Requirements include:
   A. Meet requirements for all tiered licensure applicants.
   B. A job offer with a Minnesota public school district or charter school.
   C. Meet 1 of the following requirements:
      1. Enrollment in a Minnesota state-approved teacher preparation program aligned to the licensure area,
      2. A master's degree aligned to the licensure area,
         or
      3. Meet 1 of the following requirements:
         a. Teacher preparation in the licensure area
         b. Eight upper-division credits in the licensure area
         c. Field-specific methods of training

       d.   Passing scores on the MTLE pedagogy and content tests aligned to the licensure area

       e.   Two years of teaching experience in the licensure area

  D.   For renewal, the applicant must participate in cultural competency training.

  E.   License is renewable up to 3 times, unless the school district or charter school can verify good cause for additional renewals.

IV. Tier 3 (valid for 3 years). Requirements include:

  A.   Meet requirements for all tiered licensure applicants.

  B.   Pass the MTLE pedagogy and contents tests aligned to the licensure area.

  C.   Meet 1 of the following requirements:

      1.   Completion of a Minnesota state-approved teacher preparation program

      2.   Completion of an out-of-state approved teacher preparation program with equivalent student teaching experience to that of a Minnesota teacher preparation program (currently 12 weeks)

          a.   Certifying officer of the college/university through which the state-approved program was completed must recommend the applicant for Minnesota licensure.

      3.   Recommendation for licensure through the Licensure via Portfolio process

      4.   Possession or past possession of a professional teaching license in another state and verification of 2 years of teaching experience in the licensure area

      5.   Three years of teaching experience on a Tier 2 license in the licensure area and no placement on an improvement plan by the school district or charter school

  D.   To renew, an applicant must have 75 clock hours and meet the mandatory components in place at the time of renewal.

  E.   Tier 3 licensure can be renewed indefinitely.

V. Tier 4 (valid for 5 years). Requirements include:

  A.   Meet requirements for all tiered licensure applicants.

  B.   Pass the Minnesota basic skills, pedagogy, and content exams aligned to the licensure area

  C.   Meet 1 of the following requirements:

      1.   Completion of a Minnesota state-approved teacher preparation program

      2.   Completion of an out-of-state approved teacher preparation program with equivalent student teaching experience to that of a Minnesota teacher preparation program (currently 12 weeks)

  D.   Verification of 3 years of teaching experience in Minnesota and no placement on an improvement plan by the school district

  E.   To renew, an applicant must have 125 clock hours and meet the mandatory components in place at the time of renewal.

  F.   Tier 4 licensure can be renewed indefinitely.

VI. Testing Requirements for Teacher Licensure

  A.   Minnesota accepts a variety of exam options for meeting the state's basic skills requirement. Please refer to PELSB's website at https://mn.gov/pelsb/aspiring-educators/requirements/ for full details.

  B.   The Minnesota Teacher Licensure Examinations (MTLEs) are the means of assessing the pedagogical and content area knowledge of candidates for Minnesota licensure. MTLE information can be found at http://www.mtle.nesinc.com/.

VII.   Teachers and School Administrators (outside Minnesota)

    A.   Minnesota does not have licensure reciprocity with any other state.

    B.   Applicants prepared out of state may be granted a Minnesota professional license when the following criteria are met:

        1.   The teacher preparation institution is accredited by the regional association for the accreditation of colleges and secondary schools; consult http://www.ncahlc.org.

        2.   The program leading to licensure, including alternative programs, has been recognized by the other state as qualifying the applicant completing the program for current licensure within that state.

        3.   The program leading to licensure completed by the applicant is the same as, greater than, or not more than 2 years less than the grade-level range of the Minnesota licensure field for which application is made. A restricted teaching license may be issued where the out-of-state license is more limited in content or grade levels than a similar Minnesota license.

        4.   The preparing institution verifies applicant completion of the approved licensure program and recommends the applicant for a license in the licensure field and at the licensure level.

        5.   Program completion is verified by an official transcript or equivalent issued by the recommending institution or program.

VIII. Related Services Personnel

    A.   Includes school counselors, school nurses, school psychologists, school social workers, and speech/language pathologists (see below for specific requirements).

    B.   Related Services Personnel are not eligible for a Tier 1 license. In specific instances, school counselors, school psychologists, and speech/language pathologists could qualify for a Tier 2 license. Contact PELSB for more information. Otherwise, related service licenses are granted at Tiers 3 and 4.

    C.   Applications for school counselor (if the program completed is accredited by the Council for the Accreditation of Counseling and Related Educational Programs [CACREP]), school nurse, school psychologist, school social worker, and speech/language pathologists do not require a recommending signature.

Administration

I.   Licensure for superintendent, principal, or special education director. Requirements for all 3 positions include:

    A.   Three years of successful classroom teaching experience while holding a classroom teaching license valid for the position or positions in which the experience was gained,

        or

        For applicants who do not have 3 years of classroom teaching experience, they may meet the experience requirement by completing the alternative pathway for administrative licensure (see section III, below);

        and

B. Completion of a specialist or doctoral program, or a program consisting of 60 semester credits beyond the bachelor's degree that includes a terminating graduate degree and topics preparatory for educational administration and specified Minnesota competencies.

    1. Each program must be approved by the Board of School Administrators and be offered at a regionally accredited Minnesota graduate school.

C. Additional position-specific requirements include:

    1. An applicant for licensure as a superintendent or principal must have field experience of at least 320 hours or 40 8-hour days to be completed within 12 continuous months in elementary, middle or junior high, and high schools as an administrative aide to a licensed and practicing school principal or superintendent, depending on the licensure sought.

        a. The field experience must include at least 40 hours or 1 week at each level not represented by the applicant's primary teaching experience.

            i. A person licensed as an elementary school principal must complete a field experience of at least 200 hours in secondary administration to qualify for licensure as a K–12 principal.

            ii. A person licensed as a secondary school principal must complete a field experience of at least 200 hours in elementary administration to qualify for licensure as a K–12 principal.

    2. An applicant for licensure as a director of special education must have a practicum or field experience that includes a minimum of 320 hours in an administrative position under the immediate supervision of a licensed and practicing director of special education.

        a. The field experience will include at least 40 hours or 1 week at a special education administrative unit other than the primary experience of the applicant.

II. Provisional license (valid 2 years; nonrenewable)

A. Currently licensed elementary and secondary school principals seeking entry into a position as a K–12 principal may apply for a provisional license.

    1. Applicant must provide evidence of enrollment in an approved administrative licensure program for licensure as a K–12 principal.

B. Applicants who are coming from out of state who do not meet the necessary credits, field experience, and/or human relations requirement for a full Minnesota principal license may qualify for a 2-year provisional license to allow time to enroll in a preparation program to meet the deficiencies.

III. Administrative Licensure without Teaching Experience for Superintendents, Principals, and Directors of Special Education. Requirements include:

A. Meet the degree requirement specified in I, B, directly above;

B. Satisfactorily complete a field experience in school administration as an intern in the license area sought:

    1. In a school district setting appropriate for the license sought,

    2. Under the supervision of educators from an approved college or university school administration program and a licensed practicing school administrator working in the area of the intern's field experience,

and

3. The field experience must consist of at least 320 hours, of which at least 40 must be in each school level: elementary, middle grades, and high school, and is in addition to the teaching internship requirement below;

C. Demonstrate required basic teaching knowledge and skills by:

1. Presenting a portfolio or other appropriate presentation as determined by the approved school administration program demonstrating appropriate teaching knowledge and skills;

and

D. Fulfill teaching internship requirement ensuring that applicant shall have experience and knowledge in curriculum, school organization, philosophy of education, early childhood, elementary, junior high, middle school, and senior high schools through an internship that:

1. Includes 1 school year with a minimum hour equivalency of 1,050 hours of classroom experiences, including 8 weeks of supervised teaching;
2. Is under the supervision of a licensed practicing school administrator;
3. Includes supervision provided by educators from an approved school administration program;

and

4. Is based on a written agreement between the intern, the approved school administration preparation institution, and the school district in which the internship is completed.

IV. Licensure for Directors of Community Education. An applicant recommended for licensure as a director of community education shall:

A. Hold a bachelor's degree from a regionally accredited college or university;

and

B. Satisfactorily complete a preparation program as listed in subpart 3 of Minnesota Rule 3512.0505, consisting of a minimum of 20 semester hours, or the equivalent, that provides a candidate recommended for licensure with the knowledge, skills, and dispositions in all of the subjects listed in Minnesota Rule 3512.0510, subparts 1 and 5.

C. The applicant must complete a practicum (field experience) that includes at least 320 clock hours in an administrative position under the supervision of a licensed director of community education during which the candidate shall demonstrate the ability to apply the knowledge and skills listed in Minnesota Rule 3512.0510, subparts 1 and 5.

1. A person prepared in another state as director of community education may substitute 1 year of experience as a district-wide director of community education in another state for the field experience.

School Counselor (K–12)

I. Requirements for Entrance License

A. Hold a master's degree from a college or university that is regionally accredited by the association for the accreditation of colleges and secondary schools.

B.   Complete an approved preparation program leading to the licensure of school counselors or provide evidence of having completed a preparation program in school counseling accredited by the Council for the Accreditation of Counseling and Related Educational Programs; consult www.cacrep.org.

School Nurse (K–12)

I.   Requirements for Entrance License
A.   Hold a bachelor's degree in nursing from a regionally accredited college or university.
B.   Be currently registered in Minnesota to practice as a licensed registered nurse under the Board of Nursing.
C.   Be currently registered in Minnesota as a public health nurse under the Board of Nursing.
II. Maintaining Board of Nursing Registration
A.   In order to retain school nurse license, current registration as a registered nurse and public health nurse must be maintained at all times since lapse in registration is grounds for revocation of school nurse license.

School Social Worker (K–12)

I.   Requirements for Entrance License
A.   Hold a bachelor's or master's degree in social work.
B.   Be currently licensed in Minnesota to practice as a social worker under the Board of Social Work.
II. Maintaining Board of Social Work License
A.   In order to retain school social worker license, current Minnesota Board of Social Work license must be maintained at all times since lapse in license is grounds for revocation of school social worker license.

School Psychologist (K–12)

I.   Requirements for Entrance License
A.   Complete an approved preparation program in school psychology accredited by the National Association of School Psychologists; consult http://www.nasponline.org/. *or*
B.   Provide evidence of National Certification of School Psychologists through the National Association of School Psychologists.

Speech-Language Pathologist (K–12)

I.   Requirements for Entrance License
A.   Complete an approved preparation program in speech-language pathology accredited by the Council on Academic Affairs of the American Speech-Language-Hearing Association; consult www.asha.org.

or

B. Provide evidence of a valid certificate of clinical competence from the American Speech-Language-Hearing Association.

or

C. Hold a speech-language pathology license granted by the Minnesota Department of Health.

Licensure Requirements, Levels, and Renewals

I. For the most accurate information on the approximately 34 programs approved for licensing in Minnesota, consult PELSB's website: https://mn.gov/pelsb/aspiring -educators/preparation-programs/approved-programs/.

II. For a detailed listing of the 92 teacher licensure fields, 4 administrative licenses, and 5 related licenses, contact PELSB (see Appendix 1).

III. For information on how to renew a license, contact PELSB (see Appendix 1).

Mississippi

This information was current at press time. For the most current licensure guidelines, please visit the Mississippi Department of Education Office of Educator Licensure website at https://www.mdek12.org/OTL/OEL.

Standard Educator Licenses

I. Five-year Educator License, Traditional Teacher Education Route
  A. Class A Five-Year Educator License (valid for 5 years; renewable)
    1. Bachelor's degree in teacher education from a state-approved or a National Council for Accreditation of Teacher Education (NCATE)/Council of the Accreditation of Educator Preparation (CAEP)–accredited program from a regionally/nationally accredited institution of higher learning
    2. Passing scores on Praxis II (Principles of Learning and Teaching Test)
    3. Passing scores on Praxis II (Specialty Area Test) in degree program (certain licensure areas may require more than 1 subject area assessment)
  B. Class AA Five-Year Educator License (valid for 5 years; renewable)
    1. See I, A, 1–3, directly above.
    2. Master's degree in the endorsement area in which license is requested
       or
       Master of Education degree
  C. Class AAA Five-Year Educator License (valid for 5 years; renewable)
    1. See I, A, 1–3, directly above.
    2. Specialist degree in the endorsement area in which license is requested
       or
       Specialist of Education degree
  D. Class AAAA Five-Year Educator License (valid for 5 years; renewable)
    1. See I, A, 1–3, directly above.
    2. Doctoral degree in the endorsement area in which license is requested
       or
       Doctor of Education degree
II. Five-Year Educator License, Alternate Route
  A. Class A Five-Year Educator License
    1. Route 1
      a. Bachelor's degree (non-education) from a regionally/nationally accredited institution of higher learning
      b. Passing scores on Core Academic Skills for Educators Test (Praxis Core) or an ACT composite score of at least 21
      c. Passing scores on Praxis II (Specialty Area Test) (certain licensure areas may require more than 1 subject area assessment)

       d.   Successful completion of a 1- or 3-year state-approved alternate route program (for details, consult https://www.mdek12.org/OTL/OEL/Alternate)

       e.   Application for a 5-year educator license

       or

  2. Route 2

       a.   Hold a bachelor's degree with a minor or concentration in secondary education (7–12)

       b.   Passing scores on Praxis Core Academic Skills for Educators Tests or an ACT composite score of at least 21

       c.   Passing scores on Praxis II (Specialty Area Test) (certain licensure areas may require more than 1 subject area assessment)

       d.   Documentation of completion of student teaching from a state- or NCATE-approved program

  B. Class AA, Class AAA, and/or Class AAAA Five-Year Educator License

    1. Meet the requirements for a Class A license

    2. Master's, specialist, or doctoral degree in the endorsement area in which license is requested

      or

      Master of Education degree or Specialist of Education degree

      or

      Doctor of Education degree

III. Reciprocity

  A. Class A Five-Year Educator Reciprocity License (valid 5 years; renewable)

    1. Granted to applicants who hold a valid standard out-of-state license (K–12) in an area in which Mississippi issues an endorsement if it meets minimum Mississippi license requirements or equivalent requirements

    2. Applicants must submit to the Office of Educator Licensure:

       a.   Original valid out-of-state license;

       b.   Sealed copy of all college transcripts;

       and

       c.   Documentation showing a passing score on a core subject area assessment required for certification by issuing state, or documentation that verifies the out-of-state license was obtained in a manner equivalent with current Mississippi license guidelines for that license.

  B. Class AA, AAA, or AAAA Five-Year Educator Reciprocity License

    1. Meet requirements for Class A Five-Year Educator Reciprocity License (see III, A, 1 and 2, directly above)

    2. Original valid out-of-state Standard Class AA (master's degree), Class AAA (specialist degree), or Class AAAA (doctoral degree) License in a Mississippi endorsement area

  C. Two-Year Reciprocity License (valid current teaching year plus 1 additional school year, to expire June 30; non-renewable)

    1. For applicant with a valid credential less than a standard license or certificate from another state. Applicant must submit to the Office of Educator Licensure:

        a.   See III, A, 2, a and b, directly above.

    2.   To convert this provisional license to a 5-year renewable license, the applicant must meet all requirements for a 5-year license in Mississippi.

IV.   Five-Year Educator License — Guidance and Counseling

    A.   Class AA Option One (valid 5 years; renewable)

        1.   Hold a Five-Year educator license

        2.   Complete a master's degree program in guidance and counseling

        3.   Passing score on Praxis II (Specialty Area for Guidance Counselor)

    B.   Class AA Option Two (valid 5 years; renewable)

        1.   Complete an approved master's degree program for guidance and counseling that includes a full year internship

        2.   Passing score on Praxis Core Academic Skills for Educators Tests or an ACT composite score of at least 21

        3.   Passing score on Praxis II (Specialty Area Test for Guidance Counseling)

    C.   Class AA Option Three (valid 5 years, renewable)

        1.   Hold National Certified School Counselor (NCSC) credential issued by National Board of Certified Counselors (NBCC)

    D.   Class AAA (valid 5 years; renewable)

        1.   Meet requirements for Class AA License (see IV, A–C, directly above)

        2.   Specialist degree in guidance and counseling

    E.   Class AAAA (valid 5 years; renewable)

        1.   Meet requirements for Class AA License (see IV, A–C, directly above)

        2.   Doctoral degree in guidance and counseling

V.   Five-Year Library/Media License (valid 5 years; renewable)

    A.   Class A Requirements (1 of the following):

        1.   Complete bachelor's degree program or higher in Library/Media, and attain passing scores on Praxis Core Academic Skills for Educators or an ACT composite score of at least 21; Praxis II (Principles of Learning and Teaching); and Praxis II (Specialty Area for Library/Media);
           or

        2.   Hold a Five-Year Educator license and complete an approved Library/Media program;
           or

        3.   Hold a Five-Year-Educator license and attain passing score on Praxis II (Specialty Area for Library/Media).

    B.   Class AA, AAA, or AAAA Requirements

        1.   Meet requirements for Class A license (see V, A, 1–3, directly above) and complete an approved master's (Class AA), specialist (Class AAA), or doctorate (Class AAAA) in library/media from a state-approved or regionally/nationally accredited institution of higher learning

VI.   Licenses Available

    A.   Mississippi Educator Teacher Education Route License

        1.   Five-Year Educator License

    B.   Alternate Route Licenses

        1.   MS Alternate Path to Quality Educators/Three-Year Alternate Route License

2. Teach MS Institute/Three-Year License
3. Master of Arts in Teaching/Three-Year License
4. American Board Certification/One-Year Alternate Route License
5. Five-Year Alternate Route License
C. Special Subject Five-Year Educator Licenses
1. Audiologist, Child Development, Dyslexia Therapy, Early Oral Intervention Hearing Impaired B–K, Emotional Disability, Guidance and Counseling, Library Media, Performing Arts, Psychometrist, School Psychologist, Speech/Language Clinician, Speech/Language Associate, Special Education Birth–Kindergarten, Special Education Mild/Moderate Disability K–12
D. Career Technical Educator Licenses
1. Career Technical Non-Education Degree (Associate's Degree)/Three-Year License
2. Career Technical Non-Education Degree (Bachelor's Degree)/Three-Year License
3. Career Technical Educator License Non-Degree or Non-Education Degree/Five-Year License
E. Licenses by District Request Only
1. JROTC Non-practicing
2. One-Year License for Veteran Teachers Entry Level
3. Expert Citizen Career Level
4. Special, Non-Renewable License for specific Traditional Teacher Preparation Program Completers
5. Special, Non-Renewable License for Prospective Non-Traditional Teacher Preparation Program Completers
6. Special, Non-Renewable License for Adjunct Teachers

Administrator Licenses

I. Non-practicing Administrator License (Class AA, AAA, or AAAA; 5 years renewable): issued to an educator not currently employed in an administrative position
A. Hold 5-year standard educator license
B. Verification of 3 years of education experience
C. Completion of an approved master's, specialist, or doctoral degree in educational administration/leadership from a state-approved or regionally/nationally accredited institution of higher learning
D. Successful completion of School Leaders Licensure Assessment (SLLA), Educational Testing Service
E. Institutional recommendation documenting completion of an approved planned program in educational leadership/supervision through a state-approved or regionally/nationally accredited institution of higher learning
F. Validity is based upon validity of period of standard license currently held.
II. Entry-Level Administrator License (Class AA, AAA, or AAAA; valid 5 years; non-renewable): issued to an educator employed as a beginning administrator
A. See I, A–E, directly above.

B. Application for Entry-Level license upon obtaining first job as administrator (Orientation to School Leadership—OSL)

C. Letter from District stating the administrative position and date of administrative employment

III. Standard Career-Level Administrator License (Class AA, AAA, or AAAA; 5 years renewable)

A. Complete School Executive Management Institute (SEMI) requirements

IV. Alternate Route Administrator License (Class AA, AAA, or AAAA)

A. One-Year Alternate Route Administrator License (Class AA; valid 1 year; convertible to IV, B, directly below)

1. Requirements

a. Completion of Master of Education (MED) or higher education degree

b. Passing score on Praxis Core Academic Skills for Educators Test or an ACT composite score of at least 21 and Praxis II (Principles of Learning and Teaching Test)

c. Three years teaching experience for MED

d. Successful completion of alternate route training

e. Priority will be given to Superintendent/Board recommendation for admittance into an alternate route program.

2. Conversion to Five-Year Entry-Level Alternate Route Administrator License

a. Complete Alternate Route program

b. See I, D, directly above.

B. Five-Year Entry-Level Alternate Route Administrator License (Class AA; valid 5 years; non-renewable)

1. Requirements

a. See IV, A, 1, a–e, directly above.

b. See I, D, directly above.

2. Conversion to Standard Career-Level Alternate Route Administrator License within 5 years—see III, A, directly above.

a. Completion of SEMI entry-level OSL requirements

b. Completion of 6 hours of educational leadership course work from an approved educational leadership administrator program (courses must be in school law, school finance, instructional improvement or leadership, curriculum and instruction)

C. Standard Career-Level Alternate Route Administrator License (Class AA, AAA, AAAA)

1. Requirements

a. See IV, A, 1, a–c, directly above.

b. Completion of School Executive Management Institute (SEMI) entry-level requirements

D. Five-Year Alternate Route Administrator License, Business Track (Class AA valid 5 years; non-renewable)

1. Requirements:

a. Complete 1 of the following: Master of Business Administration (MBA), or

Master of Public Administration (MPA), or Master of Public Planning and Policy (MPP), or Doctor of Jurisprudence (JD);

b. Praxis Core Academic Skills for Educators or an ACT composite score of at least 21 and Praxis II (Principles of Learning and Teaching) Tests;

c. Five years of administrative/supervisory experience, meaning direct supervision of individuals and/or programs within a business, industry, and/or organization;

d. Successful completion of SLLA-Educational Testing Service; *and*

e. Successful completion of Alternate Route training.

f. Priority will be given to Superintendent/Board recommendation for admittance into an Alternate Route program.

2. Conversion to Career-Level Standard License within 5 years—see IV, B, 2, directly above.

E. Other Administrative Licenses; for further information, consult http://www.sos.ms .gov/ACCode/00000398c.pdf.

1. Athletic Administrator

2. School District Business Administrator

Missouri

Educator Certification, Classification, and Renewals

I. General Qualifications for Certification
    Identical for all teaching certificates, except for some areas of Vocational Education
    A. Baccalaureate degree from college/university with teacher education program approved by Missouri Department of Elementary and Secondary Education (DESE) or with teacher education program approved by state education agency in states other than Missouri
        1. No formal reciprocity for certification with other states; however, graduates from approved teacher-education programs within other states may obtain Missouri certificate based on meeting certain requirements.
    B. Recommendation for certification from designated official for teacher education in college/university where program was completed; not required with possession of a valid out-of-state certificate
    C. Overall grade point average of 2.75 or higher on a 4.00 scale, with professional education and content area GPA of 3.00 or higher on a 4.00 scale
    D. Successful completion of Missouri Content Assessment
        1. Consult DESE website (see Appendix 1) for list of the Missouri Specialty Area Tests and qualifying scores.
    E. Meet educational, professional, and subject area requirements as specified
    F. Applicants are required to complete a Missouri background check, including fingerprinting; for details, consult http://dese.mo.gov/eq/cert/index.html.
II. Classifications
    A. Initial Professional Certificate (valid 4 years)
        1. Assigned to new graduates of teacher-education programs and to individuals with less than 4 years of DESE-approved teaching experience who meet the minimum requirements and qualifications
        2. See I, A–E, directly above.
        3. To advance to next level, during valid dates of classification, the teacher must meet all of following requirements:
            a. Participate in district-provided and -approved mentoring program for 2 years
            b. Successfully complete 30 contact hours of professional development that may include college credits
            c. Participate in Beginning Teacher Assistance Program
            d. Successfully participate in a yearly performance-based teacher evaluation
            e. Complete 4 years of approved teaching experience
    B. Career Continuous Professional Certificate, or CCPC
    C. Administrative Classification
        1. Elementary Principal and Secondary Principal

a. Initial Administrator Certificate (valid 4 years)
    i.   Permanent or professional Missouri teaching certificate
         or
         Baccalaureate degree and recommendation from state-approved teacher preparation program; and qualifying score on designated assessment for initial certification
    ii. Minimum of 2 years of approved teaching experience
    iii. Complete designated building-level administrator's assessment
    iv. Course in psychology and education of the exceptional child
    v.   Master's degree in educational leadership from approved college/university
    vi. Recommendation for certification from approved college/university program
b. Transition Administrator Certificate—Principal (valid 6 years)
    i.   Four years of state-approved administrator experience
    ii. Two years of designated district-provided mentoring.
    iii. Development, implementation, and completion of approved professional development plan
    iv. Annual performance-based evaluation that meets or exceeds Missouri Performance Based Principal's Evaluation
    v.   Completion of 8 semester hours towards advanced degree in educational leadership or 120 contact hours in professional development activities
c. Career Continuous Administrator Certificate—Principal
    i.   Educational specialist degree or higher in educational leadership, reading/literacy or curriculum/instruction.
    ii. Performance-based principal evaluation
    iii. Thirty contact hours of professional development annually
2. Superintendent
   a. Initial Administrator certificate (valid 4 years)
       i.   Ed.S. or Ed.D. in educational administration with recommendation from the degree-granting university
       ii. Designated district-level administrator's assessment
       iii. Minimum of 3 years of experience as a building- or district-level administrator at public or accredited non-public school
       iv. See II, C, 1, a, i–vi, directly above.
   b. Career Certificate Administrator
       i.   See II, C, 1, c, i–iii, directly above.
3. Special Education Administrator K–12
   a. Initial Administrator Certificate—Special Education Director (valid 4 years)
       i.   Professional teaching certificate for an area of special education or student services
            or
            Baccalaureate degree and recommendation from state-approved

teacher preparation program in an area of special education; and qualifying score on designated assessment

    ii. Minimum of 2 years of approved special education or student services teaching experience

    iii. See II, C, 1, a, i–vi, directly above.

  b. Transition Administrator Certificate—Special Education Director (valid for 6 years)

    i. See II, C, 1, b, i–v, directly above.

  c. Career Administrator Certificate—Special Education Director

    i. See II, C, 1, c, i–iii, directly above.

4. Career Education Director

  a. Initial Administrator Certificate—Career Education Director (valid 4 years)

    i. Permanent or professional or career education Missouri teaching certificate

    or

    Baccalaureate degree and recommendation from state-approved teacher preparation program; and qualifying score on designated assessment

    ii. See II, C, 1, a, ii–vi, directly above.

  b. Transition Administrator Certificate—Career Education Director (valid 6 years)

    i. See II, C, 1, b, i–v, directly above.

  c. Career Administrator Certificate—Career Education Director

    i. See II, C, 1, c, i–iii, directly above.

D. Student Services Classification

1. Counselor K–8 (valid 4 years)

  a. Recommendation for certification from approved college/university with a school counseling program

  b. Master's degree with major emphasis in school guidance and counseling from approved college/university based upon completion of approved program of at least 24 semester hours of approved graduate courses in guidance and counseling, with at least 12 semester hours focused upon guidance in elementary schools

  c. Qualifying score on designated assessment

2. Counselor 7–12 (valid 4 years)

  a. See II, D, 1, a–c, directly above.

3. Career Student Services (valid 99 years)

  a. Four years of state-approved school counseling experience

  b. Participation in 2 years district-provided mentoring during the first 2 years of student services experience

  c. Development, implementation, and completion of a professional development plan of at least 40 contact hours of professional development or 3 semester hours of graduate credit towards an advanced degree

      d.   Successful participation in an annual performance-based evaluation
    4.   For related certificates listed here, contact Educator Certification at Missouri's Department of Elementary and Secondary Education (http://dese.mo.gov/eq/cert/index.html).
      a.   Psychological Examiner K–12
      b.   School Psychologist K–12
      c.   Speech-Language Pathologist
E. Classifications involving district application. For detailed information on these, contact Missouri Department of Elementary and Secondary Education (http://dese.mo.gov/divteachqual/teachcert/).
    1.   Provisional (valid 2 years)
    2.   Temporary Authorization Classification (valid 1 year)
F. Career (Vocational) Classification Applicants may seek certificates below; for full details, contact Missouri Department of Elementary and Secondary Education (http://dese.mo.gov/eq/cert/index.html).
    1.   Secondary Career Education Certificate
    2.   Postsecondary/Adult Career Education Certificate
    3.   Career Continuous Career Education (CCCE) Certificate

Areas and Types of Certification

I. Certification Levels
  A. Early Childhood (Birth–Grade 3)
  B. Elementary Education (1–6)
  C. Middle School (5–9)
    1.   Language Arts
    2.   Mathematics
    3.   Science
    4.   Social Studies
    5.   Other Middle School Endorsements
  D. Secondary Education (9–12) (except as noted)
  E. Special Education (K–12)
  F. Student Services
  G. Administration
  H. Career Education (vocational)
  I. Other
II. Subject Areas
Agriculture; Art (K–12, 9–12); Blind & Partially Sighted (B–12); Building-Level Administrator; Business Education; Deaf and Hearing Impaired (B–12); District-Level Administrator (Superintendent, K–12); Early Childhood Education (B–Grade 3); Early Childhood Special Education (B–Grade 3); English; English Language Learners (K–12); Family and Consumer Science (K–12); Foreign Languages (French [K–12]; German [K–12]; Spanish [K–12]); Gifted Education (K–12); Health (K–12); Library Media Specialist (K–12); Marketing Education; Mathematics; Music (Instrumental, Vocal)

(K–12); Physical Education (K–12); Principal (K–8, 5–9, 7–12); School Counselor (K–8, 7–12); School Psychologist K–12; Science (Biology; Chemistry; Earth Science; General Science; Physics); Severely Developmentally Disabled (B–12); Social Science; Special Education Administrator; Mild/Moderate Cross-Categorical K–12; Special Reading (Remedial) (K–12); Speech and Language Pathologist (B–12); Speech/Theater; Unified Science (Biology; Chemistry; Earth Science; Physics); Technology and Engineering; Vocational School Director

Montana

Educator Licenses

For the most current information, please refer to the Montana Office of Public Instruction (OPI) website at http://opi.mt.gov/Educators/Licensure/Become-a-Licensed-Montana-Educator.

I. Class 2 Standard Teacher's License (valid 5 years)
   A. To meet Montana's requirements for a Class 2 Standard License, applicants must meet 1 of the following criteria:
      1. Completion of an educator preparation program that is accredited by the National Council for Accreditation of Teacher Education (NCATE), Council for Accreditation of Educator Preparation (CAEP), or Montessori Accreditation Council for Teacher Education (MACTE), or that is a state-approved program from a regionally accredited college or university, and completion of student teaching or a supervised teaching experience through an educator preparation program;
      or
      2. Completion of National Board Certification program;
      or
      3. Completion of a nontraditional teaching program with 5 successful years of teaching experience, along with a current, standard, unrestricted out-of-state educator license.
   B. Applicant must submit verification of all of the following:
      1. If the educator preparation program completed by the applicant is not in Montana, the applicant must provide proof of a minimum score on the Praxis II test applicable to the requested endorsement area; and
      2. Completion of the free, online course, "An Introduction to Indian Education for All in Montana."
   C. Class 2 standard teacher's license shall be renewable with verification of 60 renewal units earned during the 5 years of validity through August 31 of the year the license expires. Participation in renewal activities is equivalent to the following renewal units:
      1. One hour of attendance at a professional development activity = 1 renewal unit;
      2. One quarter college credit = 10 renewal units; and
      3. One semester college credit = 15 renewal units.
   D. A lapsed Class 2 standard teacher's license may be reinstated by showing verification of 60 renewal units earned during the 5-year period preceding the application date of the new license.
II. Class 1 Professional Teacher's License (valid 5 years)
   A. To meet Montana's requirements for a Class 1 Standard License, applicants must meet 1 of the following criteria:

1. Completion of an educator preparation program that is accredited by NCATE, CAEP, or MACTE, or that is a state-approved program from a regionally accredited college or university, and completion of student teaching or a supervised teaching experience through an educator preparation program;
   or
2. Completion of National Board Certification program;
   or
3. Completion of a nontraditional teaching program with 5 successful years of teaching experience, along with a current, standard, unrestricted out-of-state educator license.

B. Applicant must submit verification of all of the following:
   1. A master's degree in education or endorsable teaching area(s) from a regionally accredited college or university, or certification by the National Board for Professional Teaching Standards;
   2. If the educator preparation program completed by the applicant is not in Montana, the applicant must provide proof of a minimum score on the Praxis II test applicable to the requested endorsement area;
   3. Completion of the free, online course, "An Introduction to Indian Education for All in Montana"; and
   4. Verification of successful teaching experience while appropriately licensed and assigned: 3 years for applicants who completed a traditional educator preparation program and 5 years for applicants who completed a nontraditional educator preparation program.

C. Class 1 standard teacher's license shall be renewable with verification of 60 renewal units earned during the 5 years of validity through August 31 of the year the license expires.
   1. See I, Class 2 Standard Teacher's License, C, 1–3, above, for renewal unit equivalencies.

D. A lapsed Class 1 professional teacher's license may be reinstated by showing verification of 60 renewal units earned during the 5-year period preceding the application date of the new license.

Administrative Licenses

I. Class 3 Administrative License (valid 5 years)
   A. Appropriate administrative areas that may be approved for license endorsement are: elementary principal, secondary principal, K–12 principal, K–12 superintendent, supervisor, and special education supervisor.
   B. To obtain a Class 3 administrative license, an applicant must:
      1. Be eligible for an appropriately endorsed Class 1, 2, or 5 license to teach in the school(s) in which the applicant would be an administrator or would supervise;
         or
      2. Complete a non-traditional educator preparation program along with a current, standard, unrestricted out-of-state administrator license and verification of 5 years of successful administrative experience while appropriately licensed.

3. Complete required Montana course work and the online course "Indian Education for All in Montana."

C. Class 3 administrative license shall be renewable with verification of 60 renewal units earned during the 5 years of validity through August 31 of the year the license expires.

1. See I, Class 2 Standard Teacher's License, C, 1–3, above, for renewal unit equivalencies.

D. A lapsed Class 3 administrative license may be reinstated by showing verification of 60 renewal units earned during the 5-year period preceding the validation date of the new license.

II. Class 3 Administrative License—Superintendent Endorsement

A. Applicant must provide verification of all of the following:

1. An education specialist, master's, or doctoral degree in education or education leadership;

2. Completion of an accredited professional educator preparation program for superintendents;

3. A minimum of 18 semester graduate credits in a school administrator preparation program, of which 12 must be beyond the master's degree in education leadership and include 3 credits in each of the following:

   a. Montana school law,

   b. Montana school finance,
      and

   c. Montana collective bargaining and employment law;

4. A minimum of 3 years of teaching experience as an appropriately licensed teacher or specialist;

5. Licensure and endorsement as a P–12 principal;
   and

6. A minimum of 1 year of administrative experience as an appropriately licensed principal or 1 year of a supervised Board of Public Education approved administrative internship as a superintendent.

B. Applicant must also submit a recommendation for the endorsement requested from the appropriate official from an accredited professional educator program.

III. Class 3 Administrative License—Elementary Principal Endorsement

A. Applicant must provide verification of:

1. A minimum of 3 years of experience as an appropriately licensed and assigned Class 1 or 2 teacher at the elementary level;

2. A master's degree in educational leadership from an accredited professional educator preparation program or a master's degree related to education;

3. Completion of an accredited professional educator preparation program for elementary principals;

4. Completion of 3 semester credits of college course work in Montana school law, including special education law;
   and

5. Recommendation for the endorsement from the appropriate official from an accredited professional educator program.

IV. Class 3 Administrative License—Secondary Principal Endorsement
   A. Applicant must provide verification of:
   1. A minimum of 3 years of experience as an appropriately licensed and assigned Class 1 or 2 teacher at the secondary level;
   2. A master's degree in educational leadership from an accredited professional educator preparation program or a master's degree related to education;
   3. Completion of an accredited professional educator preparation program for secondary principals;
   4. Completion of 3 semester credits of college course work in Montana school law, including special education law;
      and
   5. Recommendation for the endorsement from the appropriate official from an accredited professional educator program.

V. Class 3 Administrative License—K–12 Principal Endorsement
   A. Applicant must provide verification of:
   1. A master's degree in educational leadership from an accredited professional educator preparation program as defined in ARM 10.57.102 or a master's degree related to education;
   2. Completion of an accredited educator preparation program for K–12 principals;
   3. A minimum of 3 years of experience as an appropriately licensed and assigned Class 1 or 2 teacher;
   4. Completion of 3 semester credits of college course work in Montana school law, including special education law;
      and
   5. Recommendation for the endorsement from the appropriate official from an accredited professional educator program.

VI. Class 3 Administrative License—Supervisor Endorsement
   A. Issued in specific fields such as math, music, and school counseling, or in general areas such as elementary education, secondary education and curriculum development.
   B. Applicants must submit verification of:
   1. Completion of a master's degree in the area requested for endorsement at a regionally accredited college or university;
   2. Meeting eligibility requirements for a Class 1 or Class 2 teaching license endorsed in the field of specialization;
   3. Three years of experience as an appropriately licensed and assigned teacher in a state-accredited P–K or K–12 setting;
   4. Completion of a supervised preparation program that is accredited by NCATE or CAEP, or that is a state-approved program from a regionally accredited college or university;
      and
   5. Recommendation for the endorsement from the appropriate official from an accredited professional educator program.

VII. Class 3 Administrative License—Special Education Supervisor Endorsement
   A. Issued in specific field of special education

B. Applicants must submit verification of:
   1. Completion of a supervisor preparation program that is accredited by NCATE or CAEP, or that is a state-approved program from a regionally accredited college or university in the following special education-related service fields: school psychologist, speech-language pathologist, audiologist, physical therapist, occupational therapist, registered nurse, clinical social worker, or clinical professional counselor;
   2. Meeting eligibility requirements for a Class 1 or Class 2 teaching license endorsed in the field of specialization;
   3. Completion of a master's degree in the area requested for endorsement (special education or related service area, school psychologist, speech-language pathologist, audiologist, physical therapist, occupational therapist, registered nurse, clinical social worker, or clinical professional counselor); *and*
   4. Three years of experience in an accredited school setting as an appropriately licensed and assigned teacher, or 5 years of experience in an accredited school setting as a fully licensed and assigned related services provider.

Additional Licenses

I. Class 4 Career and Technical Education License (valid 5 years)
   A. Three types of Class 4 licenses:
      1. Class 4A license issued to individuals holding a valid Montana teaching license, but without an appropriate career and technical education endorsement;
      2. Class 4B license issued to individuals with at least a bachelor's degree but who do not hold a valid Montana teaching license with the appropriate career and technical education endorsement; and
      3. Class 4C license issued to individuals who hold at least high school diploma or high school equivalency diploma and meet minimum requirements for endorsement.
   B. Class 4 license renewal requires 60 renewal units.
      1. Class 4A licenses shall be renewable by earning 60 renewal units. Endorsement-related technical studies may be accepted. The first renewal must show evidence of renewal units earned in the following content areas:
         a. Curriculum and instruction in career and technical education; *and*
         b. Safety and teacher liability.
      2. Class 4B or 4C licenses shall be renewable by earning 60 renewal units. The first renewal must show evidence of renewal units earned in the following content areas:
         a. Principles and/or philosophy of career and technical education;
         b. Curriculum and instruction in career and technical education;
         c. Learning styles/teaching styles; including serving students with special needs;
         d. Safety and teacher liability;

       e.   Classroom management;
       f.   Teaching methods;
       g.   Career guidance in career and technical education; or
       h.   Endorsement-related technical studies, with prior OPI approval.

    3.   A lapsed Class 4 license may be reinstated by showing verification of 60 renewal units earned during the 5-year period preceding the validation date of the new license, including, for Class 4A licenses, renewal units in:
       a.   Curriculum and instruction in career and technical education;
       b.   Safety and teacher liability;
           and
       c.   Endorsement-related technical studies or industry validated training.

C.   Unless otherwise noted, to obtain an endorsement on a Class 4 license, an applicant must provide verification of a minimum of 10,000 hours of documented, relevant work experience, which may include apprenticeship training, documenting the knowledge and skills required in the specific trade in which they are to teach. Acceptable documentation of relevant work experience is determined by the Superintendent of Public Instruction and may include, but is not limited to:
    1.   Work experience completed and verified by previous employers, to include detailed description of duties performed during employment;
    2.   For self-employed individuals, examples of projects completed, letters of verification from clients or customers, profit and loss statements demonstrating viability of business or self-employment;
    3.   Verification of teaching experience in area requested for endorsement, accompanied by verification of substantial work experience in area requested for endorsement; or
    4.   Certificates of completion of appropriate technical programs or related college degrees and course work, and industry certification (e.g., ASE, AWS).

D.   Class 4A, 4B, or 4C career and technical education license may be approved to teach traffic education if the license meets specific requirements; contact Montana Office of Public Instruction (OPI)—see Appendix 1—for full details.

II.   Class 6 Specialist License (valid 5 years)

A.   Class 6 specialist licenses may be issued with the following endorsements:
    1.   School psychologist
       or
    2.   School counselor
    3.   A Class 6 specialist license may also be endorsed in traffic education if the licensee meets the requirements and is approved by the Superintendent of Public Instruction.

B.   Class 6 specialist license renewal requires verification of 60 renewal units earned during the 5 years of validity through August 31 of the year the license expires.
    1.   See I, Class 2 Standard Teacher's License, C, 1–3, above, for renewal unit equivalencies.

III.   Class 6 Specialist License—School Psychologist

A.   To obtain Class 6 specialist license with school psychologist endorsement, applicant must provide verification of:

1. Current credentials as a nationally certified school psychologist (NCSP) from the National Association of School Psychologists (NASP); *and*
2. Completion of a specialist-level degree from a NASP-accredited school psychologist program that included a 1,200-hour internship, of which 600 hours were in a school setting.
3. For those applicants who did not earn at least a specialist-level school psychology degree from an NASP-accredited program:
   a. A master's degree or higher in school psychology or a related field from a regionally accredited college or university; *and*
   b. Recommendation from an NASP-accredited specialist program attesting to the applicant's qualifications being equivalent to NASP training standards, which included a 1,200-hour internship experience of which 600 hours were in a school setting.

IV. Class 6 Specialist License—School Counselor
   A. To obtain Class 6 specialist license with a school counselor endorsement, applicant must provide verification of:
      1. A master's degree; *and*
      2. Completion of a Council for Accreditation of Counseling and Related Educational Programs (CACREP)–accredited school counselor program that included an internship in a school setting of 600 hours.
      3. For those applicants who did not earn a degree from a CACREP-accredited program:
         a. A master's degree in school counseling from a regionally accredited college or university; *and*
         b. Recommendation from an accredited specialist program that included an internship in a school setting of 600 hours.

V. Class 7 American Indian Language and Culture Specialist (valid 5 years)
   A. The Superintendent of Public Instruction shall issue a Class 7 license based upon verification by the authorized representative of a tribal government that has a memorandum of understanding with the Superintendent of Public Instruction, that the applicant has met tribal standards for competency and fluency as a requisite for teaching that language and culture.
   B. The Board will accept and place on file the criteria developed by each tribe for qualifying an individual as competent to be a specialist in its language and culture.
   C. A Class 7 American Indian language and culture specialist licensee may be approved to teach traffic education if the licensee meets the requirements and is approved by the Superintendent of Public Instruction.
   D. A school district may assign an individual licensed under this rule only to specialist services within the field of American Indian language and culture under such supervision as the district may deem appropriate. No teaching license or endorsement is required for duties within this prescribed field.

VI. Class 8 Dual Credit-Only Postsecondary Faculty License (valid 5 years)

    A. Whenever a faculty member of a postsecondary institution is teaching a course for which 1 or more students will earn both high school and college credit, that faculty member is required to hold a Class 8 dual credit license, unless already licensed or eligible for licensure (as a Class 1, 2, or 4) and properly endorsed. Contact the Montana Office of Public Instruction for more details.

Nebraska

The term "certificate" will apply to Initial, Standard, and Professional (regular) certificates. Other options formerly designated as certificates will now be designated as permits. The Nebraska Certification Office sends certificates electronically as email attachments, so all applicants must have a current email address.

Teaching Certificate Types

I.   Initial Certificate (valid 5 years; renewable)
  A. Requires completion of:
    1. Bachelor's degree
        and
    2. An approved teacher education program with an endorsement recommendation from an approved institution.
      a. Six semester hours must be completed within the past 5 years.
  B. Renewable with 6 semester hours or 1 year of documented experience teaching in the past 5 years in an approved school.
II. Standard Certificate (valid 5 years; renewable)
  A. Requirements include holding a valid Initial Certificate and at least 2 consecutive years of teaching experience.
  B. Renewable with 6 semester hours or 1 year of teaching experience within the past 5 years.
III. Professional Certificate (valid 10 years; renewable)
  A. Issued with completion of master's degree in curriculum and instruction, special education, educational technology, or in the applicant's content field.
  B. Renewable with 6 approved semester hours or 1 year of teaching experience within the past 5 years.

Requirements for Teaching Certificates

I.   Professional, Standard and Initial Certificates. Requirements for all include:
  A. Completion of a bachelor's degree;
    1. Originals of all college transcripts are required.
  B. Recommendation and endorsement by college for teacher training program completed;
  C. Completion of at least 6 hours of college course work in the past 5 years or 1 year work experience as a contracted teacher half time or more, within the past immediate 5 years;
  D. Complete Praxis Series—CORE test, basic skills testing in mathematics, reading and writing;

E. Complete ETS Praxis Subject Assessment for the area of endorsement(s) the person wants to add to the certificate;

F. Human relations training—an approved human relations course addressing the 6 competencies found in statute;

G. Special education training—an approved special education course addressing the exceptional child in the classroom; *and*

H. Fingerprinting required for applicants who have not lived in Nebraska for 5 consecutive years prior to the date of application.

    1. Applicant must have no felony convictions.

II. Standard and Professional Certificates Additional Requirements:

A. Both require 2 years of teaching experience during the previous 5 years.

B. Professional certificate also requires a master's degree in curriculum and instruction, educational technology, or in the person's content area.

III. Permits with deficiencies. Consult the website for more detailed information at https://www.education.ne.gov/TCERT/.

A. Provisional Teaching Permits

    1. Provisional Teaching Permit (valid 2 years; not renewable)

        a. Issued to persons reentering the profession who do not have recent teaching experience and need to complete course hours

        b. Need to complete basic skill test and Praxis subject assessment or special education requirement

B. Alternative Program Teaching Permit

    1. Issued at the request of a school district to employ a person who has completed a bachelor's degree plus 50 percent of their pre–student teaching requirements and 75 percent of their content courses to take a difficult-to-fill position

    2. Issued to applicants with a completed bachelor's degree, an alternative certification pathway, an offer of employment from a Nebraska school, teaching employment and certification in another state, and an approved plan for addressing deficiencies

C. Substitute Teaching Permit

    1. State Substitute Permit (valid 5 years)

        a. Issued to applicants with a bachelor's degree who have completed a teacher education program

        b. Allows holder unlimited days per year to substitute in Nebraska schools

    2. Local Substitute Permit (valid 3 years)

        a. Issued to applicants with at least 60 college hours including 1 education class

        b. Allows holder to substitute only in 1 district for no more than 90 days per year

D. Temporary Teaching Certificate (valid 6 months)

    1. Issued to those persons who have not completed the human relations training but have met all other requirements for a regular certificate

E. Conditional Teaching Permit (valid for up to 1 year)

    1. Allows teaching while fingerprints are being processed or at the direction of

the Commissioner when existing deficiencies prevent the issuance of a regular certificate in a timely manner

F. Transitional Teaching Permit (valid 1 year in 1 district only) for those enrolled in the Transitional program

G. Career Education Permit (valid 3 years)
1. Issued to a person with a particular area of expertise who is offering a career education program to students in 1 Nebraska school district

H. Postsecondary Teaching Permit (valid 3 years)
1. Issued to college employees who are teaching dual credit courses for both college and high school credit
2. Human relations training requirement
3. District Permit—Post Secondary Form

I. Military Teaching Permit (valid 3 years)
1. Issued to military spouses or retired military who do not meet all Nebraska teaching requirements. Applicants must show evidence of current service by applicant or spouse, hold a teaching certificate in another state, and show 2 years of teaching experience.
2. Human relations training requirement
3. Fingerprinting required for applicants who have not lived in Nebraska for 5 consecutive years prior to the date of application
4. Nebraska district employment verification letter

Administrative Certificates

I. Professional Administrative Certificate (valid 10 years). Requirements include:
A. Two years of teaching experience;
B. Completion of a specialist degree or more than 60 hours in educational administration;
C. Six semester hours of graduate work in educational administration within 5 years of the date of application,
or
Have been serving as a school administrator for 2 or more years within the past 5;
and
D. Successful completion of Praxis CORE Test, Praxis Subject Assessment, human relations and special education (SPED) training.

II. Standard Administrative Certificate (valid 5 years). Requirements include:
A. Two years of teaching experience;
B. Completion of a master's degree in educational administration;
C. Six semester hours of graduate work in educational administration within 5 years of the date of application,
or
Have been serving as a school administrator for 2 or more years within the past 5;
and
D. Human relations, CORE, Praxis Subject Assessment, and SPED training completed.

III. Provisional Administrative Permit (valid 2 years; this is not renewable)

A. Candidate must have at least 75 percent of a superintendent's program completed or 50 percent of a principal's program completed.

B. Candidate must have employment offered by a Nebraska district

IV. Temporary Administrative Certificate (valid 6 months)

A. Issued to applicant to complete human relations training

Support Services Certificates/Permits

I. School Nurse and Educational Audiologist

A. Standard Special Services Certificate (valid 5 years). Requirements include:
1. Human relations training;
2. Additional subject-specific required training or course work;
3. Completion of an approved program in candidate's specialty; *and*
4. Six hours of college credit within the past 5 years or 1 year of valid experience.

B. Provisional Special Services Permit (valid 1 year) for Speech-Language Technician only. Requirements include:
1. Human relations training
2. Bachelor's degree in Communication Disorders
3. Letter offering employment as a Speech-Language Technician in a Nebraska district

C. Special Services Permit for Coaching
1. Human relations training
2. Courses in First Aid and Principles of Coaching completed

D. Temporary Special Services Certificate (valid 6 months)
1. Issued to applicants who have met all other requirements for a Special Services Certificate to complete human relations training

Nevada

Fingerprinting is required for all initial licenses and licensure renewals.

Teaching Certificates and Requirements

I. Standard License (valid 5 years)
   A. Bachelor's degree from a regionally accredited college/university, completion of a teacher education program that meets state-approved program standards, and completion of competency and state mandated testing in the area applied for.
   B. Renewal is based on 6 semester hours of college/university credit, or 6 Nevada approved in-service credits, or a combination of both to equal a total of 6 renewal credits.

II. Provisional License (valid 3 years)
   A. Same requirements as the Standard License except with provisions for state-mandated testing and/or up to 6 credits of course work.
   B. All provisions must be met prior to the expiration date. Once all provisions are satisfied prior to expiration date, license may be changed to Standard or Professional.

III. Professional License (valid 6 years)
   A. Meet requirements for the renewable license, submit master's degree from a regionally accredited college/university, and verify 3 years of successful teaching experience at the K–12 grade level.
   B. Renewal is based on 6 semester hours of college/university credit, or 6 Nevada approved in-service credits, or a combination of both to equal a total of 6 renewal credits.

IV. Professional License (valid 8 years)
   A. Meet requirements for the Renewable License, complete an educational specialist degree program from a regionally accredited college/university, and verify 3 years of successful teaching experience at the appropriate K–12 grade level. Renewal requirement is submission of professional development credit.

V. Professional License (valid 10 years)
   A. Meet requirements for the Renewable License, complete a doctoral degree program from a regionally accredited college/university, and verify 3 years of successful teaching experience at the appropriate K–12 grade level. Renewal requirement is submission of evidence of professional growth.

Basic Qualifications for Licensure

I. Applicants must be citizens of the United States or have legal immigration status that allows them to work in the United States.

II. Degree(s) and credits for courses must have been earned from a regionally accredited college or university.

III. Foreign transcripts must be accompanied by a course-by-course and degree equivalency evaluation done by an approved evaluator service (list available on website; see Appendix 1) before applicant applies for licensure.

IV. A license is issued based on the evaluation of the applicant's official transcript(s).

Elementary School (Kindergarten–8th Grade)

I. Standard Elementary License Requirements
  A. Bachelor's degree from accredited college or university and completion of a State Board of Education–approved program of preparation for teaching in elementary grades
  B. Completion of the following:
   1. Elementary professional education, semester hours 50
     a. Supervised student teaching 8
     b. Teaching methods of teaching basic elementary subjects, including, but not limited to, mathematics, science, and social studies 9
     c. Teaching of literacy or language arts 9
     d. Six semester hours of credit each in mathematics, science and social studies 18
     e. Professional education course work 6
     These must include special education and parental involvement/family engagement.
  C. Completion of required competency testing as specified on website (see Appendix 1)
II. Professional Elementary License Requirements
  A. Meet all requirements for Elementary License
  B. Hold a master's degree in education
  C. Have 3 years of verifiable elementary teaching experience in state-approved schools

Middle School (7th–9th Grades)

I. Requirements to teach in designated middle school or junior high school
  A. Hold bachelor's or higher degree from accredited college or university, and
   1. Complete Board-approved preparation program for teaching at this level
     or
     Complete professional education course work, semester hours 24
     Hours to include:
     a. Supervised student teaching in designated middle or junior high school, semester hours 8
     b. A course in methods and materials for teaching major or minor field of specialization at middle school, junior high school, or secondary grade level, or a middle or junior high school level integrated methods course
     c. Course of study regarding education or curricular adaptation for pupils

with disabilities and/or a course or study regarding educational foundation or methods in teaching English-language learners, semester hours 3

    d. Course work in at least 2 of following areas: Middle school foundations, history, theory or philosophy; middle school curriculum, pedagogy, or assessment; adolescent growth and development; nature and needs of the adolescent including social, emotional, and cultural concerns; classroom management strategies; school/family/community collaboration; or supervision and evaluation of programs and pupils in a middle school, semester hours 6
and

    e. Course work in any of the following subjects: English as a second language/bilingualism or biculturalism; educational technology; tests and measurement; educational psychology; education of the exceptional child; multicultural education; or educational research, semester hours 6

and

    2. Credits in a major field of endorsement or area of concentration, semester hours 24

B. Subsequent minor fields of endorsement may be added to the license upon verification of 14 semester hours of credit, or by passing a subject-matter exam in the area of endorsement.

C. Complete required competency testing as specified on the Department of Education website (see Appendix 1)

II. Endorsement areas: Art; English/language arts; foreign language (see Department of Education website in Appendix 1 for specifics); mathematics; music; science; and social science

A. Mathematics endorsement requires completion of 3 semester credits, to include a course in college algebra or concepts of calculus, including an introduction to limits, derivatives and integrals, precalculus, or differential calculus.

B. Major or minor fields of endorsement or area of concentration shall be deemed to be met if applicant holds bachelor's degree or a higher degree with a major, minor, or area of concentration identified on official transcript of record conferred by regionally accredited college or university.

III. A person who holds a valid Nevada license to teach elementary education, early childhood education, special education, or secondary education may obtain a license to teach middle school by passing a subject-matter exam in the area of endorsement the applicant wishes to teach. In such a case, the applicant would not be required to complete additional pedagogy course work.

Secondary School

I. Authorization

A. A license endorsed in a recognized teaching field is required for teaching in departmentalized seventh and eighth grades, junior high schools, senior high schools, and designated and approved middle schools. Endorsements are dependent upon the applicant's field of specialization or concentration, usually designated as majors or minors or areas of concentration.

II.   Standard Secondary License Requirements
A.   Bachelor's degree and completion of an approved program of preparation for secondary school teaching,
or
B.   Bachelor's degree and completion of the following:
   1.   A teaching field major from a regionally accredited institution
   2.   Secondary professional education, total semester hours as detailed below 22
      a.   Supervised teaching and/or teaching internship 8
      b.   A course in methods and materials of teaching in field of specialization.
      c.   A course of study regarding education or curricular adaptation for pupils with disabilities 3
      d.   A course of study regarding parental involvement/family engagement ... 3
      e.   Additional secondary pedagogy courses 8
      f.   Check with Department of Education (see Appendix 1) for specific requirements in occupational education.
   or
C.   A person who holds a valid Nevada license to teach elementary education, early childhood education, special education, or secondary education may obtain a license to teach secondary school by passing a subject-matter exam in the area of endorsement the applicant wishes to teach. In such a case, the applicant would not be required to complete additional pedagogy course work.

III.   Professional Secondary License Requirements
A.   Meet all requirements for Standard Secondary License
B.   Hold a master's degree
C.   Have 3 years of verified teaching experience in state-approved secondary schools

IV.   Available Secondary Teaching Endorsements
A.   Academic endorsements (comprehensive major/minor): art, biological science, English, general science, instrumental and vocal music, instrumental music, mathematics, physical education, physical education and health, physical science, recreational physical education, social studies, speech and drama, vocal music
B.   Secondary Business and Industry endorsements: accounting and finance; administrative services; aerospace engineering; agricultural business systems; agricultural leadership; communication and policy; agricultural mechanics technology; animal science; animation; architectural and civil engineering; architectural design; automation technology; automotive service technician; automotive technology; aviation maintenance technician; aviation technology; baking and pastry; biomedical sciences; biotechnology; business management; collision repair technology; community health science; computer science; construction technology; cosmetology; criminal justice; culinary arts; cybersecurity; dance performance; dental science; diesel technology; digital game development; drafting and design; early childhood education; electrical engineering; electronic technology; emergency medical technician; emergency telecommunication;

energy technologies; entrepreneurship; environmental engineering; environmental management; ethnic dance; ethnic music; family and consumer sciences; fashion, textiles and design; fire science; floriculture design and management; food science technology; foods and nutrition; forensic science; furniture and cabinetmaking; graphic design; health information management; hospitality and tourism; human development; information technology for networking; information technology for service and support; interior design; landscape design and management; law enforcement; manufacturing technologies; marketing; mechanical engineering; mechanical technology; medical assisting; metalworking; military science/ JROTC; natural resources and wildlife management; nursing assistant; ornamental horticulture and greenhouse management; pharmacy practice; photography; radio production; respiratory science; sports and entertainment marketing; sports medicine; teaching and training; theatre technology; veterinary science; video production; web design and development; welding technology

C. All comprehensive fields of concentration require the following:
    1. Majors, semester hours 36
    2. Minors, semester hours 24
    See the Department of Education website (see Appendix 1) for specific coursework requirements for each listed comprehensive major/minor area of endorsement.

D. Single-subject academic endorsements: anthropology, biology, botany, chemistry, composition and rhetoric, computer science, dance, dramatic or theatrical arts, earth science, economics, English or American literature, environmental science, geography, geology, health education, history of the US and world, journalism and communication, linguistics, physics, physiology, political science, psychology, reading, sociology, speech, world languages, zoology

E. Secondary Career & Technical Education endorsements: accounting and finance; administrative services; aerospace engineering; agricultural business systems; agricultural leadership, communication, and policy; agricultural mechanics technology; animal science; animation; architectural and civil engineering; architectural design; automation technology; automotive service technician; automotive technology; aviation maintenance technician; aviation technology; baking and pastry; biomedical sciences; biotechnology; business management; collision repair technology; community health science; computer science; construction technology; cosmetology; criminal justice; culinary arts; cybersecurity; dance performance; dental science; diesel technology; digital game development; drafting and design; early childhood education; electrical engineering; electronic technology; emergency medical technician; emergency telecommunication; energy technologies; entrepreneurship; environmental engineering; environmental management; ethnic dance; ethnic music; family and consumer sciences; fashion, textiles and design; fire science; floriculture design and management; food science technology; foods and nutrition; forensic science; furniture and cabinetmaking; graphic design; health information management; hospitality and tourism; human development; information technology for networking; information technology for service and support; interior design; landscape design and management; law enforcement; manufacturing technologies; marketing; mechanical engineering;

mechanical technology; medical assisting; metalworking; military science/ JROTC; natural resources and wildlife management; nursing assistant; ornamental horticulture and greenhouse management; pharmacy practice; photography; radio production; respiratory science; sports and entertainment marketing; sports medicine; teaching and training; theatre technology; veterinary science; video production; web design and development; welding technology

F. All single-subject majors and minors require the following:
   1. Majors, semester hours 30
   2. Minors, semester hours 16
   While there are no specific course work requirements for single-subject endorsements, all course work taken must be relevant to the endorsement being sought.

Early Childhood Education (Birth–Grade 2)

I. Standard Early Childhood License Requirements
   A. Bachelor's degree from accredited college or university and completion of a State Board of Education–approved program of preparation for teaching children from birth through grade 2
      or
   B. Bachelor's degree from accredited college or university and completion of the following:
      1. Course work in early childhood education, semester hours 35
         a. Supervised student teaching 8
         b. Child development and learning 6
         c. Early childhood curriculum and program implementation to include at least 1 course in each of the following areas: language and literacy; mathematics and science; social studies; and strategies for working with children with disabilities 12
         d. Family and community relations 3
         e. Assessment and evaluation for early childhood education 3
      or
   C. Hold a current license to teach elementary, middle, or junior high school, or a secondary license that is endorsed with a major in child care, including
      1. Experience teaching pupils under 6 years of age, consisting of
         a. Eight semester hours of student teaching;
            or
         b. One year of verifiable experience teaching pupils in a program of early childhood education for a public school, public agency, or licensed private school;
            or
         c. Equivalent field experience;
            or
         d. A practicum conducted by an accredited college or university;
            and

At least 6 semester hours of course work in early childhood education, consisting of courses in any of the following: early childhood curriculum; emergent language and literacy; play theory and creativity;
and
At least 6 semester hours of course work in any of the courses listed directly above, or in any of the following: child development from birth to age 8; diversity in young children; introduction to early childhood education; positive discipline and guidance for young children; working with families of young children;
or
At least 35 hours of course work in early childhood education for children who are developing typically and atypically, in specific areas mandated by state regulation; refer to the Department of Education website for details (see Appendix 1).
  D. Completion of required competency testing as specified on website (see Appendix 1).
II. Professional Early Childhood Education License Requirements
  A. Meet all requirements for Standard Early Childhood Education License
  B. Hold a master's degree or higher
  C. Have 3 years of verifiable teaching experience in state-approved schools

Special Education

Available endorsements include adaptive physical education, alternative education, autism, early childhood developmentally delayed, generalist, gifted and talented, hearing impairments, intellectual disabilities, orientation and mobility, speech and language impairments, and visual impairments. Contact the Department of Education (see Appendix 1) for more detailed information in this area.

Administration

 I. Authorization
  A. An Administrator of a School endorsement is required for the following: superintendent, associate superintendent, assistant superintendent, principal, vice principal, supervisor, administrative assistant, and program supervisor or coordinator.
  B. An Administrator of a Program endorsement is required for an individual who supervises or coordinates a program of nursing, school psychology, speech therapy, physical therapy, occupational therapy, or any other program area unless that person holds an Administrator of a School endorsement.
II. Professional Administrator of a School Endorsement: Must meet requirements A or B below.
  A. Complete the following:
    1. Master's degree

2. Five years of verified teaching experience at the K–12 level, or in an early childhood education program, in state-approved schools

3. At least 24 semester hours of graduate courses in school administration, to include: administration and organization of schools; supervision and evaluation of instruction; development of personnel; school finance; school law; curriculum; educational research; internship or field experience in school administration; and other courses considered to be part of an administrative program for educators
   and

4. Have completed 12 additional semester hours of graduate course work, which may include other courses considered to be part of an administrative program for educators
   or
   Hold a master's degree or higher in educational administration from a college or university accredited by a regional accrediting association

   or

B. Hold a master's degree or higher in educational administration from an accredited institution, and have 5 years of verified teaching experience as per section II, A, above.

III. Professional Administrator of a Program Endorsement
   A. Hold a master's degree
   B. Hold a valid license in program for which endorsement is requested
   C. Have and submit to Department evidence of 5 years of experience as licensed employee in early childhood education, kindergarten, or grades 1–12
   D. Have completed at least 27 semester hours in administration courses (which may not be taken as independent study), to include:
      1. Administration and organization of a school or the role of a program administrator in the applicant's endorsement area
      2. General principles of supervision of personnel or supervision of personnel for a program in the applicant's endorsement area
      3. Finances of a school or finances of a program in the applicant's endorsement area
      4. The laws that apply to schools
      5. The evaluation and development of personnel for a school or for a program in the applicant's endorsement area
         and
      6. Any other courses that are required for a degree in the administration of a program in the applicant's endorsement area

Other Licensed School Personnel

I. Available endorsements: reading specialist, school counselor, school library media specialist, school nurse, school psychologist, school social worker, music therapist

II. All endorsements for licensed school personnel are valid for grades K–12. For a list of specific course work/degree and professional licensure or certification requirements, refer to the Department of Education website (see Appendix 1).

Special Endorsements

I. Available special endorsements: American Sign Language, art, audiological services, bilingual education, computer applications, computer literacy, computer programming, dance, drivers education, foreign language, Great Basin language, JROTC, music, physical education, reading, teaching English as a second language (TESL)

II. For specific course work/degree requirements for each listed endorsement, refer to the Department of Education website (see Appendix 1).

III. Some special endorsements are valid for grades K–12; others are specific to the level of the applicant's base teaching license. Refer to the Department of Education website for specific information on each endorsement (see Appendix 1).

New Hampshire

For detailed information, please visit https://www.education.nh.gov/certification/.

Alternatives for Certification for Teachers, Educational and Instructional Specialists, and Administrators

I. Alternative 1—approved professional preparation programs in New Hampshire
    A. The New Hampshire State Board of Education approves programs of professional preparation in education and the chairperson of the Education Department of each institution recommends certification to Credentialing.
II. Alternative 2—For out-of-state graduates of approved professional educator preparation programs or experienced out-of-state educators:
    A. Requirements include:
        1. Graduation from an approved educator preparation program from another state or jurisdiction
            or
        2. Full, valid educator credential based on a bachelor's or higher degree from a state or jurisdiction other than New Hampshire and employment verification as a certified, full-time, regular teacher for at least 3 out of the last 7 years.
III. Alternative 3A—This rigorous portfolio and oral examination process is for candidates who have gained the necessary competencies, skills, and knowledge required for certification in a specific subject area and/or educator role (e.g., teacher, administrator, or specialist) through a means other than the completion of an approved educator preparation program.
    A. To qualify a candidate shall:
        1. Hold a bachelor's degree,
        2. Have met specific prerequisite certification testing requirements, *and*
        3. Have at least 3 months of full-time continuous educator experience in the area of endorsement for which certification is being requested.
            a. Educator experience does not have to be acquired in a public school; experience in a private school is acceptable.
IV. Alternative 3B—National/Regional Certifications, such as National Board for Professional Teaching Standards, or National Association of School Psychologists
V. Alternative 3C—Administrative Transcript Review; available only for the following endorsements: Superintendent, Principal, Curriculum Administrator, Special Education Administrator, Career and Technical Education Director, Business Administrator
VI. Alternative 4—This certification process is restricted to critical shortage areas, certain career and technical specialty areas, and business administrators. A superintendent may employ a candidate who meets eligibility requirements. The superintendent

of schools, or designee, then submits the candidate's Individualized Professional Development Plan leading to full certification. A list of critical shortage areas is available on our website.

VII.   Alternative 5 — This on-the-job training option allows an individual to attain certification in elementary and secondary teaching areas if the following requirements are met:
   A.   Candidate has a bachelor's degree with a 2.50 overall GPA and at least 30 credits in the area in which they wish to pursue certification;
   and
   B.   A local school district is willing to assume the responsibility for training and supervising the candidate.

VIII.   Additional endorsement-specific requirements include:
   A.   Superintendent
      1.   Certificate of Advanced Graduate Studies (CAGS) or doctoral degree
         and
      2.   Three years of experience as an education administrator in the K–12 setting,
         and
      3.   Three letters of recommendation (addressing leadership)
   B.   Principal
      1.   Master's degree
         and
      2.   Five years of full-time experience as an educator,
         and
      3.   Three letters of recommendation (addressing leadership)
   C.   School Counselor
      1.   Master's degree
   D.   Special Education Categorical Area
      1.   Certification in General Special Education or Early Childhood Special Education
   E.   Reading and Writing Specialist
      1.   Master's degree
         and
      2.   Three years of experience as a certified teacher
   F.   Reading and Writing Teacher
      1.   Two years of experience as a certified teacher
   G.   Elementary Education Mathematics Specialist
      1.   Master's degree in math, education, or related field
         and
      2.   Three years of experience teaching mathematics at the K–6 level
   H.   Curriculum Administrator
      1.   Master's degree in curriculum and instruction or education
         and
      2.   Five years as a classroom teacher
   I.   Special Education Administrator
      1.   Master's degree in special education or related area
         and

   2.   Five years in special education or related area,
        and
   3.   Three letters of recommendation (addressing leadership)
J.   Career and Technical Education (CTE) Director
   1.   Master's degree in educational leadership or education
        and
   2.   Three years of experience as a CTE educator,
        and
   3.   Three letters of recommendation (addressing leadership)
IX.   Other endorsement-specific requirements can be found here: https://www.education.nh
      .gov/certification/documents/codelist.pdf.

Certification rules are subject to revision. To monitor the status of any pending changes, please visit https://www.education.nh.gov/legislation/adopt_amend_repeal.htm.

New Jersey

Applicants are strongly advised to consult the New Jersey Licensing Code, available at http://www.state.nj.us/education/code/current/title6a/chap9b.pdf, for specific eligibility requirements for obtaining certificates.

Certification Overview

I. New Jersey certificates are issued under 3 categories; for detailed listings of the many certificates and specific requirements for them, go to http://www.state.nj.us/education/educators/license/.
   A. Instructional certificates for classroom teachers
   B. Administrative certificates for school administrator, principal, supervisor, and school business administrator
   C. Educational Services certificates for such positions as school social worker, school psychologist, learning disabilities teacher-consultant, substance awareness coordinator, etc.
   D. In addition, the following certificates may be issued when the appropriate requirements have been satisfied:
      1. Emergency Certificate: a substandard 1-year license issued only in limited fields of educational services
      2. County Substitute Credential: a temporary certificate issued by the county office which allows the holder to temporarily perform the duties of a fully licensed and regularly employed teacher when none is available
II. Endorsements
   A. An endorsement is an area of certification with distinct grade-level and subject matter authorizations in which a certificate holder is authorized to serve.
III. Certification Process for Novice Educators
   A. Certificate of Eligibility (CE): for applicants who did not complete a teacher preparation program. Requirements:
      1. Hold a bachelor's or advanced degree from regionally accredited college or university.
      2. Meet all minimum requirements in N.J.A.C. 6A:9B-5, including, but not limited to, citizenship, minimum age, and examination in physiology, hygiene, and substance abuse requirements.
      3. Achieve cumulative minimum GPA of 3.00 (when 4.00 GPA equals an A grade) in baccalaureate, higher degree, or state-approved post-baccalaureate certification program with at least 13 semester-hour credits.
         a. For students graduating before September 1, 2016, same requirements apply except minimum GPA is 2.75.
         b. A candidate graduating on or after September 1, 2016, with a GPA that

is below 3.00, but at least 2.75, and achieves a score on the appropriate State test of subject matter knowledge that exceeds the passing score by 10 percent or more may be deemed to meet the requirements.

    c.   A candidate graduating on or after September 1, 2016, with a GPA that is below 3.00, but at least 2.75, and is sponsored by a provisional training program may be deemed to meet the requirements.

4.   Satisfy the endorsement requirements and exceptions pursuant to N.J.A.C. 6A:9B-9–11, including, but not limited to, passing the appropriate state test(s) of subject matter knowledge and completing the required subject-area course requirements.

5.   After September 1, 2015, achieve a minimum score on a Commissioner-approved assessment of basic reading, writing, and mathematics skills

or

Achieve a minimum score on the SAT, ACT, or GRE. All minimum scores are established by the New Jersey Department of Education and are available on its website.

B.   Certificate of Eligibility with Advanced Standing (CEAS): for applicants who did complete a teacher preparation program. Requirements:

1.   The candidate shall meet the requirements in I, A, 1–5, directly above, and complete 1 of the following programs of teacher preparation:

    a.   A New Jersey college program, graduate or undergraduate, approved by the Department for the preparation of teachers;

    b.   A college preparation program included in the interstate certification reciprocity system of the National Association of State Directors of Teacher Education and Certification (NASDTEC);

    c.   An out-of-state educator preparation program approved by the National Council for the Accreditation of Teacher Education (NCATE), Teacher Education Accreditation Council (TEAC), or any other national professional education accreditation body recognized by the Council on Higher Education Accreditation approved by the Commissioner;

    d.   An educator preparation program approved for certification by the Department in a state party to the NASDTEC Interstate Contract, provided the program was completed on or after January 1, 1964, and the state in which the program is located would issue the candidate a comparable endorsement;

      or

    e.   An out-of-state college teacher education program approved by the state department of education in which the program is located.

2.   The teacher preparation programs listed in I, B, 1, a–e, directly above, must culminate in college supervised student teaching.

3.   A candidate who graduates on or after September 1, 2016, will meet the requirements in I, B, 1, a–e directly above, if they fall within the parameters in 3, a and b, directly below. For details, consult http://www.state.nj.us/education/educators/license/gpa.htm.

       a.   A GPA that is below 3.00, but at least 2.75, and a score in the appropriate state test of subject matter knowledge exceeding the passing score by 10 percent or more
           or

       b.   A GPA that is 3.50 or higher, and a score in the appropriate state test of subject matter knowledge falling below the passing score by no more than 5 percent

C. Standard Certificate Requirements:

  1. Possess a provisional certificate;
      and

  2. Successfully complete a state-approved district training program while employed provisionally in a position requiring the appropriate instructional certificate.

  3. Further eligibilities and their restrictions are available at http://www.state.nj.us/education/educators/license/.

  4. A candidate who holds National Board of Professional Teacher Standards (NBPTS) Certification and the corresponding out-of-state license or out-of-state certificate shall be eligible for the standard certificate in the NBPTS certificate field without additional requirements.

IV. Provisional Certificate

A. School-based training and evaluation program provided to all novice teachers during first year of New Jersey teaching. See N.J.A.C. 6A:9B-8.4 for full details.

B. Building principal recommends standard certification at completion of program requirements.

C. Both alternatively and traditionally prepared teacher candidates participate and receive support by veteran teachers in their school. Contact Department of Education (see Appendix 1) for full details.

D. Alternate route candidates complete 400 hours of formal instruction in professional education aligned with New Jersey Professional Standards for Teachers.

E. Effective academic year 2017–2018, provisional teachers holding a CE with a Preschool–Grade 3 endorsement must complete 400 hours of formal instruction pursuant to N.J.A.C. 6A:9A-5.4(a)1.

V. Interstate Reciprocity

A. Through reciprocity, the Certification and Induction Office shall issue an instructional CEAS to candidates who:

  1. Have a valid CEAS issued by another state in a subject area or grade level also offered by the Department, following the completion of a CEAS educator preparation program that includes clinical practice and endorsement in a subject that is also issued in New Jersey;

  2. Passed a subject matter test to receive their out-of-state endorsement or passed the appropriate New Jersey subject matter test;
      and

  3. For candidates who begin teaching academic year 2017–2018, passed a performance assessment that is approved by the state in which the certificate

was issued, unless the candidate holds National Board for Professional Teacher Standards (NBPTS) or the Meritorious New Teacher Candidate (MNTC) designation.

B. A candidate who meets all requirements in A1 and A2 above but did not take a state-approved performance assessment because it was not required for educator preparation program completion and/or for certification in that state shall be issued a CE.

1. The candidate shall meet all requirements for provisional and standard certification pursuant to N.J.A.C. 6A:9B-8.4 and 8.7, respectively, but shall be exempt from:

a. CE certification requirements pursuant to N.J.A.C. 6A:9B-8.3(a);

b. The provisional certification requirement to be enrolled in a CE educator preparation program pursuant to N.J.A.C. 6A:9B-8.4(a)4;

c. The renewal of provisional certification requirement to be enrolled in or to have completed a CE educator preparation program pursuant to N.J.A.C. 6A:9B-8.5(b)4;
    and

d. The standard certification requirement to complete a CE educator preparation program pursuant to N.J.A.C. 6A:9B-8.7(a)4ii.

Educational Services Certification

For a full listing of available endorsements, authorizations, and related requirements, see the New Jersey Department of Education website: http://www.nj.gov/njded/code/current/title6a/chap9 .pdf, beginning on page 58.

Administrator Certification

I. School Administrator Certificate of Eligibility (CE)

A. Candidate must:

1. Hold a master's or higher degree in educational leadership, curriculum, and instruction, or 1 of the recognized fields of leadership or management from a regionally accredited college or university,
    or
    Hold a master's degree from a regionally accredited college or university and complete a post-master's program resulting in a CEAS in educational administration and supervision,
    or
    Hold a master's degree from a regionally accredited college or university and complete a post-master's program in a coherent sequence of 30 semester-hour credits as they appear on the institution's transcript (the study must be completed at 1 institution in fields mentioned directly above),
    or
    Hold a master's degree from a regionally accredited college or university and complete a Commissioner-approved certification program in educational

leadership offered by a Commissioner-approved provider pursuant to N.J.A.C. 6A:9B-12.5(k)2 and (l)2,

or

Hold a master's degree in educational leadership from a nationally accredited program at an out-of-state college or university;

2. Complete a minimum of 30 graduate credits, either within the master's program or in addition to it, in the following quality components of preparation to promote student learning as set forth in the Professional Standards for School Leaders in N.J.A.C. 6A:9-3.4(a)1–6;

3. Complete a 150-hour internship in educational leadership aligned to the Professional Standards for School Leaders in N.J.A.C. 6A:9-3.4 and in accordance with the roles and responsibilities as a school administrator, independent of other course requirements (this internship either must appear on a transcript from a 4-year regionally accredited college or university or must be certified by a Commissioner-approved program for preparing school administrators);

4. Pass a state-approved examination of knowledge acquired through study of the topics listed in A2 above, aligned with the Professional Standards for School Leaders, and most directly related to the functions of superintendents as defined in N.J.A.C. 6A:9B-12.3(a);

   and

5. Complete 5 years of successful educational experience in a school district, nonpublic school, or a regionally accredited college or university.

II. For more detailed information on available administrative endorsements, authorizations, and related requirements, see the New Jersey Department of Education website: http://www.nj.gov/education/code/current/title6a/chap9b.pdf, beginning on page 104.

New Mexico

Routes to Initial Teacher Licensure

I. Option 1—Approved Program
   A. Possess a bachelor's and/or master's degree from a regionally accredited college or university;
   B. Complete an approved educator preparation program that includes student teaching; *and*
   C. Pass the National Evaluation Series (NES) tests required (for specifics, consult http://www.ped.state.nm.us/licensure/) or possess a valid certificate issued by the National Board for Professional Teaching Standards (NBPTS)

II. Option 2—Reciprocity
   A. Possess a bachelor's and/or a master's degree from a regionally accredited college or university;
   B. Possess a current valid and standard certificate/license from another state or country, or possess a valid certificate issued by the NBPTS.
   C. Provide proof of having completed an approved teacher education program (if the program is not contained on a transcript, provide documented evidence of the program completed);
   D. Provide copies of test scores for exams required to receive an out-of-state or out-of-country license; *and*
   E. Provide evidence of having satisfactorily taught under the out-of-state certificate or license from the school and/or supervisor where taught.

III. Option 3—Alternative Licensure
   A. Possess a bachelor's degree, including 30 semester hours in a particular field, *or*

   Possess a master's degree, including 12 graduate semester hours in a particular field, *or*

   Possess a doctorate degree in a particular field;
   B. Pass the NES tests required (for specifics, consult http://www.ped.state.nm.us/licensure/); *and*
   C. Complete an approved alternative program through an accredited New Mexico college or university, *or*

   Complete the NMTEACH Summative Report Requirements.

Endorsements for Teaching License

I. An endorsement is a teaching field on a teaching license.
II. Endorsements available are visual arts; technology education; health; physical education; library media; gifted; psychology; social studies language arts; reading; Teachers of English to Speakers of Other Languages (TESOL); science; information technology coordinator; business education; mathematics; modern, classical, and native language; bilingual education; family and consumer science; agriculture; and performing arts.
III. General endorsement requirements: submit an endorsement application with transcripts reflecting:
    A. A minimum of 24 semester hours of credit in the endorsement area, plus the exam for beginning teachers (teaching field):
        1. Twelve of those hours must be upper-division level, except on a special education or elementary license, where the credits can be lower division; *or*
        2. Provide proof of having passed a content knowledge assessment in the endorsement area (the teaching field).
        3. Core subject areas—language arts, social studies, science, and mathematics—are not available as endorsements to an elementary or special education license.
IV. Detailed requirements for adding each endorsement to a teacher license are available at https://webnew.ped.state.nm.us/bureaus/licensure/adding-endorsements/.

Licenses

I. Level 1 Elementary License (valid 5 years)
    A. Requirements
        1. Bachelor's degree from a regionally accredited college or university;
        2. Minimum of 30–36 semester hours in an elementary education program including student teaching;
        3. Six semester hours of credit in the teaching of reading for those who first entered any college or university on or after August 1, 2001;
        4. Minimum of 24 semester hours in 1 teaching field, such as mathematics, science, language arts, etc.; *and*
        5. Passage of the NES tests:
            a. Essential Academic Skills (Subtests I, II and III),
            b. Assessment of Professional Knowledge Elementary,
            c. Elementary Education (Subtests I and II), and
            d. Essential Components of Elementary Reading Instruction, *or*
        Possess a certificate issued by the National Board for Professional Teaching Standards.
II. Level 1 Middle Level Education, Grades 5–9 (valid 5 years)
    A. This license authorizes individuals to teach in a departmentalized setting.
        1. Individuals must be endorsed in the subject they are teaching.

B.   Requirements for Option I:
1.   Bachelor's degree from a regionally accredited college or university;
2.   Minimum of 30–36 semester hours in a middle level education program, including student teaching;
3.   Three semester hours of credit in teaching reading for those who first entered any college or university on or after August 1, 2001;
4.   Minimum of 24 semester hours in at least 1 teaching field such as mathematics, science, language arts, etc., with 12 of those hours earned at the upper division level (300 and above);
     and
5.   Passage of the NES tests:
     a.   Essential Academic Skills (Subtests I, II and III),
     b.   Assessment of Professional Knowledge Elementary or Secondary, and
     c.   Content Knowledge Assessment for first endorsement (plus course work).
C.   Requirements for Option II:
1.   Possess a New Mexico elementary, secondary, PreK–12 specialty, or special education license;
2.   Provide verification of 5 years of successful teaching experience at the middle school level;
3.   Complete a minimum of 24 semester hours of credit in each subject the teacher teaches, 6 of which must be upper-division credit;
     and
4.   Pass the National Evaluation Series Content Knowledge Assessment in each subject the teacher teaches
     or
     Possess a certificate issued by the National Board for Professional Teaching Standards.

III.   Level 1 Secondary Education, Grades 7–12 (valid 5 years)
A.   This license authorizes individuals to teach in a departmentalized setting.
1.   Individuals must be endorsed in the subject they are teaching.
B.   Requirements
1.   Bachelor's degree from a regionally accredited college or university;
2.   Minimum of 24 semester hours in a secondary education program, to include student teaching;
3.   Three semester hours of credit in teaching reading for those who first entered any college or university on or after August 1, 2001;
4.   Minimum of 24 semester hours in at least 1 teaching field, such as mathematics, science, language arts, etc., with 12 of those hours earned at the upper division level (300 and above);
     and
5.   Passage of the NES tests:
     a.   Essential Academic Skills (Subtests I, II and III),
     b.   Assessment of Professional Knowledge: Secondary, and
     c.   Content Knowledge Assessment for first endorsement (plus course work),
     or

Possess a certificate issued by the National Board for Professional Teaching Standards.

IV. Educational Administration, PreK–12 Program
  A. Bachelor's and master's degree from a regionally accredited college or university;
  B. Minimum of 18 semester hours of graduate credit in an educational administration program;
  C. Completion of an administrative apprenticeship/internship at a college/university or under the supervision of a local superintendent;
  D. Hold a Level 2 or 3A New Mexico teaching license; *and*
  E. Pass the content knowledge assessment in educational administration.

V. Approved licenses. For comprehensive requirements for each license not detailed above, consult https://webnew.ped.state.nm.us/bureaus/licensure/how-to-apply/.
  A. Administrators
    1. Education administration, PreK–12
  B. Teachers
    1. Blind and visually impaired, birth–12; birth–3 early childhood; birth–PreK; PreK–3; elementary, K–8; middle level, 5–9; PreK–12 specialty; secondary, 7–12; secondary vocational-technical, 7–12; special education, PreK–12
  C. Instructional Support Providers (PreK–12 unless otherwise noted)
    1. Alcohol, drug, and substance abuse counselor; certified occupational therapy assistant; educational diagnostician; interpreter for the deaf; licensed practical nurse; occupational therapist; orientation and mobility specialist; physical therapist; physical therapist assistant; recreational therapist; rehabilitation counselor; school counselor; school nurse; school psychologist; school social worker; speech-language pathologist; speech-language pathologist fellow; speech-language pathologist apprentice; audiologist
  D. Support providers (PreK–12 unless otherwise noted)
    1. Athletic coaching, 7–12; educational assistant; health assistant; substitute teacher

VI. Alternative Licenses. For comprehensive requirements, consult http://www.ped.state.nm.us/licensure.

VII. Three-Tiered Licensure Systems
  A. Three-tiered licensure system is designed to attach base salaries to each level of teaching licenses, and it includes annual evaluation and licensure advancement.
  B. The Professional Development Dossier (PDD) is the cornerstone of advancement for teachers in the 3-Tiered Licensure System.
    1. Teachers must complete the PDD in order to advance from Level 1 to Level 2 and to advance from Level 2 to Level 3. For specific information, consult http://www.teachnm.org.
  C. Advancement via the NMTEACH Educator Effectiveness System for teachers in the 3-Tiered Licensure System
    1. Teachers may advance from Level 1 to Level 2 if:
      a. They have taught a minimum of 3 years on their Level 1 license (including years taught on a Level 1A alternative license),

   b. They have earned a rating of Effective, Highly Effective, or Exemplary on their current summative report,

   c. They have achieved Step 2 on their current summative report with a minimum of 35 points out of 70 earned in the student achievement section, *and*

   d. They have the approval of their district.

  2. Teachers may advance from Level 2 to Level 3 if:

   a. They have taught a minimum of 3 years on their Level 2 license,

   b. They have earned a master's degree or possess a certificate issued by the National Board for Professional Teaching Standards,

   c. They have earned a rating of Effective, Highly Effective, or Exemplary on their current summative report,

   d. They have achieved Step 2 on their current summative report with a minimum of 35 points out of 70 earned in the student achievement section (teachers with National Board Certification are exempt from this requirement), *and*

   e. They have the approval of their district.

New York

Types of Certificates

I. Initial Certificate (valid 5 years)
  A. Entry-level certificate issued in specific subject areas and grade levels for classroom teaching, educational leadership, and school counselor
  B. A Conditional Initial Certificate (valid 1 year; nonrenewable; leads to Initial certificate) may be issued to applicants who hold a valid teaching certificate from another US state or territory in the subject area of the New York State certificate title sought, have completed an out-of-state teacher preparation program comparable with a New York State teacher preparation program, and have completed all Initial certificate requirements except for the edTPA.
II. Internship Certificate (valid up to 2 years; nonrenewable while applicant is matriculated in teacher education program and completing the internship requirement)
  A. Issued to a student at least halfway through a New York State–registered and approved graduate teacher education program
III. Professional Certificate (valid continuously)
  A. Certificate holders must register and successfully complete 100 clock hours of acceptable Continuing Teacher and Leader Education (CTLE) during each 5-year registration period.
  B. Advanced-level certificate issued in specific subject areas and grade levels for classroom teaching, educational leadership, and school counselor
IV. A full listing of other certificates, including Supplementary certificates and Transitional certificates, is available at http://www.highered.nysed.gov/tcert/certificate/typesofcerts.html.

Certification Pathways

Links to detailed requirements for each certification pathway are available at http://eservices.nysed.gov/teach/certhelp/CertRequirementHelp.do.

I. Approved Teacher Preparation Program—for high school and college graduates:
  A. Complete a New York State–registered teacher preparation program;
  B. Pass the appropriate New York State certification exams—see Testing, below; *and*
  C. Complete appropriate workshop requirements.
II. Individual Evaluation—for career changers, persons educated outside of the United States, and persons not graduated from a teaching program:
  A. Earn a bachelor's degree with a GPA of at least 2.5;
  B. Satisfy semester hour requirements in liberal arts and sciences general core, content core, and pedagogical core competencies for the area of the certificate title sought;

C. Pass the appropriate New York State certification exams—see Testing, below;

D. Student teach or gain paid teaching experience for at least 40 days in the area of the certificate title sought;
and

E. Complete appropriate workshop requirements.

III. Alternative Teacher Preparation Program ("Transitional B" Program)—for career changers, college graduates:

    A. Possess a bachelor's degree (minimum 3.0 GPA) with an academic major, or 30 semester hours, in the subject area of the certificate title sought, of which 12 semester hours can be in a related subject area;

    B. Enroll in a New York State–registered Transitional B program;

    C. Provide a recommendation from the institution offering the program;

    D. Pass the appropriate New York State certification exams—see Testing, below;
and

    E. For the Initial certificate, complete the Transitional B program, hold the Transitional B certificate, and pass the edTPA in the area of the certificate title sought.

IV. National Board Certification—for teachers certified by the National Board for Professional Teaching Standards (NBPTS):

    A. Hold a valid NBPTS certificate in the area of the certificate title sought;
and

    B. Complete appropriate workshop requirements.

V. Interstate Reciprocity—for certified teachers from other states who meet requirements in either A or B. For list of acceptable out-of-state certificates, see http://www.highered .nysed.gov/tcert/certificate/levelcert.html.

    A. Initial Certificate

        1. College Teacher Education Program (outside New York)

            a. Complete a comparable, approved teacher preparation program, in the subject area of the certificate title sought, at a college in another US state or territory, that leads to an institutional recommendation for certification in the state in which the college is located;

            b. Possess a bachelor's or higher degree with a 2.5 cumulative GPA;

            c. Pass the appropriate New York State certification exams—see Testing, below;
and

            d. Complete appropriate workshop requirements.
or

        2. Endorsement of Certificate

            a. Possess a valid, comparable US state or territory certificate in the subject area of the certificate title sought;

            b. Have 3 years of teaching experience out of the last 5 years, completed in a public school while holding a valid certificate in the subject area of the certificate title sought;

            c. Have evaluation ratings of Effective or Highly Effective for the teaching experience;

> > d.   Possess a bachelor's or higher degree with a 2.5 cumulative GPA; *and*
> > e.   Complete appropriate workshop requirements.
> B.   Conditional Initial Certificate (valid 1 year, during which time applicant must complete the appropriate edTPA; see Testing, below)
> > 1.   Meet the requirements for A1, with the exception of the edTPA, which is to be completed during the 1-year certificate validity period; *and*
> > 2.   Possess a valid, comparable US state or territory certificate in the subject area of the certificate title sought.

VI.   Additional Certificate—for New York State–certified teachers seeking additional certificates:
> A.   Possess a valid New York State classroom teaching certificate;
> B.   Satisfy the 30-semester-hour content core requirements and the pedagogical core requirements for the certificate title sought;
> C.   Pass the appropriate New York State Content Specialty Test(s) (CSTs); *and*
> D.   Complete appropriate workshop requirements.

VII.   Supplementary Certificate—for New York State–certified teachers seeking to teach another subject area while completing requirements for the Initial certificate in that subject area:
> A.   Possess a valid New York State classroom teaching certificate;
> B.   Satisfy the 12-semester-hour content core requirements for the certificate title sought;
> C.   Obtain a recommendation from the employing school district; *and*
> D.   Pass the appropriate New York State Content Specialty Test(s) (CSTs).

VIII.   New York State Professional License—for New York State–licensed speech-language pathologists who pursue the Speech and Language Disabilities Initial certificate:
> A.   Hold a New York State speech-language pathology license and be registered in the profession; *and*
> B.   Complete appropriate workshop requirements.

IX.   Transitional G—for college professors with appropriate credentials and experience:
> A.   Possess a master's or higher degree in the subject area of the certificate title sought;
> B.   Have completed 2 years of satisfactory teaching experience at the college level in the subject area of the certificate title sought within the past 10 years;
> C.   Obtain a recommendation from the employing school district; *and*
> D.   For the Initial certificate, pass the Educating All Students Test and complete the pedagogical core (6 undergraduate semester hours, 4 graduate semester hours, or 2 years' experience under the Transitional G certificate).

Testing

For full details of required examinations, see http://www.highered.nysed.gov/tcert/certificate/certexam.html.

I. Individuals seeking a teaching certificate must achieve qualifying scores on a set of assessments determined by the certificate title.
   A. Candidates who are certified by the NBPTS in the area of the certificate title sought are not required to take any certification exams.
   B. Candidates who meet the requirements for the Endorsement of Certificate pathway are not required to take any certification exams.

North Carolina

Licensure Categories

I. Initial Professional License (intended for teachers with 0–2 years of teaching experience; valid 3 years). Applicant must have:

   A. Completed an approved educator preparation program (EPP) from a regionally or nationally accredited college or university;

   or

   Completed another state's approved alternative route to licensure;

   and

   B. Earned at least a bachelor's degree from a regionally or nationally accredited college or university.

II. Continuing Professional License (intended for teachers with 3 or more years of teaching experience; valid 5 years). Issued to teachers who:

   A. Have 3 or more years of teaching experience;

   or

   B. Have 3 or more years of experience in another state and are fully licensed in another state,

   and

   1. Meet North Carolina's State Board of Education (NCSBE)–required licensure exam(s) (consult http://www.NCPublicSchools.org/licensure)

      or

   2. Have passed, at a satisfactory level, another state's licensure exam that the North Carolina Department of Public Instruction has determined is comparable to North Carolina's assessment

      or

   3. Have certification from the National Board for Professional Teaching Standards (NBPTS),

      and

   4. Demonstrate evidence of effectiveness by evaluation data, including student growth (where applicable), from the state in which the current license is held.

III. Lateral Entry License (valid 3 years; being phased out in the 2018–19 fiscal year)

   A. Issued to an individual who is employed in a North Carolina public school system and who affiliates with a college or university with an approved EPP in the license area or with the Regional Alternative Licensing Center in North Carolina.

   1. An individual plan of study is prescribed for the lateral entry teacher.

   B. Applicants must hold at least a bachelor's degree from a regionally accredited institution

   and

   1. One of the following:

      a.   Bachelor's degree or higher that is relevant to the subject being taught;
           or

      b.   Twenty-four semester hours of course work in core area;
           i.   English as a Second Language requires a degree in English or linguistics, *or* 24 semester hours in English *or* linguistics, *or* a passing score on the NCSBE-approved assessments.
           or

      c.   Passing score on the NCSBE-required assessment(s) for the area of license;
           or

      d.   For world languages except English, passing score on the American Council on the Teaching of Foreign Languages (ACTFL) examination;
      and

  2.   One of the following:
      a.   GPA of 2.5 or above;
           or

      b.   At least 5 years of experience considered relevant by the employing local education agency (LEA);
           or

      c.   Passing scores on Core Academic Skills for Educators;
           or

      d.   A total SAT score of 1100 on tests taken prior to March 2016 (1170 on the redesigned test taken after March 2016);
           or

      e.   A total ACT score of 24 *plus* 1 of the following:
           i.   GPA of 3.0 in the major field of study,
           or
           ii.   GPA of 3.0 in all courses in senior year,
           or
           iii.   GPA of 3.0 on a minimum of 15 semester hours of courses completed within the last 5 years after the bachelor's degree or higher.

C.   Lateral Entry License holders must pass the NCSBE-required licensure exams during the first 3 school years as a license holder if the exams were not the basis of qualifying for the license.

IV. Residency License—replaces the Lateral Entry License per NC GS 115C-270.20(a)(5)

V. Emergency License—a 1-year, nonrenewable license issued to an individual who:
  A.   Holds a bachelor's degree with 18 hours of course work relevant to the requested license area, but has not completed a recognized educator preparation program, *and*
  B.   Does not qualify for the Residency License.
  C.   All other NCSBE requirements must be met, including pre-service teacher training.

Licensure Renewal

I. Continuing Professional License must be renewed every 5 years.

II. Requirements to renew the Continuing Professional License:

    A.   NBPTS Certification

        1.   Eight credits for completion; 2 credits for 10-year renewal

III. Renewal Credits: Credits required for renewal differ based on the date of the license expiration. Please consult the website for the most accurate information: https://stateboard.ncpublicschools.gov/policy-manual/licensure/copy5_of_licensure-renewal-requirements.

    A.   Definition and equivalencies

        1.   One unit of renewal credit is equivalent to 1 quarter hour, or 1 in-service credit from a North Carolina public school system, or 10 contact/clock hours of professional development.

        2.   One semester hour is equivalent to 1.5 units of renewal credit.

    B.   Exclusions and restrictions

        1.   For a professional educator's license to remain current, all credit must be earned by the expiration date of the existing professional educator's license.

        2.   To renew an expired professional educator's license, 8 units of renewal credit must be earned within the most recent 5-year period.

IV. Activities accepted for renewal credit:

    A.   College or university courses

        1.   Official transcripts are required as documentation; grade reports and unofficial transcripts are not accepted.

    B.   Local in-service courses or workshops

        1.   The administrative unit certifies credits.

    C.   Classes and workshops approved by the school system

        1.   Documentation of completion is provided by the agency sponsoring the activity.

V. Credits required for licenses expiring on June 30, 2019:

    A.   Grades K–5: 3 subject area; 3 literacy; 2 digital learning competencies

    B.   Grades 6–12: 3 subject area; 2 digital learning competencies; 3 general

    C.   Student Services Personnel: 3 professional discipline area; 2 digital learning competencies; 3 general

    D.   Administrators: 3 executive's role; 2 digital learning competencies; 3 general

    E.   As a condition of employment per NCSBE Policy LICN-005, LEAs reserve the right to assign literacy requirements for any educator.

Administrators/Special Service Personnel

I. Requirements for administrators, Special Service, and instructional support personnel

    A.   Obtain a valid Continuing Professional License

    B.   Student services personnel who have completed an approved EPP
        and

        1.   Have satisfied North Carolina's SBE-approved testing requirements are issued a Continuing Professional License.

        2.   Have not satisfied North Carolina's SBE-approved testing requirements are issued an Initial Professional License.

            a.   Special Service personnel who are issued the Initial Professional License must attempt their NCSBE-required licensure exams in their first year of employment and pass the exam in the second year of employment.

      b.   When North Carolina's testing requirements are satisfied, the license is converted to a Continuing Professional License.

C.   Student services personnel who are fully licensed in another state and have 3 or more years of student services school experience in another state will be issued the Continuing License when they:

    1.   Meet NCSBE-required licensure exams,
or

    2.   Earn National Board Certification,
or

    3.   Provide evidence of successfully passing a comparable state-approved licensure exam(s) in the state where they completed their EPP.

License Areas and Requirements

I.   School Administrator—Superintendent
    A.   Must hold both the North Carolina principal's license (master's level or above)
       and
    B.   Superintendent's license at the advanced graduate level (6th-year degree or doctorate) issued under the authority of the NCSBE.

II.   School Administrator—Principal
    A.   Completion of an approved program in school administration at the master's level or above
    B.   No provisional principal license is issued for service as a principal.

III.   School Administrator—Assistant Principal
    A.   Completion of an approved program in school administration at the master's level or above
    B.   Provisional principal license is issued for service as an assistant principal if the local board determines there is a shortage of individuals with principal licensure.
    C.   Affiliation with a master's school administrator program must occur before the expiration of the provisional license. Provisional principal licenses shall be issued for 3 school years, during which time program requirements must be completed.

IV.   Curriculum Instructional Specialist
    A.   Completion of an approved program for a curriculum instructional specialist at the master's level or above
    B.   NTE/Praxis Educational Leadership: Administrative and Supervision required score

V.   Career-Technical Director
    A.   Completion of an approved program for a career-technical education director at the master's level or above

VI.   Exceptional Children Program Administrator (licensure is a supervisory classification)
    A.   Master's degree in an exceptional children area or an advanced (6th-year) degree in school psychology;
       and
       Three graduate semester hours of credit in each of the following:
       1.   Administration,
       2.   Curriculum development, and

       3.   Supervision;
      and
      NTE/Praxis Educational Leadership: Administrative and Supervision required score.
      or

   B.   A master's degree in administration and/or curriculum instruction,
      and
      Nine semester hours of course work in exceptional children,
      and
      NTE/Praxis Educational Leadership: Administrative and Supervision required score.

  VII. Instructional Technology Specialist—Computers
     A.   Completion of an approved college or university program in Instructional Technology Specialist Computers at the master's level or above

 VIII. Instructional Technology Specialist—Telecommunications
     A.   Completion of an approved college or university program in Instructional Technology Specialist Telecommunications at the master's level or above

   IX. Media Supervisor
     A.   Master's degree in school media
     B.   Three graduate semester hours in each of the following:
       1.   Administration
       2.   Curriculum development
       3.   Supervision
     C.   Required testing: NTE/Praxis Educational Leadership: Administrative and Supervision (for details, consult http://www.ets.org/praxis/)

    X. Media Coordinator
     A.   One of the following:
       1.   Completion of an approved program for a media coordinator at the master's level or above
          or
       2.   Completion of an approved program after July 1, 1984 allows a provisional license upon employment with requirement to update to master's level
          or
       3.   Obtain a provisional media coordinator license (consult http://www.ncpublicschools.org/licensure/administrator/)
     B.   Required testing: NTE/Praxis Library Media Specialist (for details, consult http://www.ets.org/praxis/)

   XI. School Counselor
     A.   Completion of an approved program in school counseling at the master's level or above
     B.   NTE/Praxis Professional School Counselor test required score

  XII. School Social Worker
     A.   Completion of an approved program in school social work at the bachelor's level or above

 XIII. School Psychologist
     A.   Completion of an approved program in school psychology at the sixth-year level
     B.   NTE/Praxis School Psychology required score

XIV.   School Speech-Language Pathologist
    A.   Current valid North Carolina Board of Examiners for Speech and Language Pathologists and Audiologists (NCBOESLPA) license

XV.   School Audiologist
    A.   One of the following:
        1.   Audiology Certificate of Clinical Competence (CCC-A) from the American Speech-Language-Hearing Association
           or
        2.   License from the North Carolina Board of Examiners for Speech and Language Pathologist and Audiologist
           or
        3.   Completion of an approved program in audiology at the master's level or above.
    B.   NTE/Praxis Audiology required score

North Dakota

North Dakota teachers are licensed by the state Education Standards and Practices Board (ESPB), while administrators and other school personnel are licensed by the state Department of Public Instruction (DPI).

Types of Licenses

I. North Dakota Century Code Authority
   A. Individual must hold valid North Dakota license issued by the North Dakota ESPB in order to be permitted or employed to teach in any state public school.
   B. Nonpublic schools must employ licensed teachers to be approved and in compliance with compulsory attendance laws.
II. Licensure Level
   A. Level I indicates that individual still has educational or employment requirements to meet before receiving regular Level II license, or that they are not currently maintaining contracted employment.
   B. Level II indicates that individual has met all basic requirements for regular North Dakota Educators' Professional License.
   C. Level III indicates that individual has earned advanced degrees beyond bachelor's level (master's, specialist, or doctoral) or National Board for Professional Teaching Standards (NBPTS) advanced licensure.
III. Types of Educator's Licenses and Procedures
   A. Forty-Day Provisional: Issued to applicants who have been offered a job and have completed entire application process with exception of background investigation. Letter from school administrator indicating desire to issue contract without background investigation being complete and letter from applicant indicating any criminal background history are needed by ESPB prior to issuing this license.
   B. Initial License (valid 2 years): Issued to first-time applicants who have met all state requirements for licensure
   C. Regular (valid 5 years): Issued to individuals who have met all requirements for a state Educator's Professional License and have successfully taught for 18 months (full-time equivalent) in state
   D. Alternate License (valid 1 year): Issued in documented shortage area. License is initiated by letter from local school administrator indicating search for qualified applicant and desire for this license to be issued. Requirements include:
      1. School's request letter and successful background check
      2. Bachelor's degree in appropriate content area
      3. Plan of study from college of education where applicant will complete 8 semester hours each year toward teaching degree
   E. Out-of-State Reciprocal (valid 2 years, can be renewed once): Issued to individuals

who do not hold valid license from another state and have not met this state's standards and rules. Plan of study is developed for each individual indicating course work needed. Individual has 4 years to complete all requirements.

    F.   Other State Educator's License (OSEL; valid 2 years or 5 years): Issued to individuals who hold a valid license from another state, have met that state's testing requirements, and have completed a traditional teacher education program.

    G.   Additional types of educator's licenses and procedures. For full details, consult http://www.nd.gov/espb/licensure/license-information/types-licenses.

        1.   Two-Year Renewal
        2.   Interim/Substitute (2 years)
        3.   Re-Entry (2 years)
        4.   Probationary (2 years)
        5.   Minor Equivalency Endorsement
        6.   Kindergarten Endorsement
        7.   Major Equivalency Praxis Endorsement
        8.   Thirty-Year Life License

Elementary School

I.   North Dakota Educator's Professional License

    A.   Bachelor's degree from an accredited college approved to offer teacher education
    B.   Professional requirements, credits in professional education, including student teaching, overall grade point average of 2.5, 34 semester hours
    C.   Valid for 2 years for teaching in the level of preparation
    D.   A 5-year renewal may be issued with 2 years of successful full-time teaching experience in the state. Each renewal of the 5-year license requires 6 semester hours of work.
    E.   Submission of PPST/Praxis I/Core Academic Skills for Educators scores in reading, writing, and mathematics that meet or exceed North Dakota cut scores
    F.   Submission of Praxis II content and pedagogy test scores that meet or exceed North Dakota cut scores
    G.   Background investigation, including Bureau of Criminal Investigation and the FBI

Secondary School

I.   North Dakota Educator's Professional License

    A.   Same as Elementary School, I, A–G
    B.   Thirty-two semester hours

Superintendent (Regulated by State DPI)

I.   Provisional Credential

    A.   Valid until the end of the second school year following the year in which the provisional credential is issued; not renewable

B. Issued as the initial credential to an individual who does not meet the qualifications for a professional credential

C. Issued to those who have a level I principal's credential but lack the superintendent course work, the experience, or both that are necessary for the superintendent professional credential

D. Applicant must fulfill all the following standards:
    1. Hold a valid North Dakota teaching license during the life of the credential
    2. Have at least 3 years of teaching experience, verified in a letter of recommendation by a supervisor or employer who has firsthand knowledge of the individual's professional work
    3. Have at least 2 years of administrative experience comprising at least half time as an elementary or secondary principal, a central office administrator, or an administrator of an approved school with a 12-year program. This experience is to be verified by a supervisor or employer who has firsthand knowledge of the individual's professional work.
    4. Complete the requirements for the level I elementary or secondary principal credential and 8 additional hours of designated course work specific to the superintendency (see state DPI, Appendix 1)

II. Professional Credential
    A. Issued to coincide with the period for which the individual is licensed to teach by the ESPB and may be renewed. An individual holding a lifetime educator's professional license must renew the credential every 5 years.
    and
    B. Issued upon satisfying credential standards; see I, D, 1–4, directly above.

III. Renewal Requirements
    A. Applicant must fulfill 1 of the following:
        1. Provide a copy of official transcripts showing satisfactory completion of at least 8 semester hours of graduate work in education, of which 4 semester hours are in the area of educational administration;
        or
        2. Provide a copy of official transcripts showing satisfactory completion of at least 4 semester hours of graduate work and verification of attendance or participation in at least 6 administrative educational conferences or workshops from a state-approved list with specific verification.

Secondary Principal (Regulated by State DPI)

I. Provisional Credential
    A. Issued as the initial credential to an individual who does not meet the qualifications for a level I or level II professional credential and is employed as a secondary principal; valid until the end of the second school year following the year in which the provisional credential is issued; not renewable
    B. Issued to a person enrolled in a state-approved program in educational leadership who has completed 8 semester hours of course work in that area

C. Issued upon satisfying the following credentials standards with specific verification of each:
    1. Valid North Dakota educator's professional license issued by the ESPB allowing the individual to teach at the secondary level
    2. At least 3 years of teaching or administrative experience (as defined by DPI) or a combination thereof in secondary schools:
        a. Equal to full-time equivalency: at least 6 hours for a 180-day school term
        b. Positions must have been stated on a professional contract.

II. Level I Professional Credential
    A. Issued to coincide with the period for which the individual is licensed to teach by the ESPB and may be renewed at the end of that period. An individual holding a lifetime educator's professional license must renew their credential every 5 years.
        and
    B. Issued upon satisfying the following credentials standards:
        1. See I, C, 1 and 2, directly above.
        2. The level I credential requires 1 of the following:
            a. Master's degree in educational administration from a state-approved program;
                or
            b. Master's degree with a major certifiable by the ESPB in addition to 20 semester hours of credit that include designated courses specific to the secondary level contained within a master's degree in educational administration from a state-approved program.

III. Level II Professional Credential
    A. Issued to coincide with the period for which the individual is licensed to teach by the ESPB. An individual holding a lifetime educator's professional license must renew their credential every 5 years.
    B. Renewal of the level II professional credential is available only for principals serving secondary schools with 100 or fewer students.
    C. Issued upon satisfying the following credentials standards:
        1. See I, C, 1 and 2, directly above.
        2. Level II credential requires 20 semester hours of graduate credit in a master's degree program from a state-approved program in educational administration with designated courses.

IV. Renewal Requirements
    A. To renew the level I and level II professional credentials, an individual shall submit 1 of the following:
        1. A copy of official transcripts of 8 semester hours of graduate work in education acquired after the date of the original credentialing or last renewal, of which 4 semester hours are in the area of educational administration;
            or
        2. A copy of official transcripts of 4 semester hours of graduate work in education acquired after the date of the original credentialing or last renewal and verification of attendance or participation in at least 6 educational conferences or workshops from a designated list with specific verification.

Elementary Principal (Regulated by State DPI)

I. Provisional Credential
    A. Issued as the initial credential to an individual who does not meet the qualifications for a level I or level II professional credential and is employed as an elementary principal; valid until the end of the second school year following the year in which the provisional credential is issued; not renewable
    B. Issued to a person enrolled in a state-approved program in educational leadership who has completed 8 semester hours of course work in that area
    C. Issued upon satisfying the following credentials standards with specific verification of each:
        1. A valid North Dakota teaching license issued by the ESPB allowing the individual to teach at the elementary level
        2. At least 3 years of teaching or administrative experience (as defined by DPI) or a combination thereof in elementary schools:
            a. Equal to full-time equivalency: at least 5.5 hours daily, for a 180-day school term
            b. Positions must have been stated on a professional contract.

II. Level I Professional Credential
    A. Issued to coincide with the period for which the individual is licensed to teach by the ESPB. An individual holding a lifetime educator's professional license must renew their credential every 5 years.
        and
    B. Issued upon satisfying the following credential standards:
        1. See I, C, 1 and 2, directly above.
        2. The level I credential requires 1 of the following:
            a. Master's degree in educational administration that includes designated course work specific to the elementary level from a state-approved program,
                or
            b. Master's degree with a major certifiable by the ESPB. Twenty semester hours of credit that includes designated courses specific to the elementary level contained within a master's degree in educational administration from a state-approved program.

III. Level II Professional Credential
    A. Issued to coincide with the period for which the individual is licensed to teach by the ESPB. An individual holding a lifetime educator's professional license must renew their credential every 5 years.
    B. Renewal of the level II professional credential is available only for principals serving elementary schools enrolling 100 or fewer students.
    C. Issued upon satisfying the following credential standards:
        1. See I, C, 1 and 2, directly above.
        2. Level II credential requires 20 semester hours of graduate credit in a master's degree program from a state-approved program in educational administration with designated courses.

IV. Renewal Requirements
  A. To renew the level I and level II professional credentials, an individual must submit 1 of the following:
     1. A copy of official transcripts of 8 semester hours of graduate work in education acquired after the date of the original credentialing or last renewal, of which 4 semester hours are in the area of educational administration;
        or
     2. A copy of official transcripts of 4 semester hours of graduate work in education acquired after the date of the original credentialing or last renewal and verification of attendance or participation in at least 6 educational conferences or workshops from a designated list with specific verification.

School Counselor (Regulated by State DPI)

I. School Counselor Credentials
  A. Credential designations: SC03 for grades PreK–12
  B. Credential is valid only while the individual holds a North Dakota educator's professional license or a professional school counseling restricted license.
     1. A credential must be renewed each time the individual's educator's professional license is renewed.
     2. Holders of a lifetime North Dakota educator's professional license must renew the credential every 5 years.
     3. To renew the credential, submit a copy of college transcripts documenting 6 semester hours of graduate course work in education, of which 2 semester hours must be in counseling.
        a. Two semester hours of required counseling course work may be replaced by 30 clock hours of continuing education hours in counseling with a signed verification of attendance or participation by the conference or workshop sponsor, the employer, or a school district business manager.
  C. SC03 credential standards—counselor must:
     1. Hold a valid educator's professional license from the state Education Standards and Practices Board;
        and
     2. Have a master's degree in counseling, education, or a related human service field and the following graduate core counseling course work content from a state-approved school counseling program:
        a. Elementary school counseling;
        b. Secondary school counseling;
        c. Supervised school counseling internship consisting of a minimum of 450 contact hours, of which at least 150 are at both the elementary and secondary level;
        d. Counseling program management;
        e. Counseling theories;
        f. Assessment techniques;

    g.   Group counseling;
    h.   Career counseling and assessment;
    i.   Social and multicultural counseling;
    j.   Ethics and law;
        and
    k.   Counseling techniques.
D. If a school is unable to employ a credentialed counselor, the school may employ a licensed teacher to serve as the counselor on a plan of study. Contact DPI for details at 701-328-2260.

Library Media (Regulated by State DPI)

Contact the Department of Public Instruction (see Appendix 1) for a detailed listing of required course work, official application forms, and instructions.

I. Librarian (LM03)
  A. Bachelor's degree with a licensable major or minor or an endorsement in elementary, middle-level, or secondary education
  B. Valid North Dakota Educator's Professional License
  C. Complete course work in library media from a state-approved program as detailed in Subsection 1 of Section 67-11-04-05, 15 semester hours*
  D. Validity Length
    1. Valid only while the individual holds a valid North Dakota educator's professional license
    2. Must be renewed each time professional license is renewed; 2 graduate semester hours in library media and information science from a state-approved program
      a. Individual holding a lifetime North Dakota educator's professional license must renew the credential every 5 years.

II. Library Media Specialist (LM02)
  A. See I, A, directly above.
  B. Valid North Dakota Educator's Professional License
  C. Complete course work in library media from a state-approved program as detailed in Subsection 1 of Section 67-11-04-05, 15 semester hours*
    Subsection 2 of Section 67-11-04-05, 9 semester hours*
  D. See I, D, directly above.

III. Library Media Director (LM01)
  A. Master's degree in library science, media education, education, or educational administration from a state-approved program
  B. Valid North Dakota Educator's Professional License (based on bachelor's degree with a licensable major or minor or an endorsement in elementary, middle-level, or secondary education)
  C. Complete course work in library media from a state-approved program as detailed in Subsection 1 of Section 67-11-04-05, 15 semester hours*
    Subsection 2 of Section 67-11-04-05, 9 semester hours*

Subsection 3 of Section 67-11-04-05, 6 semester hours (graduate in school library or school administration)

IV. Plan of Study Option to qualify for library media director, library media specialist, or librarian credentials

A. If school is unable to employ credentialed librarian, as required by enrollment of students served, may employ licensed teacher to serve as librarian if licensed teacher has completed at least 6 semester hours in library media course work and has submitted a written plan of study showing at least 6 graduate or undergraduate semester hours in library media course work to be completed annually until credential is earned.

B. Once plan is approved, licensed teacher must document a minimum of 6 semester hours of library media course work each year until qualified for required credential

V. Renewal Requirements (LM03, LM02, LM01): All are renewed by submitting application form and documenting completion of 2 semester hours of graduate credit in library media and information science.

*graduate or undergraduate

Ohio

Ohio's standards are performance-based and lead to licensing based on assessments (administered under the authority of the state board of education) of the performance of teachers during their participation in the Ohio Resident Educator Program. Applicants for any license or permit must complete both an Ohio and an FBI criminal background check, conducted by the Bureau of Criminal Identification and Investigation. For full details, consult Educator Licensure at education.ohio.gov.

Resident Educator

I. Resident Educator License (valid 4 years)—for applicants seeking initial teaching license:
   A. A degree required by license
   B. Evidence of good moral character
   C. Successful completion of an approved program of preparation
   D. Recommendation by dean or head of teacher education at institution approved to prepare teachers
   E. Successful completion of Ohio Assessments for Educators (OAE) examination in content and professional knowledge, or equivalent out-of-state licensure exam for out-of-state applicants
      1. For world languages, the American Council on the Teaching of Foreign Languages (ACTFL) Oral Proficiency Interview and Writing Proficiency Test are also required.
   F. Completed course work in teaching of reading, 12 semester hours
      1. For early childhood, middle childhood, and intervention specialist licenses, at least 1 separate 3-semester-hour course in teaching of phonics is required.
      2. For multi-age and adolescence to young adult licenses, 3 semester hours in teaching of reading are required.
   G. Individuals who have completed licensure programs at colleges/universities outside of the state of Ohio apply to the Ohio Office of Educator Licensure (see Appendix 1).
   H. Beginning July 1, 2017, applicants seeking a new 4- or 5-year teaching license in 1 of the following areas must pass the Ohio Assessment for Educators Foundations of Reading (OAE 090) test:
      1. Early childhood education (grades PreK–3)
      2. Middle childhood education (grades 4–9)
      3. Intervention specialist: early childhood, mild/moderate, moderate/intensive, hearing impaired, visually impaired, or gifted
      4. More information can be found at http://education.ohio.gov/Topics/Teaching/Licensure/Prepare-for-Certificate-License/FAQs-about-Foundations-of-Reading-Test-Requirement#FAQ2800.

II. Alternative Resident Educator License (valid 4 years)—provides an accelerated pathway to classroom teaching. To enroll in an approved Alternative Resident Licensure Program, candidates must:
   A. Request an alternative resident educator evaluation;
   B. Hold a bachelor's degree or higher from an accredited institution of higher education;
   C. Successfully complete the OAE examination in content and professional knowledge, or equivalent out-of-state licensure exam for out-of-state applicants;
      1. For world languages, the American Council on the Teaching of Foreign Languages (ACTFL) Oral Proficiency Interview and Writing Proficiency Test are also required.
      and
   D. Complete mandatory background checks by the FBI and the state Bureau of Criminal Identification and Investigation (BCI).
   E. To advance to a 5-year professional license, applicants must:
      1. Complete 4 years of successful teaching experience under the alternative educator license;
      2. Complete 12 semester hours of specific professional education course work from a college or university approved in teacher preparation;
         or
      3. Complete a Professional Development Institute approved by the Ohio Department of Higher Education;
      4. Successfully complete the OAE examination in content and professional knowledge;
      5. Complete all components of the Ohio Resident Educator Program.

Professional Licenses

I. Professional Teacher License (valid 5 years)—for applicants who already hold an Ohio teaching license but wish to seek licensure in a new area. For more information and a list of license areas, visit http://education.ohio.gov/Topics/Teaching/Licensure/Apply-for-Certificate-License/Educator-License-Types-and-Descriptions.
   A. Baccalaureate degree
   B. See I, Resident Educator License, B, C, and E, above.
   C. Successful completion of Ohio Resident Educator Program
   D. Alternative license holders complete additional course work or professional development work to obtain professional license.

Professional Pupil Services Licenses

I. Professional Pupil Services License (valid 5 years)
   A. Evidence of good moral character
   B. Completion of an approved program of preparation
   C. Recommendation by dean or head of teacher education
   D. Completion of examination prescribed by the state board of education

II. License Areas
   A. School audiologist
     1. Master's degree and current license to practice audiology
     2. See I, A–D, directly above.
   B. School counselor
     1. Master's degree
     2. See I, A–D, directly above.
   C. School psychologist
     1. Master's degree and approved program of preparation, successful completion of Praxis II or OAE examination, successful completion of 9-month, full-time internship in approved school setting
     2. See I, A–D, directly above.
   D. Other professional pupil personnel license areas include school social worker; school speech-language pathologist; school nurse; and orientation and mobility specialist. Please consult Educator Licensure at education.ohio.gov for details.

Professional Administrator Licenses

I. Professional Administrator License
   A. Evidence of good moral character
   B. Master's degree
   C. Recommendation by dean or head of teacher education at institution approved to prepare teachers
   D. Successful completion of an educational leadership examination prescribed by the state board of education
II. License Areas
   A. Principal License
     1. Successful completion of an approved preparation program for principal licensure and the prescribed examination
     2. Valid for working with
       a. Ages 3–12 and grades PreK–6
       b. Ages 8–14 and grades 4–9
       c. Ages 10–21 and grades 5–12
     3. A principal must have 2 years of successful teaching experience with students of the ages and grade levels for which the principal license is sought.
     4. Alternative Principal License—Ohio offers various alternative pathways to licensure for principals, detailed here: http://education.ohio.gov/Topics/Teaching/Licensure/Resident-License-Options/Alternative-Principal-License.
   B. Administrative Specialist License
     1. Valid for working in central office or supervisory capacity
     2. Prior to issuance, applicant must have completed 2 years of successful teaching experience under professional teacher's license and must have successfully completed approved program of preparation.
     3. Alternative Administrative Specialist License—Ohio offers various alternative pathways to licensure for administrative specialists, detailed here: http://

education.ohio.gov/Topics/Teaching/Licensure/Resident-License-Options/Alternative-Administrative-Specialist-License.

C. Superintendent License

1. Prior to issuance, applicant must have completed 3 years of successful experience in position requiring principal or administrative specialist license and must have successfully completed approved preparation program for superintendents.

2. Alternative Superintendent License—Ohio offers various alternative pathways to licensure for superintendents, detailed here: http://education.ohio.gov/Topics/Teaching/Licensure/Resident-License-Options/Alternative-Principal-License.

Oklahoma

Oklahoma Senate Bill #1443 waives requirements of educator residency indefinitely, thus exempting school districts from participation in a residency program. Accordingly, resident teacher programs and committees mentioned in the text below are currently on hold. Refer to the Oklahoma State Department of Education website for the most current information at https://sde.ok.gov/teacher-certification.

Traditional Licensure and Certification

I. Oklahoma Initial Teaching License (provisional, valid 2 years)
   A. Requirements for licensure
      1. Holds a bachelor's degree from an accredited institution of higher education (IHE) that has approval or accreditation for teaching education;
      2. Successfully completed a higher education teacher education program approved by the Office of Educational Quality and Accountability (OEQA)—see Appendix 1 for contact information;
      3. Has met all other requirements as may be established by the Oklahoma State Board of Education (OSBE);
      4. Has made necessary application and paid competency examination fees in amount and as prescribed by OCTP;
      5. Successfully completed 3 competency examinations, including:
         a. Oklahoma General Education Test (OGET),
         b. Oklahoma Subject Area Test(s) (OSAT), and
         c. Oklahoma Professional Teaching Examination (OPTE);
         and
      6. Has on file with the OSBE both a current Oklahoma and national criminal history record search from the Oklahoma State Bureau of Investigation (OSBI) and Federal Bureau of Investigation (FBI), respectively.
II. Oklahoma Standard Teaching Certificate (valid 5 years, renewable)
   A. Requirements for certification
      1. Has completed all requirements for the Initial license (see section I) and has completed 1 full year of successful employment in an Oklahoma accredited school district;
      2. Has made the necessary application and paid the certification fee;
         or
      3. Holds an out-of-state certificate and meets standards set by the OSBE;
         or
      4. Holds certification from the National Board for Professional Teaching Standards.

5. For those who do not have a teacher education degree, see Alternative Routes to Teaching below.

B. Additional subjects may be added to certificate by testing: contact Teacher Certification for details (see Appendix 1).

C. Special Education teachers new to the profession after December 3, 2004, are required to have a Special Education certificate as well as an appropriate certificate in 1 of the following areas: early childhood, elementary education, middle or secondary education in math, science, or language arts.

D. Credentialing for Educators with Out-of-State Licensure
1. Applicants who hold a full teaching credential in any state are eligible for a provisional Oklahoma certification in equivalent subject areas.
   a. Out-of-state teachers are exempt from Oklahoma testing requirements.
2. Oklahoma does have certification agreements limited to educator preparation program requirements with certain participating states/jurisdictions; see http://nasdtec.site-ym.com/?InterstateAgreements for full listing.
   a. Contact individual states regarding ancillary requirements such as minimum grade point average, standardized testing, mentoring experience, or graduation from an accredited institution.
3. If applicants hold a full credential in any state, they are eligible for Oklahoma certification in equivalent subject areas.
4. Following 1 full year of successful employment in an Oklahoma accredited school district, applicants will be eligible for a Standard teaching certificate (valid 5 years, renewable).

III. Specialist Certificate (valid 5 years, renewable)
A. Specialist certification is awarded for library media specialist, school counselor, school psychometrist, school psychologist, speech-language pathologist, and reading specialist.
B. In addition to meeting initial licensure requirements (see I, above), specialist certification requires completion of a graduate degree program meeting the professional education association standards specific to the profession.
1. Specialist certification may not be added through testing alone.
C. Application for certification in the specialist areas listed above should be initiated through the director of teacher education at the recommending IHE.

IV. Administrator Certificate
A. Principal Standard Certificate (valid 5 years, renewable)
1. Holds a standard master's degree,
2. Completed an Oklahoma-approved building-level leadership skills program in educational administration,
3. Achieved a passing score on principal specialty areas of the principal OSATs, *and*
4. Completed 2 years of successful teaching experience in an OSBE-accredited Oklahoma public or private school.
B. Superintendent Standard Certificate (valid 5 years, renewable)
1. Holds principal certification

or

Completed an Oklahoma-approved building-level leadership skills program in educational administration that includes a standard master's degree;

2. Achieved a passing score on superintendent OSAT;
3. Completed an Oklahoma-approved district-level leadership skills program in educational administration;
    and
4. Completed 2 years of administrative experience in an OSBE-accredited Oklahoma public or private school.

C. For alternative administrator certification for principal or superintendent (valid 3 years, non-renewable)
1. Holds a standard master's degree,
2. Completed 2 years of relevant work experience in a supervisory or administrative capacity,
3. Achieved passing scores on the required administrator OSAT(s),
    and
4. Has on file with the director of teacher education at an Oklahoma-accredited IHE a declaration of intent to earn standard certification through completion of an approved alternative administrative preparation program within 3 years.

Alternative Routes to Teaching

I. Alternative Placement Program
A. Provides an opportunity for individuals with non-teaching degrees to teach in Oklahoma-accredited schools.
B. Eligibility requirements:
1. Minimum of a baccalaureate degree from an accredited college/university recognized by Oklahoma State Regents for Higher Education (OSRHE);
    a. A master's degree is required to be licensed as a school counselor, reading specialist, and library media specialist.
2. Major in a field of study corresponding to an area of Oklahoma certification for secondary, elementary/secondary, or career and technology education certificate—contact the OSDE (see Appendix 1) for full listing;
3. At least a 2.5 grade point average;
    and
4. Two years of post-baccalaureate work experience relevant to the desired certification area,
    or
5. Terminal degree (PhD, EdD, MD, DO JD, etc.) recognized by the United States Department of Education.
C. Applicants must demonstrate competency in field that corresponds to the area of specialization they seek by providing documentation of:
1. Academic major in a field that corresponds to a certification area (30 or more relevant credit hours on a higher education transcript),

or

2. Academic minor (15 or more relevant credit hours on a higher education transcript) plus 1 year qualified work or volunteer experience verified by a reference,
   or
3. Relevant work or volunteer experience for 3 or more years, plus a written recommendation from an employer or volunteer coordinator,
   or
4. Publication of a relevant article in a peer-reviewed academic or trade journal,
   or
5. Other documentable means of demonstrating competency, subject to approval of the State Department of Education.

D. Once approved to seek an alternative license, applicant must:
   1. Complete the OGET and desired OSAT tests—contact OCTP (see Appendix 1) for details;
      and
   2. Have on file with the OSBE a current approved OSBI/FBI criminal history fingerprint check.

E. Once the OSDE issues license, applicant must:
   1. Within 3 years, pass the OPTE and complete a professional education component as follows:
      a. Complete between 6 and 18 college credit hours* of professional education, or between 90 and 270 hours of professional development approved by an Oklahoma school district.
         *One college credit course in classroom management and 1 college credit course in teaching methods are mandatory.

II. American Board for Certification of Teacher Excellence (ABCTE)
   A. Funded with a US Department of Education grant, ABCTE offers a flexible and cost-effective certification program designed to inspire career changers to enter teaching.
   B. Requirements
      1. Hold a bachelor's degree from accredited IHE,
      2. Have been accepted by the ABCTE,
      3. Pass ABCTE-desired middle-level or secondary-level subject test and professional teacher test,
         and
      4. Have on file with the OSBE a current approved OSBI/FBI criminal history fingerprint check.
   C. When requirements are completed, the OSDE issues middle-level or secondary-level license (valid 1 year).
      1. Licensee must participate in 1-year mentoring program and apply for a standard certificate. See Oklahoma State Department of Education website for the most current information on resident teacher programs and committees at https://sde .ok.gov/teacher-certification.

III. Teach for America (valid 2 years)
   A. This is a national corps of outstanding recent college graduates and professionals of all academic major and career interests who commit 2 years to teach in urban and rural public schools and become leaders in the effort to expand educational opportunity. For full details, go to http://www.teachforamerica/org.
   B. Once accepted into the program, applicant could be assigned to teach in Oklahoma.
IV. Additional Alternative Certificates
   Oklahoma also offers alternative certificates in the following programs; contact the OSDE (see Appendix 1) for full details.
   A. Four-Year-Olds and Younger Certificate
   B. Career Development Program for Paraprofessionals to be Certified Teachers
   C. Troops to Teachers Defense Authorization Act
   D. Non-Traditional Special Education Provisional

Oregon

In July 2015, Oregon began a phased-in approach to a complete redesign of licensure terminology and requirements. That redesign is complete for teaching licenses, and the administrative license redesign will be completed in 2019. Work has yet to be completed on personnel services licenses. Please contact the Oregon Teacher Standards and Practices Commission (TSPC) (see Appendix 1) for the most current information, which is also available at https://www.oregon.gov/tspc/Pages/index.aspx.

Teaching Licenses

I. Preliminary Teaching License (valid 3 years), issued to new teachers who have completed a Commission-approved teacher preparation program. Note: If you completed an out-of-state teacher preparation program, you must first apply for the Reciprocal Teaching License. Applicants for the Preliminary Teaching License must:
   A. Be at least 18 years old
   B. Hold a bachelor's degree or higher from a regionally accredited institution or a foreign equivalent
   C. Complete a Commission-approved teacher preparation program (official verification of completion is required)
   D. Pass a subject matter test for your teaching content area(s) if necessary
   E. Pass the required Protecting Student and Civil Rights in the Educational Environment exam
   F. Pass a criminal background clearance, including fingerprints, if necessary
II. Professional Teaching License (valid 5 years), issued to experienced teachers who have successfully demonstrated an advanced level of educator knowledge, skills and dispositions. Applicants for this license must:
   A. Hold an Oregon Preliminary, Reciprocal, Basic, Initial or Initial II teaching license
   B. Have 4 full years or more of teaching experience or 6 full years of teaching experience in a .50 FTE or greater teaching assignment
   C. Pass a criminal background clearance, including fingerprints, if necessary
   D. Complete 1 of the following advanced professional education programs. Exceptions: Applicants who currently hold an Initial II, Continuing, Standard or Basic Teaching License do *not* need to complete an advanced professional education program.
      1. Advanced Professional Development Program: New teachers work with their school districts to design a program to complete at least 150 Professional Development Units (PDUs) of advanced professional development specifically tailored to their performance goals as novice teachers.
      2. Advanced Degree Program: Complete any advanced degree program reasonably related to improving an educator's teaching skills (e.g., a master's degree in the applicant's content area)

       3.   Endorsement Program: Complete a Commission-approved program to add new subject matter areas (e.g., English for Speakers of Other Languages [ESOL], Elementary Education, Music, etc.)

       4.   Specialization Programs: Complete a program to add new specialized areas (e.g., Bilingual, TAG, Dual Language, Autism, American Sign Language, etc.)

       5.   Advanced Licensure Program: Teacher Leader, School Counselor, School Psychology, School Social Worker, Administrator, or Professional Teaching licensure programs

       6.   National Board of Professional Teaching Standards Certification

III.   Reciprocal Teaching License (valid 1 year; nonrenewable), issued to teachers who have completed an educator preparation program and hold an active and valid non-provisional teaching license from another state. Applicants for this license must:

    A.   Hold a valid and active non-provisional teaching license from another state

    B.   Never have held an Oregon educator license or charter school registration nor have completed an Oregon educator preparation program

    C.   Hold a bachelor's degree or higher from a regionally accredited institution or foreign equivalent

    D.   Have completed an approved out-of-state teacher preparation program (official verification of completion required)

    E.   Pass a criminal background clearance, including fingerprints, if necessary

    F.   Apply for and meet the requirements for a Preliminary or Professional teaching license before the Reciprocal license expires, including:

       1.   Qualifying for an Oregon endorsement by receiving a passing score on Oregon-approved subject matter tests (unless applicant qualifies for reciprocity or waiver of subject matter tests as provided in OAR 584-220-0015)

       2.   Passing the required Protecting Student and Civil Rights in the Educational Environment exam

IV.   Restricted Teaching License (valid 1 year; renewable twice), issued to qualified individuals who have at least a bachelor's degree and who have substantial preparation in the subject matter in their teaching area, but have not completed a teacher preparation program. Note: Applicants who have failed to complete an Oregon teacher preparation program are not eligible. Applicants for this license must:

    A.   Have a letter of sponsorship provided by the employing school district directly to the Teacher Standards and Practices Commission

    B.   Be at least 18 years old

    C.   Never have previously held a Restricted Teaching License

    D.   Hold a bachelor's degree or higher from a regionally accredited institution or foreign equivalent

    E.   Provide evidence of substantial preparation or work experience in the requested teaching area

    F.   Pass the required Protecting Student and Civil Rights in the Educational Environment exam

    G.   Pass a criminal background clearance, including fingerprints, if necessary

V.   Substitute Teaching License (valid 3 years), issued to educators who have completed a teacher preparation program but do not hold a regular Oregon teaching license.

Applicants for this license must:
- A.   Hold a bachelor's degree or higher from a regionally accredited institution or foreign equivalent
- B.   Have a valid and active non-provisional teaching license from another state

  or

  Have completed an Oregon teacher preparation program that resulted in eligibility for a non-provisional Oregon teaching license
- C.   Pass the required Protecting Student and Civil Rights in the Educational Environment exam (not required for applicants who have ever held an Oregon Basic or Standard License or have ever successfully taken and passed the exam)
- D.   Pass a criminal background clearance, including fingerprints, if necessary

VI.   Other teaching licenses and registrations available in Oregon include American Indian Languages Teaching License; Career and Technical Education Licenses (Restricted CTE, Preliminary CTE, Professional CTE); Charter School Teacher Registration; Emergency Teaching License; International Visiting Teacher License; Legacy Teaching License; License for Conditional Assignment; Limited Teaching License; Restricted Substitute Teaching License; and Teacher Leader License. For information on the requirements for obtaining these licenses, contact TSPC (see Appendix 1).

Teaching Authorizations

All licenses are authorized in grades PreK–12. Limits on what licensees can teach are controlled by the endorsement(s) held and the NCES course codes associated with the endorsement(s).

Subject Matter Endorsements

I.   Educators must receive the currently specified passing score on each of 1 or more tests of subject mastery for license endorsement.
- A.   Oregon Educator Licensure Assessments (ORELA) exams in advanced mathematics, art, biology, general business, chemistry, Chinese, early childhood education, elementary education, English, English for Speakers of Other Languages (ESOL), family and consumer sciences, foundational English language arts for middle grades, foundational mathematics for middle grades, foundational science for middle grades, foundational social studies for middle grades, French, German, health, integrated science, library media, music, physical education, physics, social studies, Spanish, special education
- B.   Praxis/ETS exams in agriculture, early intervention, hearing impaired, marketing, reading, speech communication, speech-language pathology, technology education, vision impaired
- C.   Since there are no Praxis exams in drama, Latin, Russian, and Japanese, contact TSPC (see Appendix 1) for requirements.

Personnel Licenses

I. Preliminary School Counselor License (valid 3 years; renewable twice), issued to educators who have completed a school counselor preparation program and hold a master's degree. Applicants for this license must:
   A. Hold a bachelor's degree or higher from a regionally accredited institution or foreign equivalent
   B. Hold a master's or higher degree in counseling, education, or related behavioral sciences from a regionally accredited institution or foreign equivalent
   C. Have completed an initial program in school counseling as part of the master's degree or separately in an approved school counseling program
   D. Pass the required Protecting Student and Civil Rights in the Educational Environment exam
   E. Pass a criminal background clearance, including fingerprints, if necessary

II. Professional School Counselor License (valid 5 years), issued to school counselors who possess advanced school counseling preparation and experience. Applicants for this license must:
   A. Meet all requirements for the Preliminary School Counselor License
   B. Hold a master's or higher degree in the behavioral sciences or their derivative therapeutic professions from a regionally accredited institution or foreign equivalent
   C. Have completed an initial graduate program in school counseling
   D. Have 5 years of school counseling experience at least half-time or more on any non-provisional license appropriate for the assignment
   E. Pass a criminal background clearance, including fingerprints, if necessary
   F. Demonstrate minimum school counselor competencies by completing 1 of the following:
      1. An advanced program in counseling competencies in a Commission-approved Professional School Counselor program
      2. Validation of all advanced counseling competencies through assessment by a Commission-approved professional development program offered by an institution, an employer, or the two working together
         or
         A doctoral degree in educational, vocational, or clinical counseling; or in clinical or counseling psychology from a regionally accredited institution or foreign equivalent

III. Reciprocal School Counselor License (valid 1 year; nonrenewable), issued to qualified applicants who have held an out-of-state school counselor license or who have completed an out-of-state program in school counseling. Applicants for this license must:
   A. Have held a non-provisional school counselor license from another state
   B. Never have held an Oregon educator license or charter school registration nor have completed an Oregon educator preparation program
   C. Hold 1 of the following: a master's or higher degree in counseling, education, or related behavioral sciences from a regionally accredited institution or foreign equivalent
   D. Pass a criminal background clearance, including fingerprints, if necessary

E.   Apply for and meet the requirements for a Preliminary School Counselor License before the Reciprocal license expires

IV.   Restricted School Counselor License (valid 1 year; renewable twice), issued to qualified individuals who have a bachelor's degree and have either completed at least half of an approved School Counselor program or worked 3 full academic years as a Child Development Specialist. Applicants for this license must:

A.   Have a letter of sponsorship from employing school district, provided by your sponsoring district directly to TSPC

B.   Hold a bachelor's degree or higher from a regionally accredited institution or foreign equivalent

C.   Never have held a Restricted School Counselor license

D.   Meet 1 of the following qualifications:
   1.   Be enrolled in a School Counselor program approved for school counseling licensure by any state and have completed approximately one-half of the program
   2.   Have been a full-time certified Child Development Specialist (CDS) for at least 3 academic years

   or

   Have a master's degree in a counseling-related field
   3.   Pass the required Protecting Student and Civil Rights in the Educational Environment exam
   4.   Pass a criminal background clearance, including fingerprints, if necessary

V.   Other personnel licenses and certificates available in Oregon include: Emergency School Counselor License; Emergency School Nurse; Emergency School Social Worker; Limited Student Service; Preliminary School Psychologist; Preliminary School Social Worker; Professional School Nurse; Professional School Psychologist; Professional School Social Worker; Reciprocal School Psychologist; Reciprocal School Social Worker; and Restricted School Social Worker. For information on the requirements for obtaining these licenses, contact TSPC (see Appendix 1).

Administrative Licenses

I.   Preliminary Administrator License (valid 3 years; renewable twice), issued to educators who have completed an administration preparation program and hold a master's degree. Applicants for this license must:

A.   Have 3 academic years of experience as a full-time licensed educator

B.   Hold a master's or higher degree in the arts and sciences or an advanced degree in the profession from a regionally accredited institution or a foreign equivalent

C.   Complete, as part of the master's degree or separately, an initial graduate program in school administration at an institution approved for administrator education

D.   Complete course on Oregon School Law and Finance or demonstrate equivalent competency (Oregon program completers automatically meet this requirement, as the course is embedded into all approved Oregon administrator programs.)

E.   Pass the required Protecting Student and Civil Rights in the Educational Environment exam

F.   Pass a criminal background clearance, including fingerprints, if necessary

II. Professional Administrator License (valid 5 years), issued to educators who have completed an initial administrator preparation program and have advanced preparation beyond a master's degree. Applicants for this license must:

A. Hold a master's or higher degree in the arts and sciences or an advanced degree in the profession from a regionally accredited institution or a foreign equivalent

B. Have 3 years of 1 half-time or more experience on any administrator license appropriate for the assignment in a public or accredited private school setting

C. Complete, beyond the master's degree and the initial graduate program in school administration, an advanced program in administrative competencies consisting of at least 18 semester hours or 27 quarter hours of graduate credit or the equivalent

D. Pass a criminal background clearance, including fingerprints, if necessary

III. Reciprocal Administrator License (valid 18 months; nonrenewable), issued to educators who have completed an out-of-state administrator preparation program and are licensed as a school administrator in another state. Applicants for this license must:

A. Hold a valid and active non-provisional license for school administration from another state

B. Never have held an Oregon educator license or charter school registration nor have completed an Oregon educator preparation program

C. Hold a master's or higher degree in the arts and sciences or an advanced degree in the profession from a regionally accredited institution or foreign equivalent

D. Pass a criminal background clearance, including fingerprints, if necessary

E. Apply for and meet the requirements for a Preliminary or Professional Administrator license before the Reciprocal license expires, including the following:

1. Complete an Oregon School Law and Finance course

2. Pass the required Protecting Student and Civil Rights in the Educational Environment exam

IV. Restricted Administrator License (valid 1 year; renewable twice), issued to qualified individuals who have at least a master's degree and who have substantial administrative preparation but have not completed an administrator preparation program. Applicants for this license must:

A. Have a letter of sponsorship from the employing school district, provided by the district directly to TSPC

B. Hold a master's or higher degree in the arts and sciences or an advanced degree in the profession from a regionally accredited institution or a foreign equivalent

C. Never have held a Restricted Administrator license

D. Pass the required Protecting Student and Civil Rights in the Educational Environment exam

E. Provide official transcripts and other evidence of substantial completion of academic preparation or substantial work experience in administration

F. Pass a criminal background clearance, including fingerprints, if necessary

V. Other administrative licenses and registrations available in Oregon include Charter School Administrator Registration; Distinguished Administrator; Emergency Administrator License; Exceptional Administrator; and the Reciprocal Superintendent License. For information on the requirements for obtaining these licenses, contact TSPC (see Appendix 1).

Pennsylvania

Level I Certification

I.   Instructional and Educational Specialist I (valid 6 years of service; nonrenewable)
   A.   Hold a bachelor's degree and complete an approved education preparation program in the area requested with a cumulative grade point average of 3.0 on a 4.0 scale.
   B.   Receive the recommendation of the preparing entity.
   C.   Meet all Pennsylvania testing requirements.
      1.   All applicants must take the Pennsylvania tests required for certification unless they hold National Board for Professional Teaching Standards Certification.
      2.   Applicant should consult the www.education.pa.gov website for testing information (see Appendix 1).
   D.   Meet citizenship and good moral character requirements.
II. Vocational Instructional I (valid 8 years of service; nonrenewable)
   A.   Minimum of 2 years of wage-earning experience in addition to the learning period required to establish competency in the occupation to be taught.
   B.   Successful completion of the occupational competency examination or evaluation of credentials for occupations where examinations do not exist.
   C.   Eighteen credit hours in an approved program of vocational teacher education.
      1.   For Vocational I certificates issued on or after January 1, 2013, the 18 credit hours must include the equivalent of at least 3 credits in accommodations and adaptations for diverse learners in an inclusive setting.
   D.   Receive the recommendation of the preparing entity.
   E.   Present evidence of satisfactory achievement on the assessment of basic skills. Consult the www.education.pa.gov website for testing information (see Appendix 1).
   F.   Meet citizenship and good moral character requirements.
III. Administrative I: Principal PK–12 (valid 5 years of service; nonrenewable) or Administrative: Vocational Director (valid 99 years)
   A.   Hold a bachelor's degree.
   B.   Complete 3 years of professional experience in an educational setting related to the instructional process.
   C.   Complete an approved graduate-level education preparation program including an internship in the area requested with a cumulative grade point average of 3.0 on a 4.0 scale.
   D.   Receive the recommendation of the preparing entity.
   E.   Meet testing requirements listed on the www.education.pa.gov website (see Appendix 1).
   F.   Meet citizenship and good moral character requirements.
IV. Administrative Provisional (valid 5 years of service; nonrenewable)
   A.   Hold a bachelor's degree.

B. Complete 3 years of professional experience in an educational setting related to the instructional process.
C. Verification of an employment offer from a Pennsylvania public school, specifically for a position as a principal, vice principal, assistant principal, or vocational administrative director.
D. Meet citizenship and good moral character requirements.
E. Must complete additional education and testing requirements within the first 2 years of employment.

V. Supervisory (valid 99 years)
A. Hold a bachelor's degree.
B. Complete 5 years of satisfactory service relevant to the area for which the Supervisory certificate is sought.
  1. Supervisor Pupil Personnel Services requires certified education specialist service.
  2. Supervisor Curriculum & Instruction requires certified instructional service.
C. Complete an approved education preparation program including an internship in the area requested with a cumulative grade point average of 3.0 on a 4.0 scale.
D. Receive the recommendation of the preparing entity.
E. Meet testing requirements listed on the www.education.pa.gov website (see Appendix 1).
F. Meet citizenship and good moral character requirements.

VI. Vocational Supervisor (valid 99 years)
A. Complete 3 years of satisfactory certified vocational teaching experience.
B. Complete an approved graduate-level education preparation program including an internship in the area requested with a cumulative grade point average of 3.0 on a 4.0 scale.
C. Receive the recommendation of the preparing entity.
D. Meet testing requirements listed on the www.education.pa.gov website (see Appendix 1).
E. Meet citizenship and good moral character requirements.

Level II Certification

I. Instructional Certificates
A. Complete 3 years of satisfactory service on a Level I certificate.
B. Complete a Pennsylvania Department of Education–approved induction program for educators initially certified on or after June 1987.
C. Meet credit requirements:
  1. Educators awarded their initial baccalaureate degree after October 1, 1963, must provide evidence of 24 semester-hour post-baccalaureate credits.
  2. Effective September 1, 2011, educators issued a Level I certificate after September 22, 2007, must earn at least 6 post-baccalaureate credits of collegiate study in the area(s) of certification and/or designed to improve professional practice as part of the 24 post-baccalaureate credits requirement. See CSPG No. 7 on the www.education.pa.gov website (see Appendix 1) for details.

D. All instructional areas of certification simultaneously convert to a Level II certificate.

II. Education Specialist Certificates

A. Educators awarded their initial baccalaureate degree after October 1, 1963, must provide evidence of 24 semester-hour post-baccalaureate credits.

B. Complete 3 years of satisfactory service on the Level I certificate.

C. Complete a Pennsylvania Department of Education–approved induction program for certificates issued on or after September 1, 2001.

D. Most educational specialist areas of certification must be independently converted to a Level II certificate when all requirements are met. Elementary and secondary school counselor converts to a PK–12 school counselor certificate.

III. Vocational Instructional Certificates

A. Effective July 1, 2018, educators holding a Vocational Instructional Level I certificate may be recommended for Level II certification by their Pennsylvania-approved preparatory entity after completing a total of 60 semester-hour credits earned in Vocational I programs, including:

1. At least 6 credits, or 180 hours, or an equivalent combination thereof, regarding accommodations and adaptations for students with disabilities in an inclusive setting; and

2. At least 3 credits, or 90 hours, or an equivalent combination thereof, in teaching English-language learners.

B. Requires a minimum of 3 years of satisfactory service in Pennsylvania in any occupational competency area(s) for which the certificate was issued.

C. Requires completion of a Pennsylvania Department of Education–approved induction program.

D. Meet testing requirements listed on the www.education.pa.gov website (see Appendix 1).

E. All vocational areas of certification will simultaneously convert to a Level II certificate provided all requirements are met.

IV. Administrative and Supervisory Certificates

A. Educational requirements

1. The holders of Administrative certificates issued in accordance with regulations established prior to September 1999 and who have served in the capacity of principal, assistant principal, or vice principal in a Pennsylvania public school prior to January 1, 2008, have no additional educational requirements for Level II.

2. Educators granted Administrative certificates prior to January 1, 2008, but who are employed for the first time in a position of principal, assistant principal, or vice principal in a Pennsylvania public school on or after January 1, 2008, must complete the Principal's Induction Program within 5 years of service to retain the certificate.

3. An Administrative (principal) certificate issued on or after January 1, 2008, requires the completion of an approved Principal's Induction Program. No individual may serve as principal, vice principal, or assistant principal on an

Administrative I certificate for more than 5 service years in Pennsylvania public schools.
4. Supervisory certificates have no additional educational requirements.
B. Service requirements
1. Administrative I and Supervisory I certificates issued in accordance with regulations established prior to September 1, 1999, are made permanent by completion of 3 years of satisfactory service in Pennsylvania in each Administrative/Supervisory certificate area.
2. Administrative and Supervisory certificates issued in accordance with September 1, 1999, regulations are valid for 99 years.
3. Administrative I certificates issued in accordance with Act 45 of 2007 require 3 years of satisfactory Administrative I service in Pennsylvania.
V. Program Specialist Certificate
A. Program Specialist certificates do not have a Level II. Their validity is tied to a Pennsylvania Instructional certificate.
1. Service on a Program Specialist certificate is creditable toward the experience requirements for Level II Instructional certification. This service is charged against the period of validity of the Level I Instructional certificate.
2. Once an educator has completed 3 years of combined satisfactory service on the Instructional certificate and/or Program Specialist certificate and has satisfied all educational requirements for Level II certification, the educator may convert the prerequisite Level I Instructional certificate to a Level II certificate.
B. Program Specialist certificates issued to candidates completing an out-of-state program that is not tied to a Level I Instructional certificate are valid for 99 years.

Types of Certificates

I. Instructional Certificates
A. Elementary: Grades PK–4; Grades 4–8 with a concentration in English, mathematics, science and/or social studies.
B. Special education (PK–8); special education (7–12). Both require content certificates as a pre-requisite.
C. Secondary Grades 7–12: Citizenship Education; Communication; Cooperative Education; English; Marketing (Distributive) Education; Mathematics; Safety/Driver Education; Biology; Chemistry; Earth and Space; General Science; Physics; Social Studies.
D. Grades PK–12 certificates: Agriculture; Arabic; Art Education; Business, Computer and Information Technology; Chinese; Environmental Education; Family and Consumer Science; French; German; Greek; Health Education; Health and Physical Education; Hebrew; Hindi; Italian; Japanese; Latin; Library Science; Marketing (Distributive) Education; Music Education; Portuguese; Reading Specialist; Russian; Spanish; Special Education: Visually Impaired; Special Education: Hearing Impaired; Special Education: Speech/Language Impaired; Technology Education.
II. Educational Specialist certificates (PK–12): Dental Hygienist; Elementary and

Secondary School Counselor; Home and School Visitor; Instructional Technology Specialist; School Nurse; School Psychologist; School Speech-Language Pathologist.

III. Supervisory certificates (PK–12 unless otherwise indicated): Curriculum and Instruction; Pupil Personnel Services; Vocational Education (7–12); Single Instructional Area and Pupil Service Areas.

IV. Administrative certificate: Principal (PK–12); Vocational Administrative Director (7–12); Administrative Provisional I (PK–12).

V. Letter of Eligibility (PK–12): Superintendent; Intermediate Unit Executive Director.

VI. Vocational certificate (7–12): See www.education.pa.gov for a complete list of subjects.

Rhode Island

Certification Overview

I. Three-Tier Certification System provides multi-year certificates that demonstrate the educator has met all Rhode Island requirements for certification.
   A. Initial Educator Certificate (valid 3 years; renewable). Held by all educators when they are certified for the first time in Rhode Island.
   B. Professional Educator Certificate (valid 5 years; renewable). Awarded to holders of Initial Educator certificates once they demonstrate acceptable levels of performance while working under their certificate.
   C. Advanced Educator Certificate (valid 7 years; renewable). Held by educators who consistently demonstrate highly effective practice.
II. Preliminary Educator Certificate (valid 1 year). Allows educators who are not fully certified to serve as educators of record while pursuing certification.
   A. Alternate Route Preliminary Certificate (valid 1 year; renewable). For prospective educators who:
      1. Are enrolled in a Rhode Island–approved alternate route preparation program; *and*
      2. Have been offered a position in a district to serve as an educator of record while completing certification requirements.
   B. Career and Technical Education/School Nurse Teacher Preliminary Certificate (valid 3 years; renewable). For prospective educators who:
      1. Have met specified requirements; *and*
      2. Have demonstrated that they have appropriate work experience in their respective fields.
      3. Holders can seek employment as teachers of record in employing agencies that are willing to employ them while the individuals pursue full certification.
   C. Emergency Preliminary Certificate (valid 1 year; renewable). For prospective educators at the request of employing agency when a fully certified and qualified educator who meets the criteria for the position cannot be secured.
   D. Expert Residency Preliminary Certificate (valid 1 year; renewable). For prospective educators who:
      1. Demonstrate sufficient preparation in subject matter, administrative expertise, or other certificate area specific requirements to be considered for positions as educators while pursuing certification.
         a. Certified educators seeking to add new certification areas may also use this certificate as part of a route to certification in that area.
   E. Temporary Initial Educator Preliminary Certificate (valid 1 year; nonrenewable). For prospective educators who:
      1. Seek certification through reciprocity;

and

2. Meet all requirements for the Rhode Island Initial Educator certificate except for the Rhode Island certification testing requirements, including the English Language Competency Test, when applicable.

3. This certificate allows the prospective educator time to meet the Rhode Island certification testing requirements while working in Rhode Island public schools.

F. Visiting Lecturer Preliminary Certificate (valid 1 year; renewable). For individuals who:

1. Have distinctive qualifications and therefore a unique capacity to enhance educational programs in districts;
    and

2. Have been offered employment in districts.

3. This certificate is not a route to full certification.

III. Certificates Available

A. Teacher Certificates

1. Early Childhood Certificates (PK–Grade 2, unless otherwise specified)
    a. Early Childhood Education; Early Childhood Special Education (Birth–Grade 2); Early Childhood English as a Second Language Education (PK–2); Early Childhood Bilingual and Dual Language Education (Birth–Grade 2; PK–2)

2. Elementary Certificates (Grades 1–6)
    a. Elementary Education; Elementary Special Education; Elementary English as a Second Language Education; Elementary Bilingual and Dual Language Education

3. Middle Grades Teacher Certificates (Grades 5–8)
    a. English; English as a Second Language; Mathematics; Science; Social Studies; Middle Grades Bilingual and Dual Language Education; Middle Grades Special Education Teacher

4. Secondary Grades Teacher Certificates (Grades 7–12)
    a. Agriculture; Bilingual and Dual Language; Biology; Business Education; Career and Technical Education; Chemistry; English; English as a Second Language; General Science; Mathematics; Physics; Social Studies; Secondary Grades Special Education Teacher

5. All Grades Teacher Certificates (PK–12)
    a. Adapted Physical Education; Art; Bilingual and Dual Language; Dance; English as a Second Language Specialist; English as a Second Language Teacher; Family and Consumer Science; Health; Library Media; Music; Physical Education; School Nurse Teacher; Technology Education; Theatre; World Languages

6. Special Education Teacher Certificates
    a. Elementary/Middle Special Education (Grades K–8); Secondary Special Education Teacher (Grades 7–12); All Grades Special Education—Visually Impaired (PK–12); All Grades Special Education—Deaf and Hard of Hearing Teacher (PK–12); All Grades Special Education—Severe Intellectual Disability Teacher (PK–12)

B. Administrator Certificates
   1. Building Level Administrator (PK–12); District Level Administrator—Curriculum, Instruction, and Assessment; and Administrator of Curriculum and Instruction; District Level Administrator—Special Education; School Business Administrator; Superintendent of Schools
C. Support Professionals
   1. Instructional Leader; School Counselor; School Psychologist; School Social Worker, Speech and Language Pathologist
D. Specialists/Consultants
   1. English as a Second Language; Mathematics; Reading

Requirements for Certificates

I. Early Childhood (PK to Grade 2) and Elementary (Grades 1–6)
   A. Initial Educator Certificate (valid 3 years)
      1. Hold a bachelor's degree from a regionally accredited institution
      2. Complete a Rhode Island–approved program in the appropriate field at specific Rhode Island institutions of higher education, meet reciprocity requirements, or pass transcript analysis
      3. Complete a minimum of 12 weeks of student teaching in this area and a minimum of 60 hours field experience prior to student teaching
      4. Meet the professional competencies of the Rhode Island Professional Teaching Standards (RIPTS)
      5. Meet specified content competencies
         a. These may include those prescribed by National Association for the Education of Young Children (NAEYC) or by the Association for Childhood Education International (ACEI) and content specific standards.
         b. For Special Education, these may include those prescribed by the Council for Exceptional Children (CEC).
         c. For language certifications, these may include those prescribed by Teachers of English to Speakers of Other Languages (TESOL).
      6. Meet all pedagogy and subject matter testing requirements for this certification area
      7. For certificate-specific information, consult Rhode Island's Office of Educator Quality and Certification at http://www.ride.ri.gov/TeachersAdministrators/EducatorCertification.aspx.
II. Middle Grades Certificates (Grades 5–8)
   A. Educators can attain middle grades certification in the following 3 ways:
      1. Option 1: Earn a Middle Grades English, Mathematics, Science, or Social Studies Certificate, independent of any other certificate.
      2. Option 2: Extend an Elementary Education Teacher Certificate.
      3. Option 3: Extend a Secondary Grades Biology, Chemistry, English, General Science, Mathematics, Physics, or Social Studies certificate.
      4. For certificate-specific information, consult Rhode Island's Office of Educator

Quality and Certification at http://www.ride.ri.gov/TeachersAdministrators/EducatorCertification.aspx.

III.   Secondary Grades Certificates (Grades 7–12). For certificate-specific information, consult Rhode Island's Office of Educator Quality and Certification at http://www.ride.ri.gov/TeachersAdministrators/EducatorCertification.aspx.

IV.   Administrators and Support Professionals Certificates. For certificate-specific information, consult Rhode Island's Office of Educator Quality and Certification at http://www.ride.ri.gov/TeachersAdministrators/EducatorCertification.aspx.

South Carolina

Steps to Certification

To access step-by-step instructions for required materials, specific forms, and information on how to submit them for each of the categories below, consult https://ed.sc.gov/educators/certification/.

I. Uncertified Applicants. For those who have completed an approved teacher-education program but have not yet been certified:
   A. Submit an official transcript from each college or university attended, as well as a college recommendation form signed by designated college official; and
   B. Submit the required teaching content area examination score(s) and the required score on the examination of general professional knowledge (pedagogy) as adopted by the South Carolina Board of Education for purposes of certification.

II. Reciprocal Applicants
   A. Applicants with a valid standard certificate issued by another state, a United States territory, or the Department of Defense Dependents Schools (DODDS) may be eligible for certification through South Carolina's reciprocity agreement.
      1. Interstate reciprocity does not apply to Career and Technology Education Work-Based certification.
   B. To evaluate status of existing credentials, review South Carolina's current reciprocity agreement with the states, territories, and countries on website, see Appendix 1.
   C. Individuals with certification from the National Board for Professional Teaching Standards (NBPTS), upon application and presentation of a valid standard out-of-state certificate, will receive a professional certificate in their field.
   D. Reciprocal Certificate Types
      1. Reciprocal Initial Certificate (valid for 3 academic school years)
         a. Certificate is for those with less than 3 years of teaching experience or those who do not have 27 months of full- or part-time PreK–12 school teaching experience in the last 7 years on that valid standard certificate.
         b. Requirements
            i. Must present valid standard out-of-state certificate.
            ii. Subject(s) shown on the certificate must be considered comparable to the subject(s) issued in South Carolina.
            iii. All certification areas issued in that state will also be issued on the South Carolina certificate provided the areas are initially requested on the application. Areas not requested initially would have to meet South Carolina's add-on requirements at the date of the request.
            iv. The appropriate level of Principles of Learning and Teaching (PLT) and successful summative evaluation on the state-approved teacher evaluation model must be presented during the life of the Initial certificate and before the Professional certificate is issued.

    2.   Reciprocal Professional Certificate (valid for 5 academic school years)
        a.   Must present verification of 27 months of full-time PreK–12 school teaching experience in the last 7 years on that valid standard certificate.
        b.   See 1, Reciprocal Initial Certificate, b, directly above.
    3.   Reciprocal Professional Certificate (National Board Certification: will be valid for the remainder of the NBC)
        a.   Must present valid National Board Certificate and valid standard out-of-state certificate.
        b.   Subject(s) shown on the National Board Certificate must be considered comparable to the subject(s) issued in South Carolina.
        c.   Applicant will be given a professional certificate in the National Board Certification area only; or, if the reciprocal professional requirement applies, a certificate can be issued in those areas for the remainder of the NBC period.

Required Credentials

For complete requirements for each position, consult website; see Appendix 1.

   I.   District professional staff, including district administrators and district consultants, curriculum specialists, and coordinators
      A.   Master's degree and certification in the area of primary responsibility
   II.   School administrators and professional support staff
      A.   Master's degree and certification in the area of primary responsibility
  III.   Teachers of special education
      A.   Acceptable certification, determined by the area of disability in which all or the majority of the teacher's students are classified.
         1.   Acceptable certification for a resource or itinerant special education teacher is determined by the area of disability in which the majority of the teacher's students (i.e., caseload) are classified.
  IV.   Teachers of PreK–Grade 6; Grades 7–8; Grades 9–12
      A.   Acceptable certification and all mandatory attendant training
      B.   Teachers of credit-bearing courses in grades 7 and 8 must hold either middle-level certification in the content area or secondary certification in the content area.
         1.   Additionally, these teachers must have passed either the middle-level or secondary Praxis II exam in the content area or the National Teacher's Examination in the content area.
      C.   Teachers of Career and Technology Education must have acceptable certification and all mandatory attendant training.

South Dakota

Teacher Certification

Information about South Dakota educator certification rules can be found at http://doe.sd.gov/certification/.

I. Initial Certification (valid 5 years):
   A. Licensure candidates require the following:
      1. Bachelor's degree or higher from a regionally accredited institution of higher education,
      2. Passing score on state-designated pedagogy test,
      3. Completion of a 3-credit South Dakota Indian Studies course, *and*
      4. Written verification of completed teacher education program from a regionally accredited institution of higher education.
         a. Applicants from a foreign country must provide a transcript evaluation completed by an approved agency.
   B. Preparation types for initial licensure include Early Childhood (birth–grade 3), Elementary (K–grade 8), Secondary (grades 5–12), Career and Technical Education (grades 7–12), K–12 (music, art, health, etc.), Early Childhood Special Education (birth–grade 3), and K–12 Special Education.
II. Alternative Certification:
   A. Alternative Preliminary Certificate (2-year; renewable) is required for applicants applying for alternative certification through the following programs:
      1. General Education alternative certification
      2. Teach for America alternative certification
      3. Career and Technical Education (CTE) alternative certification
      4. Administrator alternative certification (if applicant does not have an educator certificate)
      More information is available at http://www.doe.sd.gov/certification/#AltCert.
   B. Once an individual meets the requirements for an alternative certification program, they receive a 5-year standard educator certificate.
   C. General Education Alternative Certification
      1. Applicant may teach grades 5–8, secondary, and K–12 general education areas while pursuing alternative certification. Requirements include:
         a. A valid alternative preliminary certificate,
         b. An offer of employment from a public school or South Dakota Department of Education–accredited school, *and*
         c. Bachelor's degree or higher.

      d.   Applicant must add subject-area endorsements based on the requirements for each endorsement.

      e.   Certificate holder may not teach grades or content areas beyond the endorsements listed on certificate.

  2.   Applicant receives a 1-year certificate that can be renewed twice; after 3 years the certificate is invalid if all requirements have not been completed.

  3.   Requirements to move to a Teaching Certificate include:

      a.   Complete 15 transcripted credits in classroom management, teaching methods and differentiated instruction, adolescent psychology, and South Dakota Indian Studies;
and

      b.   Pass a state-designated pedagogy test.

D.   Career and Technical Education Alternative Certification

  1.   Applicant may teach grades 7–12 CTE endorsement areas while pursuing alternative certification. Requirements include:

      a.   A valid alternative preliminary certificate,

      b.   An offer of employment from a public school or Department-accredited school,
and

      c.   An associate of applied science degree or higher in a relate CTE field, 4,000 hours of work in a related CTE field, or national certification in a related CTE field.

      d.   Certificate holder may not teach grades or content areas beyond the endorsements listed on the certificate.

  2.   Applicant receives a 1-year certificate that can be renewed twice; after 3 years the certificate is invalid if all requirements have not been completed.

  3.   Requirements to move to a Teaching Certificate include:

      a.   Complete a 4-credit mentored internship experience,

      b.   Complete a 3-credit South Dakota Indian Studies course,

      c.   Complete a 3-credit course in human relations, adolescent psychology, classroom management, student assessment, or differentiated instruction;

      d.   Pass a state-designated pedagogy test,

      e.   Adhere to the South Dakota Code of Professional Ethics,
and

      f.   Receive sign-off from the employing district.

E.   Teach for America Alternative Certification

  1.   Applicant may teach as an elementary teacher, secondary teacher, or K–12 teacher while pursuing alternative certification. Requirements include:

      a.   A valid alternative preliminary certificate,

      b.   An offer of employment from a public school or Department-accredited school,

      c.   Bachelor's degree or higher,
and

      d.   Participation in the Teach for America program.

     e.   Certificate holder may not teach grades or content areas beyond the endorsements listed on the certificate.

  2.   Applicant receives a 1-year certificate that can be renewed twice; after 3 years the certificate is invalid if all requirements have not been completed.

  3.   Requirements to move to a Teaching Certificate include:

     a.   Complete 15 transcripted credits in classroom management, teaching methods and differentiated instruction, adolescent psychology, and South Dakota Indian Studies;
       and

     b.   Pass a state-designated pedagogy test.

F.   Special Education Alternative Certification

  1.   Provides general education teachers an alternative pathway to receive the special education endorsement. Applicant may teach Early Childhood Special Education or K–12 Special Education while pursuing the alternative certificate. Requirements include:

     a.   A valid teaching certificate,

     b.   Minimum 3 years of teaching experience in the past 5 years,
       and

     c.   Verification of employment by the qualifying district.

  2.   Applicant receives a 1-year certificate that can be renewed twice; after 3 years the certificate is invalid if all requirements are not completed.

  3.   Requirements to move to a Teaching Certificate include:

     a.   Complete a 6-credit, year-long practicum,

     b.   Complete 9 credits of coursework in special education law, assessment, and a special education-related course,

     c.   Pass a state-designated pedagogy test,

     d.   Pass a state-designated content test,
       and

     e.   Receive sign-off from the applicant's employing school.

Endorsements

I.   To be certified to teach an assignment or act as an administrator or education specialist, certified educators must have the appropriate endorsement that meets state certification.

II.   An educator must request an endorsement to be added to a certificate. Endorsements will not be added automatically after passing the state-designated test or completing the requirements of the endorsement.

III.   As of July 1, 2019, South Dakota will adhere to the following philosophy for adding endorsements:

  A.   Individuals with early childhood preparation may add endorsement for early childhood–grade 12 and K–12 endorsements (music, health, etc.) by demonstrating content and pedagogical knowledge.

  B.   Individuals with elementary preparation may add endorsement for early childhood–

grade 12 and K–12 endorsements by demonstrating content and pedagogical knowledge.

C. Individuals with secondary preparation may add endorsement for grades 5–12 and K–12 by demonstrating content and pedagogical knowledge.

D. Individuals with K–12 preparation may add endorsement for grades 5–12 and K–12 endorsements by demonstrating content and pedagogical knowledge.

E. Individuals with early childhood special education (SPED) preparation may add endorsement for early childhood–grade 12 and K–12 endorsements by demonstrating content and pedagogical knowledge. The K–12 special education endorsement may be added by demonstrating content and pedagogical knowledge.

F. Individuals with K–12 SPED may add endorsements for grades 5–12 and K–12 endorsements by demonstrating content knowledge. The early childhood special education endorsement may be added by demonstrating content and pedagogical knowledge.

Administration

I. Initial Certification Requirements (valid 5 years):

A. As of July 1, 2019, superintendent, assistant superintendent, principal, or assistant principal applicants require all of the following:
   1. Bachelor's degree or higher from a regionally accredited institution of higher education,
   2. Completion of a school superintendent or principal program from a regionally accredited institution of higher learning,
   3. Completion of a 3-credit South Dakota Indian Studies course,
      and
   4. Written recommendation from a regionally accredited institution of higher education verifying completion of the approved program.
      a. Applicants from a foreign country must provide a transcript evaluation completed by an approved agency.

B. Preparation types:
   1. School superintendent is eligible to be a school superintendent or assistant superintendent in an educational setting from early childhood through grade 12.
   2. K–12 principal is eligible to be a principal or assistant principal in an educational setting from early childhood through grade 12.

II. Administrator Alternative Certification—Principal

A. Allows applicant to perform the duties as a principal completing the administrator alternative certification. Requirements include:
   1. Alternative preliminary administrator certificate (if the applicant does not have an educator certificate),
   2. Employment by a qualifying district,
   3. Bachelor's degree or higher,
   4. Completion of a state-approved teacher education program or alternative certification program,

5. Three or more years of teaching experience,
and

6. Passing score on the state-designed school leadership assessment.

B. Applicant receives a 1-year certificate that can be renewed 4 times; after 5 years the certificate is invalid if all requirements have not been completed.

C. Requirements to move to a standard administrator certificate with a principal endorsement include completion of 18 transcripted credits with a grade of "C" or higher in instructional leadership, ethical and inclusive leadership, cognitive coaching and facilitation skills, creating a safe and inclusive school environment, process management, systems management, educational law and policy, and a 3-credit South Dakota Indian Studies course.

III. Administrator Alternative Certification—Superintendent

A. Allows applicant to perform the duties as a superintendent completing the administrator alternative certification. Requirements include:

1. Alternative preliminary administrator certificate (if the applicant does not have an educator certificate),

2. Employment by a qualifying district,

3. Master's degree or higher,

4. Three or more years of experience in a management role in a business or district, or as a teacher with a leadership role,
and

5. Passing score on the state-designed school superintendent assessment.

B. Applicant receives a 1-year certificate that can be renewed 4 times; after 5 years the certificate is invalid if all requirements have not been completed.

C. Requirements to move to a standard administrator certificate with a superintendent endorsement include completion of 21 transcripted credits with a grade of "C" or higher in leadership and district culture, organizational management, values and ethics of leadership, educational policy and law, communication, community relations, curriculum planning and development, school finance, instructional management, and a 3-credit South Dakota Indian Studies course.

Certificate Renewal

I. Individuals who wish to renew a current South Dakota teaching certificate or update a lapsed certificate need specific items to complete an online application; for more information, visit http://doe.sd.gov/certification/renewal.aspx.

A. All certificates are valid until the expiration date of the certificate.

B. Educator certificates are valid from the date of issuance until June 30 of the year of expiration.

C. If renewal requirements are not completed by July 1, the certificate is expired.

D. A certificate becomes invalid if all renewal requirements are not met before October 1 of that year.

E. State statute requires all applicants for any initial certificate or renewal to meet a minimum of 1 clock hour of suicide awareness and prevention training.

F.   All renewal applicants must complete and document 6 credits, which can be a combination of continuing education contact hours and university credits.

Reciprocity

I.   South Dakota offers reciprocity based on the following conditions:
   A.   Approved Educator Program license-holder applicants must:
      1.   Hold a teacher, administrator, or educator specialist license from an approved program at a regionally accredited university;
      2.   Provide verification of a successful student teaching, internship, or field experience;
         and
      3.   Provide verification from licensing state that there are no ethics violations or disciplinary action.
   B.   Alternative Certification license-holder applicants must:
      1.   Have completed the alternative certification process in another state,
      2.   Provide verification of 3 years of teaching within the past 5 years,
      3.   Provide verification of a valid educator's license from the issuing state,
         and
      4.   Provide verification from licensing state that there are no ethics violations or disciplinary action.
II.   All reciprocity applicants must provide a sign-off from the university from which they obtained their degree along with supporting transcript documentation.
III.   All reciprocity applicants must complete a 3-credit South Dakota Indian Studies course and 1 clock hour of suicide awareness and prevention training.
IV.   Applicants may request a 1-year provisional certificate, during which time they may complete the South Dakota Indian Studies course. This certificate may be renewed 1 time.
V.   Applicants who have an active certificate in another state may receive endorsements based on a review of the out-of-state certificate and the equivalent South Dakota endorsements. Unless otherwise stipulated, no additional content or pedagogy requirements apply.
VI.   Information about reciprocity based on completion of an approved education program can be found at https://doe.sd.gov/certification/documents/RECIPROCITY-%20ED.pdf. Information about reciprocity based on completion of an alternative certification program can be found at https://doe.sd.gov/certification/documents/RECIPROCITY-ALT.pdf.

Tennessee

For full details on current licensure requirements, consult https://www.tn.gov/education/licensing.html.

License Requirements for Teachers and School Service Personnel

I. Practitioner License (valid 3 years; renewable once)
   A. Initial license issued to applicant who meets the following criteria:
      1. Holds a bachelor's degree from a regionally accredited college or university;
      2. Is enrolled in or has completed a state-approved educator preparation program;
      3. Is recommended by the state-approved educator preparation program; *and*
      4. Has submitted qualifying scores on required assessments or has content knowledge verified by a program, based on content major.
   B. To renew or advance the practitioner license, all educators must complete an approved education preparation program and pass all required assessments.

II. Professional License (valid 6 years; renewable)
   A. Issued to applicant who meets the following criteria:
      1. Accrues a minimum of 3 years of acceptable experience; *and*
      2. Receives the recommendation of the Director of Schools, *or* Submits documentation of 30 professional development points.
   B. License is renewed based on the following criteria:
      1. Submits documentation of 60 professional development points

III. Practitioner Occupational License (valid 3 years; renewable once)
   A. In most cases, proof of current industry certification is an additional requirement for the practitioner occupational license. (For specific information, see Tennessee's Educator Licensure Policy 5.502 at https://www.tn.gov/sbe/rules--policies-and-guidance/policies.html.)
   B. Educators seeking a practitioner occupational license must adhere to the following:
      1. Prior to enrollment in a preparation program, qualifications—such as industry certification—shall be reviewed by the Tennessee Department of Education staff. Individuals applying for this license must meet the following criteria:
         a. Hold a high school diploma or higher;
         b. Be admitted to or have completed a state-approved educator preparation program;
         c. Have 5 years of full-time work experience out of the past 8 years;
         d. Be recommended by state-approved preparation program;

      e.   Meet industry-specific requirements;

      f.   Meet the endorsement experience requirements.

IV. Professional Occupational License (valid 6 years; renewable)

    A. Issued to applicant who meets the following criteria:

      1. Has accrued a minimum of 3 years of acceptable experience;
and

      2. Has received the recommendation of the Director of Schools,
or
Submits documentation of 30 professional development points.

      3. Has completed an approved educator preparation program;

      4. Has attended 5 total days of new teacher training sponsored by the Department of Education's Career and Technical Education division during the first year of teaching;

      5. Has observed 3 experienced teachers within their endorsed teaching area and 1 experienced teacher outside the endorsed teaching area;

      6. Has an assigned mentor teacher during the first 3 years of teaching;
and

      7. Has current valid industry certification required by the teacher endorsement area.

V. Additional Requirements for Out-of-State Applicants

    A. Educators applying from out of state will apply for a practitioner license (valid 3 years; renewable once) and must meet the following criteria:

      1. Hold a bachelor's degree from a regionally accredited college or university;

      2. Submit proof of a full and valid license (comparable to the Tennessee Professional license) from a state with which Tennessee has reciprocity,
or
Submit a recommendation from the out-of-state provider where the educator completed an approved program (all out-of-state educator preparation programs must meet conditions stipulated in Tennessee State Board Rule 0520-02-03);
and

      3. Submit qualifying scores on required content assessments.

VI. Additional Requirements for Occupational Education Licenses

    A. In most cases, proof of current industry certification is an additional requirement for the Occupational License. (See Tennessee's Educator Licensure Policy for more specific information.)

    B. Educators seeking an occupational license must adhere to the following:

      1. Prior to enrollment in a preparation program, qualifications—such as industry certification—shall be reviewed by the Tennessee Department of Education staff. The teacher may advance to the professional occupational education license provided that he/she has completed the following requirements:

        a. Attended during the first year of teaching a total of 5 days at new teacher training sponsored by Career & Technical Education Division, Department of Education;

        b. Received four days of release time to observe 3 experienced teachers

within the endorsed teaching area and 1 experienced teacher outside of the teaching area;
and

c. Assigned a teacher mentor during the first 3 years of teaching.

License Requirements for Administrators

Please visit https://www.tn.gov/education/licensing.html for the most current license information.

I. Instructional Leader License—Aspiring (valid 3 years; not renewable)
   A. Issued to applicant who will serve as assistant principal and meets the following criteria:
      1. Enrolled in an approved instructional leader preparation program.
II. Instructional Leader License—Beginning (valid 3 years; renewable)
   A. Issued to applicant who meets the following criteria:
      1. Completed an approved instructional leader preparation program;
      2. Submitted passing scores on state-required assessment;
         and
      3. Received recommendation by an approved instructional leader preparation program.
III. Instructional Leader License—Professional (valid 6 years; renewable)
   A. Issued to applicant who meets the following criteria:
      1. A director of schools must certify that the applicant exhibits:
         a. A minimum of 2 years of successful experience as a principal, assistant principal, or an instructional supervisor in a Tennessee Academy for School Leaders (TASL)–mandated position,
            and
         b. Performance at the professional level on the Tennessee Instructional Leadership Standards (TILS).
         c. The TASL director must certify that the applicant has successfully completed:
            The Beginning Principals' Academy,
            or
            The Beginning Supervisors' Academy,
            or
            An Individual Professional Learning Plan, in cooperation with a Tennessee institution of higher education with an approved leadership preparation program.

License Requirements for Library Information Specialists

I. Candidates seeking endorsement as a school library information specialist must complete a graduate program of studies in library information science that leads to a master's degree and is approved by the State Board of Education.
II. Candidates who already hold a master's degree must complete an approved course of

study at the graduate level meeting the appropriate knowledge and skills for a school library information specialist.

Endorsements Issued

The most current information about license endorsements can be found at https://www.tn.gov/education/licensing/licensure-resources/endorsement-code-listings.html.

Administrator: Instructional Leadership (Aspiring PreK–12, Beginning PreK–12, Professional PreK–12, Exemplary PreK–12); Agriculture Education 6–12; Agriscience 6–12; Arabic 6–12 and PreK–12; Bible; Biology 6–12 and 7–12; Business Education 6–12; Business Technology 6–12; Early Child Care Services 6–12; Chemistry 6–12 and 7–12; Chinese 6–12, 7–12, and PreK–12; Dance K–12; Driver Education 7–12; Early Childcare Services 9–12; Early Childhood Education PreK–3; Early Development/Learning PreK–K; Earth Science 6–12 and 7–12; Economics 6–12 and 7–12; Education Interpreter; Elementary K–6; English 6–12 and 7–12; English as Second Language PreK–12; Family & Consumer Sciences 6–12; Food Production & Management Services 6–12; Food Service Supervisor; Foreign Language Other 7–12 and PreK–12; French 6–12, 7–12, and PreK–12; Geography 6–12 and 7–12; German 6–12, 7–12, and PreK–12; Gifted Education PreK–12; Greek 6–12 and PreK–12; Government 6–12 and 7–12; Health & Wellness K–12; History 6–12 and 7–12; Interventionist K–8 and 6–12; Japanese 6–12 and PreK–12; Latin 6–12, 7–12, and PreK–12; Library Information Specialist PreK–12; Marketing 6–12; Mathematics 6–12 and 7–12; Middle Grades Education 4–8; Middle Grades Language Arts 6–8; Middle Grades Mathematics 6–8; Middle Grades Science 6–8; Middle Grades Social Studies 6–8; Music (Instrumental/General K–12; Vocal/General K–12); Physical Education K–12; Physics 6–12 and 7–12; Psychology 9–12; Reading Specialist PreK–12; Russian 6–12, 7–12, and PreK–12; School Counselor PreK–12; School Psychologist PreK–12; School Audiologist PreK–12; Speech-Language Pathologist PreK–12; School Social Worker PreK–12; Sociology 9–12; Spanish 6–12, 7–12, and PreK–12; Special Education (Comprehensive K–12, Early Childhood Education PreK–3, Hearing PreK–12, Modified K–12, Speech/Language Teacher PreK–12, Vision PreK–12); Speech Communications 6–12 and 7–12; Superintendent; Supervisor of Attendance; Technology/Engineering Education 6–12; Theatre K–12; Visual Arts K–12

Texas

The rules adopted by the State Board for Educator Certification (SBEC) are part of a larger body of state agency rules that are collected and published as the Texas Administrative Code. The SBEC may adopt new rules or amendments to or repeals of existing rules at any time. Visit the Texas Education Agency website at http://www.tea.texas.gov for the most recent rule changes.

Certification Overview

I. General Certification Requirements
   A. Hold bachelor's degree from institution of higher education that at the time was accredited or otherwise approved by an accrediting organization recognized by the Texas Higher Education Coordinating Board.
      1. Texas institutions do not offer a degree in education, so every teacher must have an academic major as well as teacher-training courses.
         a. Only exemption is for individuals seeking Career and Technical Education certification to teach certain courses, such as welding or computer-aided drafting.
   B. Complete teacher training through an approved program, offered through colleges and universities, school districts, regional service centers, community colleges, and other entities.
   C. Successfully complete appropriate teacher certification tests for subject and grade level. Specific Texas Examinations of Educator Standards (TExES) and other tests are required, depending on applicant's background and certification sought; contact the Texas Education Agency (TEA) at http://www.tea.texas.gov for list of certification tests and information on which tests are required.
      1. Teachers certified in another state or country must submit an application for a review of credentials to initiate the certification process.
II. Routes to Educator Certification
   A. University-based Programs
      1. Undergraduate certificate earned as part of baccalaureate degree program
      2. Post-baccalaureate programs designed to prepare baccalaureate degree holders seeking educator certification
   B. Alternative Programs for Educator Preparation
      1. TEA-approved programs available at some institutions of higher education. These may involve university course work or other professional development experiences as well as intense mentoring and supervision during candidate's first year in role of educator.
      2. Some regional education service centers, large school districts, and private entities offer alternative programs of preparation.

C. Additional Certification Based on Examination: for teachers holding a classroom teaching certificate and bachelor's degree
    1. Such teachers may add classroom certification areas by successfully completing appropriate certification examination(s) for area(s) sought.
    2. Certification by examination not available for:
        a. Initial certification
        b. Certification other than classroom teacher (e.g., school counselor, principal, superintendent, school librarian, educational diagnostician, reading specialist, master teacher)
        c. Certificate for which no certification examination has been developed

D. Certification Based on Credentials from Another Jurisdiction
    1. Applicants holding an acceptable certificate or credential from another state, US territory, or country may apply for a Texas certificate. Credential must be equivalent to a certificate issued by TEA and must not have been revoked, suspended, or pending such action.
    2. One-Year Certificate in 1 or more subject areas may be issued to applicant who holds a standard credential issued by jurisdiction outside Texas and who meets specified requirements as determined by TEA credentials review. Applicants certified outside the state may apply for exemption of Texas tests by submitting the required documentation and following the process outlined here: https://tea.texas.gov/Texas_Educators/Certification/Out-of-State_Certification/Out-of-State_Test_Exemptions/.

Certificate Types, Classes, and Renewal

I. Types of Certificates: Designates period of validity, personnel, and requirements for each certificate (CPE stands for continuing professional education)
  A. Standard (valid 5 years; renewable with 150 CPE hours)
    1. Replaced lifetime provisional and professional certificates, and educators holding lifetime certificates have been exempted from renewal process.
        a. Lifetime certificates were issued through September 1, 1999. Individuals are now issued standard certificates that must be renewed every 5 years. Many Texas educators may hold both lifetime and standard certificates.
    2. Standard teacher certificate requirements
        a. See Certification Overview, I and II, above.
  B. One-year (nonrenewable)
    1. Issued for out-of-state or out-of-country candidates.
  C. Probationary (valid 1 year; renewable for up to 2 more years through August 31, 2017; effective September 1, 2017, limited to 1 renewal year)
    1. Issued to individual enrolled in educator preparation program and serving in supervised internship to satisfy field experience requirements of the certificate.
        a. Holder must be employed by accredited Texas public or private school in position appropriate for certificate sought.
    2. Probationary principal certificate eligibility requirements
        a. Hold at least a bachelor's degree,

        b.   Meet admission requirements of educator preparation program,
and

        c.   Qualify for internship as defined by the program.

    3.   Probationary superintendent eligibility requirements

        a.   Hold a Texas standard principal certificate or its equivalent from another state or country, provided applicant passed TEA-approved principal certificate examination,
and

        b.   Hold at least a master's degree.

    4.   Renewal contingent on enrollment of applicant in educator preparation program and employment in appropriate position, with mentoring and supervision throughout validity period.

    5.   Effective September 1, 2017, holder must pass all required content examinations for the certificate area and a pedagogy and professional responsibilities examination.

  D. Emergency Permit (valid for 1 school year, with options for reissuance for Junior Reserve Officer Training Corps [JROTC] instructors and options for renewal limited to individuals serving as teachers of students with visual impairments)

    1.   Issued to degreed individual who does not have any appropriate certificate required for assignment.

  E. Non-Renewable Permit (valid for 1 year only)

    1.   Issued to degreed individual who has completed educator preparation program but has not yet passed TExES test(s).

  F. Intern Certificate—new September 2017 (valid for 1 year only)

    1.   Individual must pass all required content certification examinations.

II. Classes of Certificates

  A. Superintendent (valid 5 years; renewable with 200 CPE hours)

  B. Principal (valid 5 years; renewable with 200 CPE hours)

  C. Classroom teacher (valid 5 years; renewable with 150 CPE hours)

  D. Student Services, for instructional educator other than classroom teacher, including reading specialist (valid 5 years; renewable with 200 CPE hours)

  E. Master teacher, including master reading, math, science, and technology teacher (valid 5 years; renewable with 200 CPE hours)

  F. School librarian (valid 5 years; renewable with 200 CPE hours)

  G. School counselor (valid 5 years; renewable with 200 CPE hours)

  H. Educational diagnostician (valid 5 years; renewable with 200 CPE hours)

III. Certificate Renewal

  A. Standard Requirements

    1.   Hold a valid Standard Certificate that has not been, nor is in the process of being, sanctioned by TEA,

    2.   Successfully complete a criminal history review,

    3.   Not be in default on a student loan or in arrears of child support,

    4.   Complete the required number of CPE clock hours,
and

    5.   Submit online application to TEA with appropriate renewal fee.

Administrator Certification

I. Principal Certificate (valid 5 years; renewable with 200 CPE hours)
   A. Requirements for certificate
      1. Successfully complete a TEA-approved principal preparation program and be recommended for certification by that program.
      2. Successfully pass TExES Principal certification exam.
      3. Hold master's degree from institution of higher education that at the time was accredited or otherwise approved by an accrediting organization recognized by the Texas Higher Education Coordinating Board.
      4. Hold a valid classroom teaching certificate.
      5. Have 2 years of creditable teaching experience as classroom teacher.

II. Superintendent Certificate (valid 5 years; renewable with 200 CPE hours)
   A. Requirements for certificate
      1. Satisfactorily pass TExES superintendent certification exam.
      2. Successfully complete a TEA-approved superintendent preparation program and be recommended for certification by that program.
      3. Hold master's degree from an accredited institution of higher education that at the time was accredited or otherwise approved by an accrediting organization recognized by the Texas Higher Education Coordinating Board.
      4. Hold a principal certificate or the equivalent issued under this title or by another state or country,
         or
         Have at least 3 credible years of managerial experience in a public school district, which must include responsibility for:
         a. Supervising or appraising faculty or staff;
         b. Conducting district-level planning and coordination of programs, activities, or initiatives; and
         c. Creating or maintaining a budget.
      5. Candidate must submit an application to TEA staff for the substitution of managerial experience as defined above. TEA staff will review the application and will notify the applicant, in writing, of approval or denial within 60 calendar days from date of receipt.
   B. Induction for New Superintendents
      1. One-year mentorship for first-time superintendents (including those new to state)
         a. Include at least 36 clock hours of professional development directly related to identified standards.
      2. Mentorship program must be completed within the first 18 months of employment as superintendent.

Utah

To be licensed as an educator in Utah, you must complete a university teacher preparation program, the Utah State Board of Education (USBE) Alternative Route to Licensing (ARL) program, or the Academic Pathway to Teaching (APT) program. Many Utah universities offer post-graduate ARL programs; visit individual university websites for more information.

For information about the USBE ARL and APT programs, visit https://www.schools.utah.gov/curr/licensing.

If you have already been hired by a Utah school district or a charter school, there may be additional pathways to licensure at your employer's discretion.

License Levels

I. Level 1 License (valid 3 years)
   A. Issued upon completion of an approved preparation program, an alternative preparation program, or pursuant to an agreement under the National Association of State Directors of Teacher Education (NASDTEC) Interstate Contract, to candidates who have also met all ancillary requirements established by law or rule. These include the following:
      1. Bachelor's degree or higher from an accredited institution,
         and
      2. Passing score on Praxis II content test.
II. Level 2 License (valid 5 years; renewable)
   A. Issued after satisfaction of all requirements for a Level 1 license as well as any additional requirements established by law or rule relating to professional preparation or experience. These include the following:
      1. Completion of the Entry Years Enhancement (EYE) requirements (for details, consult the Utah Administrative Code at https://rules.utah.gov/publicat/code/r277/r277-522.htm);
         and
      2. Recommendation of employing district/charter school.
III. Level 3 License (valid 7 years; renewable)
   A. Issued to an educator who holds a current Utah Level 2 license and has also received, in the educator's field of practice, National Board Certification, a doctorate from an accredited institution or a Certificate of Clinical Competence from the American Speech-Language-Hearing Association (ASHA).

Licensure Areas of Concentration

Licensure Areas of Concentration designate what grade level(s) an applicant is qualified to teach in Utah. Educators with a current license may attach additional License Areas to their Utah Educator License by meeting eligibility requirements for each area. For certificate-specific detailed requirements, consult https://www.schools.utah.gov/curr/licensing/areasconcentration.

I. Administrative/Supervisor
II. Career and Technical Education
III. Communication Disorders (Audiology)
IV. Early Childhood (K–3)
V. Elementary Education (K–6 or 1–8)
VI. School Counselor
VII. School Psychologist
VIII. School Social Worker
IX. Secondary Education
   A. Secondary (Grades 6–12). Secondary license areas carry endorsements for the areas in which the holder is qualified to provide instruction.
X. Special Education
   A. Special Education license area of concentration (K–12). Special Education areas of concentration carry endorsements in at least 1 of 6 specific areas.

Requirements for Licensure Candidates

For certificate-specific detailed requirements, consult https://www.schools.utah.gov/curr/licensing. Up-to-date information on licensure for early childhood, elementary, secondary, special education (K–12), and preschool special education (Birth–Age 5) is also available in the Utah Administrative Code at https://rules.utah.gov/publicat/code/r277/r277-504.htm#T3.

I. Meet the Utah Effective Teaching Standards in R277-511
II. Prepare to teach the Utah Core Standards, the Utah Early Childhood Core Standards, and the Essential Elements as appropriate to the area of licensure as established by the Board
III. Maintain a cumulative university GPA of 3.0 and receive a C or better in all education-related courses and major-required content courses, for all candidates admitted to the program after January 1, 2015
IV. Study areas required include:
   A. Content and content-specific pedagogy appropriate for the area of licensure
   B. Knowledge and skills designed to assist in the identification of students with disabilities and to meet the needs of students with disabilities in the regular classroom
   C. A student teaching culminating experience that:
      1. Requires a minimum of 400 clock hours with at least 200 clock hours in a single placement
      2. Requires that student teachers meet the same contract hours as licensed teachers in the same local education agency (LEA)

3. Requires that the student teacher not be employed in any capacity by the LEA where he or she is placed except as provided in R277-504-7B
4. Includes placement in all content or licensure areas in which the candidate shall be licensed
5. Includes intermittent supervision and evaluation by institution personnel
6. Includes direct supervision of the candidate by a classroom teacher
7. Includes meaningful self-reflection with review and feedback from both the classroom mentor teacher and institution personnel

or

An internship culminating experience that:

1. Consists of full-time employment as an educator for 1 school year with a minimum of 1,260 clock hours at a single school site
2. Requires that interns meet the same contract teaching hours as licensed teachers in the same LEA
3. Includes placement in the major content or licensure area in which the candidate shall be licensed (where possible, includes placement in all content or licensure areas in which the candidate shall be licensed)
4. Includes intermittent supervision and evaluation by institution personnel
5. Includes an LEA-assigned mentor
6. Includes meaningful self-reflection with review and feedback from both the assigned mentor and institution personnel

Early Childhood Education (K–3) and Elementary (K–6) License Areas

For certificate-specific detailed requirements, consult https://www.schools.utah.gov/curr/licensing.

I. Teacher preparation programs for Early Childhood Education (K–3), Elementary (K–6), and Elementary (1–8) license holders must:
   A. Align with the 2010 National Association for the Education of Young Children (NAEYC) Standards for Initial and Advanced Early Childhood Professional Preparation Programs or the 2007 Association for Childhood Education International (ACEI) Standards for Elementary Level Teacher Preparation, as appropriate;
   B. Require study and experiences that provide appropriate content knowledge needed to teach, including:
      1. Literacy including listening, speaking, writing, and reading,
      2. Mathematics,
      3. Physical and life science,
      4. Health and physical education,
      5. Social studies, and
      6. Fine arts;
      and
   C. Include course work specifically designed to prepare teachers:
      1. In the science of reading instruction including phonemic awareness, phonics, fluency, vocabulary and comprehension;

2. In the science of mathematics instruction including quantitative reasoning, problem solving, representation, and numeracy;

3. With the technical skills to utilize common education technology;

4. To integrate technology to support and meaningfully supplement the learning of students;

5. To facilitate student use of software for personalized learning;

6. To teach effectively in traditional, online-only, and blended classrooms;

7. To design, administer, and review educational assessments in a meaningful and ethical manner; and

8. In early childhood development and learning, if it is an Early Childhood Education (K–3), or Elementary (K–6); and in a specific content area resulting in an endorsement added to the license area, if it is an Elementary (1–8) program.

D. The standards shall be applied to the specific age group or grade level for which the program of preparation is designed.

1. An Early Childhood Education (K–3) program shall focus primarily on early childhood development and learning.

2. An Elementary (K–6) shall include both early childhood development and learning and elementary content and pedagogy.

3. An Elementary (1–8) shall focus primarily on elementary content and pedagogy.

II. A teacher holding an Elementary (1–8) license area may earn an Early Childhood (K–3) license area by completing specific course work requirements established by the Utah State Office of Education (USOE).

III. An Elementary (1–8) license permits the teacher to teach in any academic area in self-contained classes in grades 1–8.

IV. An Elementary (1–8) license permits the teacher to teach specific content courses at the 7th or 8th grade level only if the teacher's license includes the appropriate endorsement.

Secondary (6–12) License Area

For certificate-specific detailed requirements, consult https://www.schools.utah.gov/curr/licensing.

I. A Secondary (6–12) license area requires a major or major equivalent in a content area, but the teacher cannot teach in an elementary self-contained class.

II. The secondary educator preparation program of an institution must:

A. Be an undergraduate-level program and require candidates to have completed:

1. An approved content area or teaching major consistent with subjects taught in Utah secondary schools, and

2. Content course work reasonably equivalent to that required for individuals completing a nonteaching degree in the subject;

or

Be a graduate-level program and require candidates to have completed:

1. A bachelor's degree or higher from an accredited university, and

2. Course work equivalent to the minimum requirements for an endorsement as established by USOE, including the appropriate content knowledge assessment; *and*

B. Include course work specifically designed to prepare candidates:
1. With the technical skills necessary to utilize common education technology;
2. To integrate technology to support and meaningfully supplement the learning of students;
3. To facilitate student use of software for personalized learning;
4. To teach effectively in traditional, online-only, and blended classrooms;
5. To design, administer, and review educational assessments in a meaningful and ethical manner; and
6. To include literacy and quantitative learning objectives in content specific classes in alignment with the Utah Core Standards.

III. After completing a Board-approved Secondary (6–12) educator preparation program, the license shall be endorsed for all subjects in which the candidate has met the course requirements for the endorsement as established by USOE.
A. A content area or teaching major requires not fewer than 30 semester hours of credit in 1 content area.
B. An endorsement requires not fewer than 16 semester hours of credit in 1 content area.

Special Education (K–12) and Preschool Special Education (Birth–Age 5)

For certificate-specific detailed requirements, consult https://www.schools.utah.gov/curr/licensing.

I. The special education teacher preparation program must be aligned with the 2011 Council for Exceptional Children Special Education Standards for Professional Practice and focused in 1 or more of the following special education areas:
A. Mild/Moderate Disabilities
B. Severe Disabilities
C. Deaf and Hard of Hearing
D. Blind and Visually Impaired
E. Deafblind
F. Preschool Special Education (Birth–Age 5)

II. Teachers who hold Special Education (K–12+) licenses may secure additional endorsements if all endorsement requirements are met. Teachers who hold only a Special Education (K–12+) license may only be assigned as a teacher of record of students with disabilities.

III. A special education preparation program must include course work specifically designed to train candidates to:
A. Understand the legal and ethical issues surrounding special education;
B. Comply with the Individuals with Disabilities Education Act of 2004 (IDEA) and Utah State Board of Education Special Education Rules;
C. Work with other school personnel to implement and evaluate academic and positive

behavior supports and interventions for students with disabilities within a multi-tiered system of supports;

D. Train and monitor education teachers, related service providers, and paraeducators in providing services and supports to students with disabilities; *and*

E. Provide the necessary specialized instruction, as per individual education plans (IEPs), to students with disabilities, including:

1. Core content from the Utah Early Childhood Core Standards and the Essential Elements and content-specific pedagogy;

2. Skills in assessing and addressing the educational needs and progress of students with disabilities;

3. Skills in implementing and assessing the results of research and evidence-based interventions for students with disabilities; and

4. Skills in the implementation of an educational program with accommodations and modifications established by an IEP for students with disabilities.

IV. Preschool Special Education (Birth–Age 5) license holders who teach children who are hearing impaired (Birth–Age 5) or vision impaired (Birth–Age 5) or both, in self-contained, categorical classrooms shall hold an endorsement for Deaf and Hard of Hearing (Birth–Age 5) or Blind and Visually Impaired (Birth–Age 5) or both.

Vermont

Those applying for an initial educator license who hold a current educator license in a state that has signed the National Association of State Directors of Teacher Education and Certification (NASDTEC) Interstate Agreement are waived of meeting Vermont testing requirements. All educators approved for initial licensure are issued a comparable Level I Vermont Educator License.

Vermont no longer accepts paper applications. To apply for licensure, educators must use the Vermont Online Licensing System for Educators found at https://alis.edlicensing.vermont.gov/login.aspx. Finally, the Rules Governing the Licensure of Educators and the Preparation of Educational Professionals were revised in the summer of 2018. To access the current rules, go to the Vermont Agency of Education website: https://education.vermont.gov/documents/educator-quality-licensing-rules.

Pathways to Initial Licensure

I. Initial Licensure
   A. An applicant who is not licensed and has successfully completed a state-approved or Council for the Accreditation of Educator Preparation (CAEP)–approved program in a state that has signed the NASDTEC Interstate Agreement will be considered for licensure as if the applicant has completed an approved educator preparation program in Vermont.
      1. The applicant will be subject to the same requirements for initial licenses awarded in Vermont, including testing, criminal background checks, and affirmations.
      2. The applicant shall meet requirements for updated knowledge and skills as established by Vermont Standards Board for Professional Educators (VSBPE) policy when there is a time lapse of 10 or more years between the time of recommendation for licensure and application for licensure.
   B. An applicant who is not licensed and has successfully completed a state-approved or CAEP-approved program in a state that has *not* signed the NASDTEC Interstate Agreement may apply for licensure though transcript review. An applicant who meets the requirements and Jurisdiction-Specific Requirements as specified in these rules shall be issued a comparable license and/or endorsement(s) according to the provisions of these rules.
      1. The applicant shall meet requirements for updated knowledge and skills as established by VSBPE policy when there is a time lapse of 10 or more years between the time of recommendation for licensure and application for licensure.
   C. An applicant for initial licensure in Vermont who holds a professional license in another state that has signed the NASDTEC Interstate Agreement, and holds

the degree required for the endorsement, and meets the Jurisdiction-Specific Requirements specified in these rules shall be issued a Level I Professional Educator's License with a comparable endorsement(s) according to the provisions of these rules.

D. An applicant for Vermont licensure who holds a professional license in a state that has not signed the NASDTEC Interstate Agreement, or an applicant whose category of licensure is not covered by the agreement, shall be evaluated by the VSBPE on an individual basis by transcript review to establish whether the applicant meets the competency requirements.

1. Only course work that appears for credit on an official transcript and for which the applicant received a grade of B or better may be counted toward the requirements for initial licensure through transcript review.

2. The applicant shall meet requirements for updated knowledge and skills as established by VSBPE policy.

E. An applicant for Vermont licensure who is certified by the National Board for Professional Teaching Standards shall be issued a license in the comparable endorsement area.

F. Alternative Routes to Licensure

1. Peer Review (Vermont's approved Alternative Program) for Individual seeking Licensure as a Teacher or Administrator

a. An individual who holds at least a bachelor's degree from a regionally accredited or state-approved institution and who has successfully completed a major, or its equivalent, in the liberal arts and sciences, or in the content area of the endorsement sought, may be licensed by completing an alternate preparation process, Peer Review, approved by the VSBPE.

b. For endorsement areas requiring an advanced degree, the individual must hold the specified advanced degree in order to be deemed eligible to proceed through peer review.

2. Transcript Review for Individual Seeking Licensure as a Teacher or Administrator

a. For endorsements for which Vermont does not have an approved preparation program, an applicant for a Vermont license who has not completed an approved preparation program may be evaluated by the VSBPE, or its designee, on an individual basis by transcript review of course work appearing on an official transcript for which the applicant received graduate credit to establish whether the applicant meets the competency requirements of these rules.

b. An applicant seeking initial licensure in an endorsement area for which Vermont has an approved preparation program may choose to seek a recommendation for initial licensure through Vermont's Peer Review Alternative Licensure program.

c. Administrator candidates must also meet the degree, internship, examination, and requirements for updated knowledge and skills as established by the VSBPE.

d. An applicant for Vermont licensure who is certified by the National

Board for Professional Teaching Standards shall be issued a license in the comparable endorsement area.

II. General Requirements for All Licensure Candidates

    A. The applicant must hold a baccalaureate degree from a regionally accredited or Vermont-approved institution and must have successfully completed a major, or its equivalent, in the liberal arts and sciences or in the content area of the endorsement sought.

        1. Exceptions include an applicant for a Career and Technical Education endorsement or an educator who holds a Career and Technical Education endorsement; however, an applicant who currently holds a Career and Technical Education endorsement and would like to add a sub-endorsement must provide documentation of work experience in the sub-endorsement area. Documented work experience of 6 years (12,000 hours) or 4 years (8,000 hours) is required if educator held an associate's degree or the equivalent.

        2. Applicants for the Junior ROTC Instructor endorsement must have current certification as a Junior Reserve Officer Training Corps Instructor by the United States Department of Defense.

        3. Candidates for a school nurse endorsement must hold a Vermont Clinical RN License and a baccalaureate degree from a nationally accredited 4-year nursing program.

            a. Candidates for an associate school nurse endorsement must hold a Vermont Clinical RN License and an associate degree.

    B. Demonstrated ability to communicate effectively in speaking, writing, and other forms of creative expression, and ability to apply basic mathematical skills, critical thinking skills, and creative thinking skills

    C. Documentation of the specified content knowledge, performance standards, and additional requirements, if any, for the endorsement(s) being sought

    D. Documentation of required student teaching or administrative internship experience

        1. Student Teaching: Evidence of at least 13 consecutive weeks of supervised, concentrated field experience required for initial licensure, including an internship, or other concentrated field experience in which the candidate shall gradually assume the full professional roles and responsibilities of an educator in the initial endorsement area sought.

        2. Administrator Internship: a minimum of 300 hours of supervised, substantive field experience in 2 or more types of school settings.

    E. The educator has knowledge and skills in the content of his or her endorsement(s) at a level that enables students to meet or exceed the standards represented in both the fields of knowledge and the vital results of *Vermont's Framework of Standards and Learning Opportunities, Common Core, and/or Next Generation Science Standards*.

    F. The educator fulfills general competencies in teaching, Vermont's Core Teaching Standards, and, if an administrator, the Core Leadership Standards.

    G. Testing requirements

        1. Praxis Core Academic Skills Test is required for all educators for initial licenses, excluding Junior ROTC Instructors, School Nurses, Social Workers,

School Psychologists, Driver and Traffic Safety Education—In-Vehicle Only, and Work-based Learning Coordinator.

    a.   Meet scores on 3 individual core tests (reading—156, writing—162, and mathematics—150)

  2. Praxis II for applicants seeking initial license or additional endorsement in any of the following areas:

    a.   Mathematics, social studies, English, science, early childhood education, elementary education, art, music, physical education, modern or classical languages, reading, ESL audiologists, school psychologists, American sign language (ASL), and speech language pathologists.

    b.   Additional requirements for speech language pathologists: clinical licensure as a speech language pathologist in Vermont, and a minimum of a practicum in an educational setting in the diagnosis and management of individuals with communication delays and disorders under the supervision of a licensed educational speech language pathologist or ASHA-certified speech language pathologist.

    c.   For middle grades: English, mathematics, science, or history/social science

  3. Exemptions from Praxis testing requirements are available only if applicant is currently licensed from a state that has signed the NASDTEC Interstate Agreement.

Licensure Levels and Types with Renewal Requirements

I. Level I: Professional Educator License (valid 3 years; renewable)

  A. Issued to an applicant who has satisfactorily met all requirements for licensure

    1. See II, General Requirements for All Licensure Candidates, A–G, above.

  B. To renew a Level I License an educator must complete 45 hours of professional learning per the VSBPE Rules Governing the Licensure of Educators. (See VI, Renewal Requirements, below.)

II. Level II: Professional Educator License (valid 5 years; renewable)

  A. Issued, upon recommendation of a local or regional standards board, to educator who has:

    1. Successfully practiced in endorsement area for 3 years under Level I license, *and*

    2. Provided verification from a supervising administrator that the educator has demonstrated the competencies required by the endorsement at a professional level.

  B. To renew a Level II License, an educator must:

    1. Complete 135 hours of professional learning if renewing a Level II license that was held for 7 years. (See VI, Renewal Requirements, below)

    2. Complete 90 hours of professional learning if renewing a Level II license that was held for 5 years. (See VI, Renewal Requirements, below)

III. Apprenticeship License for individuals seeking Career Technical Education Endorsements (valid 4 years, not renewable). An Apprenticeship License is not a Professional Educator License.

IV. Provisional License or Endorsement (valid 2 years)
    A. A superintendent, director, headmaster of an independent school, or career technical director may apply to the Vermont Agency of Education for a provisional license or endorsement when the local district is unable to find an appropriately licensed and/or endorsed applicant after making all reasonable efforts to do so.
    B. The application for a provisional license or endorsement shall include a plan for obtaining a Level I license or endorsement and an explanation of how the applicant will be mentored and supervised during the 2-year period of the provisional license.
    C. Qualifications
        1. Possess a baccalaureate degree (except for those seeking the associate school nurse license, which requires an associate's degree, and the Junior ROTC license, for which applicant must hold Department of Defense certification as a Junior ROTC instructor) and meet at least 1 of the following criteria:
            a. Possess any valid educator license from Vermont or another state,
               or
               Possess any expired Vermont educator license or any expired license from another state, provided the license expired no fewer than 2 years and no longer than 10 years ago,
               or
               Have a major or the equivalent in the content area of the provisional endorsement sought,
               or
               Have successfully completed the Praxis II licensure content assessment for the provisional endorsement sought.
    D. If extenuating circumstances prevented an individual from completing the approved plan for Level I licensure, a new 1-year provisional license (formally known as an extension) may be granted.
V. Emergency Licenses and Endorsements (valid for school year issued and only for the assignment for which it was issued; cannot be extended for a second year, nor can an individual be issued an emergency license for any endorsement more than once)
    A. See IV, A, directly above, except for emergency license or endorsement.
    B. Emergency licenses and endorsements shall be issued only to individuals who hold a baccalaureate degree or its equivalent (except career and technical education) but do not meet the qualifications for a provisional license (see IV, C, directly above).
    C. The application for an emergency license shall include an explanation of how the applicant will be mentored and supervised.
    D. No emergency endorsements will be issued for the following: Assistant Director for Adult Education, Career Technical Center Director, Career Technical Education School Counseling Coordinator, Career Technical Education Special Needs Coordinator, Director of Curriculum, Director of Special Education, Driver and Traffic Safety Education, Early Childhood Special Educator, Educational Speech Language Pathologist, Intensive Special Education Teacher, Junior ROTC Instructor, Principal, School Nurse, Associate School Nurse, School Counselor, School Psychologist, School Social Worker, Special Educator, Special Education Consulting

Teacher, Superintendent, Teacher of the Deaf and Hard of Hearing, and Teacher of the Visually Impaired.

VI. Renewal Requirements

    A. Level I Renewal

        1. To receive a 3-year renewal, the educator shall show professional growth through completion of a minimum of 3 credits or 45 hours of professional learning in the endorsement area.

        2. Level I endorsement holders who have practiced in Vermont in the endorsement area after 3 years shall seek a recommendation from their local or regional standards board for a Level II endorsement.

            a. An educator who does not receive a recommendation for a Level II endorsement upon initial application shall renew the Level I endorsement after 3 years of professional practice and reapply for a Level II license prior to the expiration of the renewal.

            b. Level I endorsement of an educator who does not receive a recommendation for a Level II endorsement after another 3 years of professional practice shall become lapsed.

            c. Level I license holders employed as educators in Vermont but who have not practiced in a particular endorsement area for 3 years shall seek a recommendation for renewal of that Level I endorsement through their local or regional standards board.

            d. Educators may renew Level 1 endorsements under which they are not currently teaching by completing 3 credits or 45 hours of professional learning for each renewal. There is no limit to the number of times these endorsements may be renewed.

            e. An educator shall present evidence of any required additional licenses or credentials specific to a particular endorsement.

    B. Level II Renewal

        1. Level II license holders shall seek a recommendation for renewal of their Level II license and endorsement(s) from their local or regional standards board, or agency of education if not employed in a Vermont school served by a local or regional standards board.

        2. The local or regional standards board shall recommend renewal of a Level II endorsement if the applicant presents:

            a. Documentation of a minimum of 9 credits or 135 hours of professional learning, at least 3 credits or 45 hours of which must address the specific content knowledge and performance standards of each endorsement recommended for renewal if renewing a Level II license that was held for 7 years,

               or

               Documentation of a minimum of 6 credits or 90 hours of professional learning, at least 2 credits or 60 hours of which must address the specific content knowledge and performance standards of each endorsement recommended for renewal if renewing a Level II license that was held for 5 years.

b.   Evidence of any required additional licenses or credentials specific to a particular endorsement

Endorsements

I.   In order to be valid, each professional educator's license shall have 1 or more endorsements.

II. Endorsements limited in time, grade level, or scope may be issued by the VSBPE based on the applicant's background and experience, permitting practice in a specialized area within a broader endorsement field.

III. The holder of any license who wishes to qualify for an additional endorsement via transcript review shall present evidence of meeting the content knowledge and performance standards and additional requirements, if any, of the endorsement.

   A.   A minimum of 18 credit hours in the endorsement field is required.

IV. Endorsements may be obtained in the following areas:

   A.   Administrator Endorsements
       1.   Assistant Director for Adult Education
       2.   Career Technical Center Director
       3.   Director of Special Education
       4.   Principal
       5.   Superintendent
       6.   Director of Curriculum

   B.   Art (Grades PreK–8, 5–12, or PreK–12); Associate School Nurse (Grades PreK–12); Bilingual Education (Grades PreK–12); Business Education (Grades 5–12); Career Technical Education Coordinator (Grades 7–12); Career Technical Education School Counseling Coordinator (Grades 7–12); Computer Science (Grades 7–12); Dance (Grades PreK–6, 7–12, PreK–12); Design and Technology Education (Grades 5–12); Driver & Traffic Safety Education (Grades 9–12); Early Childhood Education (Birth to PreK, Grades PreK–3, Birth–Age 3); Educational Technology Specialist (Grades PreK–12); Elementary Education (Grades K–6); English (Grades 7–12); English as a Second Language (ESL) (Grades PreK–6, 7–12, or PreK–12); Family and Consumer Sciences (Grades 5–12); Health Education (Grades PreK–6, 7–12, or PreK–12); Junior Reserve Officer Training Corps (ROTC) Instructor (Grades 9–12); Mathematics (Grades 7–12); Middle Grades (with 1 or more of the required content areas of Mathematics, English/ Language Arts, Science, and Social Studies) (Grades 5–9); Modern and Classical Languages (Grades PreK–6, 7–12, or PreK–12); Music; Physical Education (Grades PreK–6, 7–12, or PreK–12); Reading/English Language Arts Coordinator (for holder of endorsement in either Early Childhood, Elementary Education, Middle Grades, Secondary Education, or Special Education) (Grades PreK–12); Reading/English Language Arts Specialist (for holder of endorsement in either Early Childhood, Elementary Education, Middle Grades, Secondary Education, or Special Education) (Grades PreK–12); School Counselor (Grades PreK–12); School Librarian (Grades PreK–12); School Nurse (Grades PreK–12); School Psychologist (Grades PreK–12); School Social Worker (Grades PreK–12); Science (Grades

7–12); Social Studies (Grades 7–12); Theater Arts (Grades PreK–12); Work-Based Learning Coordinator (Grades 9–12); Career and Technical Special Needs Coordinator (Grade 8–Age 21); Early Childhood Special Educator (Birth–Age 6); Intensive Special Education Teacher (Ages 3–21); Special Educator (Grades K–8, Grade 7–Age 21, or K–Age 21); Educational Speech-Language Pathologist (Ages 3–21); Teacher of the Visually Impaired (Ages 3–21); Teacher of the Deaf and Hard of Hearing (Ages 3–21); Online Teaching Specialist (Grades PreK–12).

Virginia

General Requirements for Licensure

I. Applicants for licensure must:
   A. Be at least 18 years of age
   B. Pay the appropriate fees as determined by the Virginia Board of Education and complete the application process
   C. Have earned a baccalaureate degree (with the exception of the Technical Professional License) from a regionally accredited college or university and meet requirements for the license sought. Persons seeking initial licensure through approved programs from Virginia institutions of higher education shall only be licensed as instructional personnel if the education endorsement programs are approved by the Virginia Board of Education.
      1. Individuals who have earned a degree from an institution in another country shall hold the equivalent of a regionally accredited college or university degree in the United States, as verified by a Virginia Department of Education–approved credential evaluation agency for the degree required for the license.

   and

   D. Possess good moral character and be free of conditions outlined in Part VII of VAC20-23-720 et seq., available at https://law.lis.virginia.gov/admincode/title8/agency20/chapter23/section720/.

II. All candidates who hold at least a baccalaureate degree from a regionally accredited college or university and who seek an initial Virginia teaching license must obtain passing scores on professional teacher's assessments prescribed by the Virginia Board of Education.
   A. With the exception of the career switcher program, which requires assessments as prerequisites, individuals must complete the professional teacher's assessments within the 3-year validity of the initial provisional license.
   B. Candidates seeking a Technical Professional License, the International License, the School Manager License, or the Pupil Personnel Services License are not required to take the professional teacher's assessments.
   C. Individuals who hold a valid out-of-state license (full credential with no deficiencies) and who have completed a minimum of 3 years of full-time, successful teaching experience in a public or accredited nonpublic school (K–12) outside Virginia are exempt from the professional teacher's assessment requirements. Documentation must be submitted to verify the school's status as a public or accredited nonpublic school.

III. All individuals seeking an initial endorsement in early/primary education PreK–3, elementary education PreK–6, special education—general curriculum, special education—deaf and hard of hearing, special education—blindness and visual impairments, and individuals seeking an endorsement as a reading specialist must obtain passing scores on a reading instructional assessment prescribed by the Virginia Board of Education.

IV. Licensure by reciprocity is set forth in 8VAC20-22-100. A school leader's assessment prescribed by the Virginia Board of Education must be met for all individuals who are seeking an initial endorsement authorizing them to serve as principals and assistant principals in the public schools.

V. Individuals seeking an initial administration and supervision endorsement who are interested in serving as central office instructional personnel are not required to take and pass the school leader's licensure assessment prescribed by the Virginia Board of Education.

VI. Individuals seeking initial licensure must:

A. Demonstrate proficiency in the use of educational technology for instruction

B. Complete study in child abuse recognition and intervention in accordance with curriculum guidelines developed by the Virginia Board of Education in consultation with the Virginia Department of Social Services

C. Receive professional development in instructional methods tailored to promote student academic progress and effective preparation for the Virginia Standards of Learning end-of-course and end-of-grade assessments

D. Provide evidence of completion of certification or training in emergency first aid, cardiopulmonary resuscitation (CPR), and the use of automated external defibrillators (AED). The certification or training program shall be based on the current national evidence-based emergency cardiovascular care guidelines for cardiopulmonary resuscitation and the use of an AED, such as a program developed by the American Heart Association or the American Red Cross. The Virginia Board of Education shall provide a waiver of this requirement for any person with a disability whose disability prohibits such person from completing the certification or training.

E. The teacher of record for verified credit courses for high school graduation must hold a Virginia license with the appropriate content endorsement.

F. Every teacher seeking an initial license in the Commonwealth with an endorsement in the area of career and technical education shall have an industry certification credential, as defined in 8VAC20-22-10, in the area in which the teacher seeks endorsement. If a teacher seeking an initial license in the Commonwealth has not attained an industry certification credential in the area in which the teacher seeks endorsement, the Virginia Board of Education may, upon request of the employing school division or educational agency, issue the teacher a provisional license to allow time for the teacher to attain such credential.

G. Effective July 1, 2017, every person seeking renewal of a license must provide evidence of completion of dyslexia awareness training, provided by the Virginia Department of Education, on the indicators of dyslexia as defined by the Virginia Board of Education pursuant to regulations and the evidence-based interventions and accommodations for dyslexia.

Types of Licenses

Unless otherwise indicated, licenses are valid for 10 years and renewable. For full information on the licenses listed below, refer to the *Virginia Licensure Regulations for School Personnel* (8VAC20-23) at https://law.lis.virginia.gov/admincode/title8/agency20/chapter23/.

I. Provisional License (valid up to 3 years; nonrenewable). Requirements include:

   A. A baccalaureate degree or higher from a regionally accredited college or university, *and*

   B. Completion of the requirements for a regular 5-year license within the validity period of the provisional license.

II. Collegiate Professional License (valid 10 years; renewable). Requirements include:

   A. A baccalaureate degree or higher from a regionally accredited college or university, *and*

   B. Satisfactory completion of the professional teacher's assessments prescribed by the Virginia Board of Education.

III. Postgraduate Professional License (valid 10 years; renewable). Requirements include:

   A. Completion of all requirements for the Collegiate Professional License, *and*

   B. Graduate degree or higher from a regionally accredited college or university.

IV. Technical Professional License (valid 10 years; renewable). This license can be issued in Career and Technical Education, Education Technology, and Military Science. Requirements include:

   A. Diploma from an accredited high school or Virginia Board of Education–approved high school equivalency credential;

   B. Academic proficiency, skills in literacy, communication, technical competency, and occupational experience;

   C. Demonstrated competency in the endorsement area sought;

   D. Completion of 9 semester hours of specialized professional studies credit from a regionally accredited college or university (must include 3 semester hours of human development, 3 semester hours of curriculum and instruction, and 3 semester hours of instructional technology or classroom and behavior management);

   E. Successful completion of a 1-year, full-time teaching experience in a public school or accredited nonpublic school in the area of endorsement;

   F. Individuals seeking an endorsement to teach military science must have the appropriate credentials issued by the US military; *and*

   G. A license issued by the appropriate Virginia board for those program areas requiring a license and a minimum of 2 years of satisfactory experience at the journeyman level or an equivalent, *or*

   Completion of a registered apprenticeship program and 2 years of satisfactory experience at the journeyman level or an equivalent level in the trade, *or*

   Four years of work experience at the management or supervisory level or equivalent, or a combination of 4 years of training and work experience at the management or supervisory level or equivalent.

V. School Manager License (valid 10 years; renewable). Requirements include:
- A. A baccalaureate degree from a regionally accredited college or university,
- B. Three years of successful managerial experience, *and*
- C. Recommendation for the license by a Virginia school division superintendent.

VI. Pupil Personnel Services License (valid 10 years; renewable). Requirements include:
- A. An appropriate graduate degree from a regionally accredited college or university, *and*
- B. An endorsement for guidance counselor, school psychologist, school social worker, or vocational evaluator.
- C. This license does not require teaching experience unless otherwise outlined under the specific endorsement's requirements.

VII. Division Superintendent License (valid 10 years; renewable). Requirements include:
- A. A graduate degree from a regionally accredited college or university that meets the requirements specified in 8VAC20-22-600.
- B. The individual's name must be listed on the Virginia Board of Education's list of eligible division superintendents.

VIII. International Educator License (valid up to 5 consecutive years; nonrenewable). This license provides a cultural exchange opportunity for Virginia students and international teachers. Applicants must:
- A. Be employed by a Virginia public or accredited nonpublic school;
- B. Hold non-US citizenship and be a nonpermanent resident;
- C. Serve as an exchange teacher for a time period not to exceed 5 consecutive years; *and*
- D. Meet the following requirements as verified by a state-approved, federally designated exchange visitor program:
  1. Be proficient in written and spoken English,
  2. Demonstrate competence in the appropriate academic subject areas by meeting credential requirements for a qualified teacher in the exchange country,
  3. Hold the US equivalent of a baccalaureate degree or higher as determined by an approved credential evaluation agency, *and*
  4. Hold US or foreign educator credentials and have completed at least 1 year of successful teaching experience that enables the educator to fulfill a similar requirement in their home country.

IX. Teach For America License (valid 2 years; nonrenewable). Requirements include:
- A. A baccalaureate degree or higher from a regionally accredited college or university;
- B. Meets requirements prescribed by the Virginia Board of Education for all endorsements sought, or has met the qualifying scores on the content area assessment prescribed by the Board for the endorsements sought;
- C. Possesses good moral character according to criteria developed by the Virginia Board of Education;
- D. Has been offered and has accepted placement in Teach For America;

E.   Has successfully completed pre-service training and is participating in the professional development requirements of Teach For America, including teaching frameworks, curricula, lesson planning, instructional delivery, classroom management, assessment and evaluation of student progress, classroom diversity, and literacy development;

F.   Has an offer of employment from a local school board to teach in a public elementary or secondary school in the Commonwealth or in a preschool program that receives state funds pursuant to subsection C of 22.1-199.1 of the Code of Virginia;
and

G.   Receives a recommendation from the employing school division for a Teach For America License in the endorsement area in which the individual seeks to be licensed.

H.   The Virginia Board of Education may extend a Teach For America license for 1 additional year upon request of the employing school division; no Teach For America license shall exceed a total of 3 years in length.

I.   Upon completion of at least 2 years of full-time teaching in a public elementary or secondary school, an individual holding a Teach For America license shall be eligible to receive a renewable license if the applicant has:
1.   Achieved satisfactory scores on all professional teacher's assessments required by the Virginia Board of Education;
and
2.   Received a satisfactory evaluation at the end of each year of employment.

X.   Online Teacher License (valid 10 years; renewable). Valid only for teaching online courses. Teachers who hold a 10-year renewable license issued by the Virginia Board of Education may teach online courses for which they are properly endorsed and do not have to seek this license. Requirements include:
A.   Meet requirements for endorsement in a content area and achieve the qualifying scores on the content area assessment prescribed by the Virginia Board of Education;
and
B.   Complete a 3-semester-hour course in online instructional methods.
C.   Online teaching experience is not acceptable to meet the full-time teaching requirements for other license types.

Alternate Routes to Licensure

I.   Career Switcher alternate route to licensure for career professions:
A.   Available to career switchers who seek teaching endorsements PreK through grade 12 with the exception of special education.
B.   An individual seeking a Provisional License through the career switcher program must meet the following prerequisite requirements:
1.   Completed application;
2.   A baccalaureate degree from a regionally accredited college or university;
3.   Completion of requirements for an endorsement in a teaching area or the equivalent through verifiable experience or academic study;

4. A minimum of 3 years of full-time work experience or its equivalent; *and*

5. Qualifying scores on the professional teacher's assessments as prescribed by the Virginia Board of Education.

C. The Provisional Career Switcher License is awarded at the end of Level I preparation, is valid for 1 year, and may be issued for a period not to exceed 3 years. The candidate must complete all components of the career switcher alternate route for career professions.

D. Level I requirements must be completed during the course of a single year and may be offered through a variety of delivery systems, including distance learning programs. Career Switcher programs must be certified by the Virginia Department of Education. If an employing agency recommends extending the Provisional License for a second year, the candidate will enter Level III of the program.

1. Level I preparation includes:
   a. Minimum of 180 clock hours of instruction, including field experience

2. Level II preparation during first year of employment includes:
   a. Seeking employment in Virginia with the 1-year Provisional Career Switcher License
   b. Continued Level II preparation during the first year of employment with a minimum of 5 seminars that will include a minimum of 20 cumulative instructional hours
   c. One year of successful, full-time teaching experience in a Virginia public or accredited nonpublic school under a 1-year Provisional License, under the direction of a trained mentor
   d. Upon completion of Levels I and II of the Career Switcher alternate route to licensure program and submission of a recommendation from the Virginia educational employing agency, the candidate will be eligible to apply for a 5-year renewable license.

3. Level III preparation, if required, includes:
   a. Postpreparation, if required, to be conducted by the Virginia employing educational agency to address the areas where improvement is needed as identified in the candidate's professional improvement plan
   b. Upon completion of Levels I, II, and III of the Career Switcher alternate route to licensure program and submission of a recommendation from the Virginia educational employing agency, the candidate will be eligible to receive a 10-year renewable license.

E. Verification of program completion will be documented by the certified program provider and the division superintendent or designee.

F. Certified providers implementing a Career Switcher program may charge a fee for participation in the program.

II. Other Alternate Routes to Licensure are available to those seeking a teaching endorsement in PreK–12, experiential learning, special education, and other areas. For more information, refer to section 8VAC20-23-90 of the *Virginia Licensure Regulations for School Personnel* at https://law.lis.virginia.gov/admincode/title8/agency20/chapter23/.

Requirements

I. General requirements:
   A. Completion of an approved program, including:
      1. A degree from a regionally accredited college or university in the liberal arts and sciences (or equivalent);
      2. Professional teacher's assessments as prescribed by the Virginia Board of Education;
      3. Specific endorsement requirements; and
      4. Professional studies requirements, including supervised classroom experience in the endorsement area.

      or

   B. If employed by a Virginia public or nonpublic school, completion of the Alternate Route to Licensure.

II. Professional studies requirements—which may be met through integrated course work or modules—total 18 semester hours for adult education, PreK–12 endorsements, and secondary grades 6–12 endorsements; for early/primary PreK–3, elementary education PreK–6, and special education, the total is 21 semester hours.
   A. Human growth and development and learning (birth through adolescence): 3 semester hours
   B. Curriculum and instruction: 3 semester hours
   C. Classroom and behavior management: 3 semester hours
   D. Assessment of and for learning: 3 semester hours
   E. Foundations of education and the teaching profession: 3 semester hours
   F. Language and literacy:
      1. Early/primary PreK–3 and elementary education PreK–6, language acquisition, and reading and writing: 6 semester hours
      2. Middle education, language acquisition and reading development: 3 semester hours; and literacy in the content area: 3 semester hours
      3. Special education, language acquisition, and reading and writing: 6 semester hours
      4. Secondary education, literacy in the content area: 3 semester hours
   G. Supervised classroom experience:
      1. Supervised clinical experience shall be comprised of early field experience and a minimum of 10 weeks of successful student teaching in the endorsement area sought.
      2. Full-time classroom experience for a minimum of 300 clock hours (including pre- and post-clinical experiences) with at least 150 clock hours spent supervised in direct teaching activities at the level of endorsement
      3. One year of successful full-time teaching experience in the endorsement area in a public or accredited nonpublic school may be accepted in lieu of the supervised teaching experience.

Endorsements for Early/Primary Education, Elementary Education, and Middle Education

The Alternate Route requirements apply to individuals seeking licensure outside of state-approved programs and through the Alternative Route to Licensure. Institutions of higher education (IHEs) with approved programs in Virginia are not subject to specific semester-hour requirements since they incorporate state competencies into their programs.

I. Early/primary education PreK–3 endorsement requirements:
    A. Graduation from an approved teacher preparation program in early/primary education PreK–3
        or
    B. A degree from a regionally accredited college or university in the liberal arts and sciences (or equivalent) and completed course work that covers the early/primary education PreK–3 competencies and fulfills the following 48 semester-hour requirements: English (must include composition, oral communication, and literature): 12 semester hours; mathematics: 9 semester hours; science (including a laboratory course): 12 semester hours in at least 2 science disciplines; history (must include American history and world history): 6 semester hours; social science (must include geography and economics): 6 semester hours; and arts and humanities: 6 semester hours

II. Elementary education PreK–6 endorsement requirements:
     A. Graduation from an approved teacher preparation program in elementary education PreK–6
         or
     B. A baccalaureate degree or higher from a regionally accredited college or university in the liberal arts and sciences (or equivalent) and fulfilling the following semester-hour requirements: English (must include composition, oral communication, and literature): 12 semester hours; mathematics: 15 semester hours; science (including a laboratory course): 15 semester hours in at least 2 science disciplines; history (must include American history and world history): 6 semester hours; social science (must include geography and economics): 6 semester hours; and arts and humanities: 3 semester hours

III. Middle education 6–8 endorsement requirements:
      A. Graduation from an approved teacher preparation discipline-specific program in middle education 6–8 with at least 1 area of academic preparation from the areas of English, mathematics, science, and history and social sciences
          or
      B. A degree from a regionally accredited college or university in the liberal arts and sciences (or equivalent), completion of a minimum of 21 semester hours in at least 1 area of academic preparation (concentration) that will be listed on the license, and completion of the minimum requirements for those areas in which the individual is not seeking an area of academic preparation. Areas: English (21 semester hours), mathematics (24 semester hours), science (21 semester hours), history and social sciences (21 semester hours). The requirements for each subject area are detailed in the *Virginia Licensure Regulations for School Personnel*.

Endorsements for PreK–12 and Secondary Grades 6–12, Special Education, and Adult Education

The Alternate Route requirements apply to individuals seeking licensure outside of state-approved programs and through the Alternative Route to Licensure. IHEs with approved programs in Virginia are not subject to specific semester-hour requirements since they incorporate state competencies into their programs.

I. Individuals seeking licensure with PreK–12 endorsements, special education, secondary grades 6–12 endorsements, and adult education may meet requirements through the completion of an approved program or, if employed by a Virginia public or nonpublic school, through the Alternative Route to Licensure. Components of the licensure program include a degree in the liberal arts and sciences (or equivalent), professional teacher's assessments as prescribed by the Virginia Board of Education, specific endorsement requirements, and professional studies requirements. For endorsement-specific requirements, refer to the *Virginia Licensure Regulations for School Personnel*.

Washington

General Certificate Information

I. The teacher certificate authorizes service in the primary role of teacher.

II. The administrator certificate authorizes service in the primary role of building-level administration (principal), program administration (program administrator), or district-wide general administration (superintendent).

III. The educational staff associate (ESA) certificate authorizes service as school psychologist, counselor, social worker, school nurse, physical therapist, occupational therapist, or speech-language pathologist or audiologist.

IV. Levels of Certificates available to first-time applicants:
- A. Teaching Certificates
  1. Residency Teaching Certificate
  2. Professional Teaching Certificate
- B. Administrator Certificates
  1. Residency Administrator Certificate—Principal and Program Administrator
  2. Professional Administrator Certificate—Principal and Program Administrator
  3. Initial Administrator Certificate—Superintendent Only
- C. Educational Staff Associate Certificates
  1. Residency ESA Certificate—School Counselor, Psychologist
  2. Professional ESA Certificate—School Counselor, Psychologist
  3. Initial ESA Certificate—School Nurse, Occupational Therapy, Physical Therapy, School Speech-Language Pathologist or Audiologist, Social Worker
  4. Continuing ESA Certificate—School Nurse, Occupational Therapy, Physical Therapy, School Speech-Language Pathologist or Audiologist, Social Worker, School Psychologist, Counselor

V. Candidates for all professional, continuing, and first 5-year residency renewal certificates must complete course work in issues of abuse, which must include information related to:
- A. Identification of physical, emotional, sexual, and substance abuse;
- B. The impact on learning and behavior;
- C. The responsibilities of a teacher, administrator, or ESA to report abuse or to provide assistance to victimized children;
  and
- D. Methods of teaching about abuse and its prevention.
- E. School nurses, counselors, psychologists, and social workers must also complete a suicide prevention training every 5 years.

Teaching Certificates

I. Residency Teaching Certificate
- A. Baccalaureate degree or higher from an accredited institution

B. Completion of a state-approved teacher education program or alternate route program

    or

    Three years of out-of-state P–12 teaching experience and a regular out-of-state teaching certificate

C. Passing score on the WEST-B (Washington Educator Skills Test-Basic skills reading, writing, and math), or approved alternative, and a WEST-E/NES (Washington Educator Skills Test-Endorsements/National Evaluation Series) content test in each endorsement area or approved alternative. For a list of all approved alternatives, visit the department website (see Appendix 1).

D. Residency teacher (First Issue) certificate is issued without a defined expiration date. Once certificate holders are employed and reported as teachers by a Washington school district on the Washington State personnel report (S-275) with 1.5 FTE experience, their certificate will expire on the following June 30. Those teachers will need to submit a residency reissuance application to have a new certificate issued with a 5-year expiration date. Until this takes place, the certificate is valid without a defined expiration date.

E. Certificate Endorsements

    1. Endorsements indicate the content area(s) and/or specializations for which the teacher is prepared.

    2. Teachers may obtain endorsements on their Washington certificate in several ways:

        a. Program + Test. Complete a college/university program approved to offer the endorsement. This can be in-state or out-of-state.

        b. National Board for Professional Teaching Standards. Earn National Board Certification in a Washington endorsement area. (A list of NBPTS-eligible endorsements can be found here: https://www.pesb.wa.gov/preparation -programs/assessments/content-knowledge-assessment-wcst-c-and-nes/ west-enes-exemption/.)

        c. Testing. Pass WEST-E/NES or an approved alternative test for a qualifying endorsement. (Test-only endorsements and an overview of how to add an endorsement can be found here: http://www.k12.wa.us/certification/ teacher/Endorsement.aspx.)

        d. Migration Chart. Certain endorsements may be added by means of migration to align previously issued endorsements with current standards.

II. Professional Teacher Certificate (valid for 5 years; renewable)

    A. As of September 1, 2011, to earn a professional certificate, teachers must:

        1. Have 1.5 years of teaching experience

        2. Pass the professional certificate assessment (ProTeach). Teachers can register to take the assessment any time prior to the expiration of their residency certificate, but typically do so during their third or fourth year of teaching in Washington schools.

            or

            Hold a certificate from the National Board for Professional Teaching Standards (NBPTS)

        a.   For full details about the portfolio of evidence requirements, visit www
           .pesb.wa.gov.
    3.   Complete an issues of abuse course
B. Existing professional certificates will remain valid until the expiration date stated on the certificate.
    1.   Renewal requires 100 clock hours, credits, PGPs, a renewed National Board Certificate, or a combination of these options every 5 years.

Administrator Certificates

I. Residency Administrator Certificate—Principal and Program Administrator (valid until completion of 2 years of service in the role in Washington)
    A. Master's degree from regionally accredited institution
    B. Completion of an administrator preparation program in the administrative role or 3 years of successful experience in another state in the administrative role while holding a regular certificate in the role issued by another state
    C. For Principal: Hold or have held a regular teaching certificate, career and technical education (CTE) certificate, or ESA certificate
    D. For Principal: Verification of 3 years of successful school-based instructional experience in an educational setting
II. Professional Administrator Certificate—Principal and Program Administrator
    A. Completion of an approved Continuing Administrator License (CAL) program in Oregon State
III. Initial Administrator Certificate—Superintendent Only (valid 7 years)
    A. Master's degree from an accredited institution
    B. Completion of an administrator preparation program for superintendent or 3 years of successful experience as a superintendent, deputy superintendent, or assistant superintendent while holding a superintendent certificate issued by another state
    C. Must hold a valid regular teaching, ESA, principal, or program administrator certificate
IV. Continuing Administrator Certificate—Superintendent Only (valid for 5-year periods; renewed upon completion of 100 clock hours, credits, PGPs or a combination of these options)
    A. Completion of all requirements for the Initial Superintendent's Certificate
    B. Master's degree plus 60 quarter hours (40 semester hours) of graduate-level course work in education completed after the baccalaureate degree, or a doctorate in education
    C. Completion of 180 days of service as a superintendent, deputy superintendent, or assistant superintendent, 30 days of which must have been in the same school district

Educational Staff Associate Certification

I. Residency Educational Staff Associate (ESA) Certificate for school counselor, school psychologist
    A. Completion of master's degree with major in the appropriate specialization

B. Completion of state-approved program for certification in the appropriate ESA role,
    or
    If no program, must have completed 3 years of out-of-state K–12 experience in the ESA role under that certificate,
    or
    For school psychologist only: must hold Nationally Certified School Psychologist (NCSP) Certificate issued after December 31, 1991, by the National School Psychology Certification Board; if the other state didn't require a certificate, must have 3 years of out-of-state experience in that role.

C. Completion of a comprehensive examination required in the master's degree program. If a candidate has been awarded a master's degree without a comprehensive examination, the candidate, as a condition for certification, must arrange to take such an examination with any accredited college or university and provide the superintendent of public instruction with an affidavit from the chair of the department of the academic field that he or she has successfully completed this comprehensive examination.

   1. School Counselor
       a. Successful completion of a proctored, comprehensive examination of the knowledge included in the course work for the required master's degree, given by an accredited institution of higher education
           or
       b. Passing score on the Praxis II guidance and counseling examination administered by Educational Testing Service (ETS)
   2. School Psychologist
       a. Successful completion of a proctored, comprehensive examination of the knowledge included in the course work for the required master's degree, given by an accredited institution of higher education,
           or
       b. Passing score on the Praxis II school psychology examination administered by ETS

II. Professional ESA Certificate for school counselor and school psychologist (valid minimum of 5 years). Requirements:
    A. Hold a certificate from the NBPTS if a school counselor (Professional ESA school counselor certificate issued on the basis of holding a valid NBPTS school counselor certificate will have a validity of 5 years or the validity of the NBPTS certificate, whichever is greater)
        or
        Hold a valid certificate from the National Association of School Psychologists (NASP) if a school psychologist
    B. Course on issues of abuse (see III, A, 5, immediately below, for full description of required course content)
    C. Completion of an approved suicide prevention course (see III, A, 6, immediately below, for full description of required course content)

III. Continuing Educational Staff Associate (ESA)
    A. For school psychologist

1. Candidate must have completed 180 days of experience in the role (or the equivalent of 180 days of full-time service), of which 30 days must be in the same district.
2. Candidate must hold a master's degree with a major or specialization in school psychology and must have completed at least 15 quarter (10 semester) credit hours of graduate work offered by a college or university with a state-approved school psychologist program,

    or

    150 clock hours of study, which meet the state continuing education clock-hour criteria pursuant to WAC 181–85,

    or

    A combination of credits and clock hours equivalent to the above.
3. The above academic study shall be:
   a. Based on the school psychologist performance domains included in WAC 181-78A-270(5)(a);
   b. Taken subsequent to the issuance of the initial or residency school psychologist certificate; and
   c. Determined in consultation with and approved by the candidate's employer or the administrator of a state-approved school psychologist preparation program.
4. Candidate must have completed a comprehensive exam relevant to the field of specialization. For those who did not complete such an exam as part of a master's degree program, there are acceptable alternatives; for more information, visit http://www.k12.wa.us/certification/ESA/pubdocs/WRITTENCOMPEXAM.pdf.
5. Candidates must have taken course work in issues of abuse, which must include information related to identification of physical, emotional, sexual, and substance abuse; the impact on learning and behavior; the responsibilities of an ESA to report abuse or to provide assistance to victimized children; and methods of teaching about abuse and its prevention.
6. Effective July 1, 2015, candidates shall attest to the completion of a Professional Educator Standards Board–approved suicide prevention training within the previous 5 years, per RCW 28A.410.226.

B. For school nurse, school occupational therapist, school physical therapist, school social worker and school speech-language pathologist or audiologist
   1. Continuing ESA is the advanced level regular certificate available for these positions. For full details, see http://www.k12.wa.us/Certification/ESA/UpgradeInitial-ContinuingR.aspx.

IV. Initial Educational Staff Associate (ESA) for school counselor, school psychologist, school social worker, school nurse, school occupational therapist, school physical therapist, and school speech-language pathologist or audiologist
   A. Initial ESA is the first-level regular certificate for these positions. For full details, see http://www.k12.wa.us/Certification/ESA/ESAFirstTime.aspx#content.

West Virginia

West Virginia educator certification rules were in the process of review at press time. The most current information can be found in Policy 5202 at http://wvde.state.wv.us/policies/.

General Information and Requirements

I. West Virginia licenses include:
   A. Professional Certificate
   B. Alternative Teaching Certificate
   C. Temporary Certificate
   D. Provisional Certificate
   E. Career/Technical Education Certificate
   F. Temporary Career/Technical Education Certificate
   G. First-Class/Full-Time Permit
   H. Adult Permit
   I. Authorization
   J. Paraprofessional Certificate (granted to service personnel)
   K. Special Education Content Endorsement
   L. Advanced Credential
II. Valid grade levels
   A. Preschool Education (PreK)
   B. Preschool to Adult (PreK–Adult)
   C. Kindergarten to Grade 12 (K–12)
   D. Early Education (PreK–K)
   E. Early Childhood (K–4)
   F. Elementary Education (K–6)
   G. Middle Childhood (5–9)
   H. Adolescent (9–12)
   I. Adult (Adult)
   J. Middle to Adult (5–Adult)

Licenses for Professional Educators

I. General requirements for all applicants for certificates detailed in this section:
   A. Applicant must be a US citizen, unless otherwise noted; of good moral character; physically, mentally, and emotionally qualified to perform the duties of a teacher; and 18 years old.
   B. FBI background check for initial certificates
   C. State background check for initial certificates
II. Provisional Teaching Certificate (valid 1 year). For out-of-state applicants who have

met all requirements except West Virginia tests if all tests in another state have been completed. Requirements:

A. Bachelor's degree or master's degree from an accredited institution of higher education (IHE) or an equivalent degree from an IHE in a foreign country

B. Out-of-State applicants must submit proof of:
1. Successful completion of an out-of-state approved teacher education program from an accredited IHE,
or
2. Evaluated foreign academic credentials,
or
3. Valid out-of-state certificate (if applying for Administrative Certificate).

III. Initial Professional Certificate (valid 3 years). Requirements:

A. Minimum proficiency levels in state board–approved tests:
1. Basic skills: Praxis (CORE)—Pre-Professional Skills in Reading, Writing, and Mathematics
2. Content specialization(s): appropriate Praxis II test(s)
3. Professional knowledge: Praxis II that includes at least a portion of the grade levels indicated on license sought

B. Successful completion of a regionally accredited IHE's state-approved program and the recommendation of the designated official at the college or university through which the program was completed
or
A valid out-of-state professional certificate (no tests are required under this option),
or
Successful completion of a state-approved alternative delivery program that incorporates the pre-professional skills, content, and professional education standards approved by the state board, including a student teaching experience or documentation of an "in lieu" experience

C. Requirements for renewal of any Professional Teaching Certificate:
1. Six semester hours of appropriate college/university course work, with a minimum 3.0 GPA, related to the public school program
   a. The 6 semester hours must meet 1 of the following criteria:
      i. Courses relevant to a master's degree in a curriculum related to the public school program
      or
      ii. Courses related to improvement of instruction and the applicant's current endorsement area
      or
      iii. Courses needed to qualify for an additional endorsement
      or
      iv. Credit prescribed by the county as a result of an applicant's evaluation
or
Master's degree plus 30 Salary Classification
or
Has reached 60 years of age and presents a photocopy of the birth certificate

2. Recommendation of the employing county's superintendent
IV. Professional Five-Year Teaching Certificate (valid 5 years). Requirements:
   A. Successful completion of the Beginning Educator Internship for classroom, unless the applicant holds a valid out-of-state certificate and has 5 years of teaching experience in another state, or received the Initial West Virginia Teaching Certificate prior to January 1, 1992
   B. Six semester hours of appropriate college/university course work reflecting a 3.0 GPA and related to the public school program, unless the applicant holds a minimum of a master's degree plus 30 Salary Classification based on the awarding of a master's degree
   C. Two years of experience, 1 of which must be completed in West Virginia, within 1 endorsement or a combination of the endorsements, on the Initial Professional Teaching Certificate
   D. Recommendation of superintendent in the county in which the educator teaches or last taught
V. Permanent Professional Teaching Certificate (valid unless surrendered, suspended, or revoked). Requirements:
   A. Hold or be eligible for the Five-year Professional Teaching Certificate;
   and
   Master's degree related to the public school;
   and
   Five years of educational experience, including 2 within the specialization(s) for which the permanent certificate is requested.
   or
   B. Hold a valid Professional Five-Year Teaching Certificate,
   and
   Renew the Professional Five-Year Teaching Certificate once based on:
     1. Six semester hours of appropriate renewal credit reflecting a 3.0 GPA,
     or
     2. Minimum of a master's degree plus 30 Salary Classification based on the awarding of a master's degree,
     or
     3. Age 60,
   or
   Hold certification through the National Board for Professional Teaching Standards (NBPTS).
VI. Individuals who hold a valid out-of-state teaching certificate, have completed a state-approved educator preparation program, and hold a bachelor's degree from a regionally accredited IHE should visit http://wvde.state.wv.us/certification for specific information.

Specializations

I. Recognized Programmatic Level
   A. Preschool Education (PreK–PreK), Early Education (PreK–K), Early Childhood (K–4), Middle Childhood (5–9), Adolescent (9–12), Adult (Adult)

II. Grade-Level Options for General Education Specializations Current Programs:
   A. Agriculture (5–Adult); American Sign Language (PreK–Adult, 5–Adult), any Modern Foreign Language (PreK–Adult, 5–Adult); Art (PreK–Adult, 5–Adult, 5–9); Biology (9–Adult); Business Education (5–Adult, 9–Adult); Chemistry (9–Adult); Chemistry/Physics (9–Adult); Chinese (PreK–Adult, 5–Adult); Computer Science Education (PreK–Adult); Dance (PreK–Adult, 5–Adult); Driver Education (9–Adult); Earth and Space Science (5–Adult); Early Childhood Education (K–4); Early Education (PreK–K); Elementary Education (K–6); Elementary Math Education (K–6); Elementary Math Specialist (K–6); English (5–Adult, 5–9); English as a Second Language (PreK–Adult); Family & Consumer Science (5–Adult); French (PreK–Adult, 5–Adult); General Integrated Math (5–Adult); General Math through Algebra I (5–9); General Science (5–Adult, 5–9); German (PreK–Adult, 5–Adult); Health (PreK–Adult, 5–Adult); Instructional Technology (PreK–Adult); Japanese (PreK–Adult, 5–Adult); Journalism (5–Adult, 9–Adult); Latin (PreK–Adult, 5–Adult); Marketing (9–Adult); Mathematics Comprehensive (5–Adult); Middle Childhood Education (MCE) (5–9); Music (PreK–Adult); Oral Communications (5–Adult, 9–Adult); Physical Education (PreK–Adult, 5–Adult, 5–9); Physics (9–Adult); Preschool Education (PreK–PreK); Reading (PreK–K, K–6, 5–Adult); Reading Specialist* (PreK–Adult); Russian (PreK–Adult, 5–Adult); School Library/Media (PreK–Adult); Social Studies (5–Adult, 5–9); Spanish (PreK–Adult, 5–Adult); Technology Education (5–Adult); Theater (PreK–Adult); Wellness (Health–Physical Education) (PreK–Adult)

III. Grade-Level Options for Special Education Specializations:
   A. Autism (PreK–PreK, K–6, 5–Adult); Emotional/Behavior Disorders (K–6, 5–Adult); Gifted (1–12); Deaf and Hard of Hearing (PreK–Adult); Mentally Impaired Mild/Moderate (K–6, 5–Adult); Multi-Categorical (E/BD, MI, SLD) (K–6, 5–Adult); Preschool Special Needs (PreK–K); Severe Disabilities (K–Adult); Specific Learning Disabilities (K–6, 5–Adult); Visually Impaired (PreK–Adult)

IV. Grade-Level Options for Student Support Specializations (all are PreK–Adult):
   A. Counselor,* School Nurse, School Psychologist,* Social Services and Attendance, Speech-Language Pathologist,* Speech Assistant

V. Grade-Level Options for Administrative Specializations (all are PreK–Adult):
   A. General Supervisor,* Principal,* Superintendent*

*Master's degree required

Administrative Certificates

I. Initial Professional Administrative Certificate (valid for 5 years)
   A. The Initial Professional Administrative Certificate shall be endorsed for Superintendent, Principal, and/or Supervisor of Instruction and shall indicate the specialization(s) and grade levels in which the holder can be legally assigned within the public schools.

B. General Requirements:
   1. Successful completion of an IHE's state-approved program and the recommendation of the designated official at the college or university through which the program was completed,
   or
   Applicants holding a valid out-of-state Administrative Certificate need only present the official transcripts evidencing completion of a state-approved administration preparation program at a regionally accredited college or university and a copy of their valid out-of-state Administrative Certificate.
   2. Minimum GPA of 3.0
   3. Three years of teaching/management experience
   4. Complete Evaluation Leadership Institute (ELI)
   5. Passing scores on Praxis II
   6. Master's degree required
C. See Licenses for Professional Educators, III, C, 1 and 2, above.

II. Permanent Professional Administrative Certificate (remains valid unless surrendered, suspended, or revoked for just cause)
   A. Requirements for converting the Initial Professional Administrative Certificate to the Permanent Professional Administrative Certificate:
      1. Six semester hours of appropriate renewal credit related to the public school program
      or
      Master's degree plus 30 Salary Classification
      2. Five years of educational experience.
         a. Two years of experience must be in any, or a combination of, the specializations reflected on the Professional Administration Certificate.
         b. One year of experience must be completed in West Virginia.
      3. Recommendation of Superintendent

III. Temporary Administrative Certificate (out-of-state applicants)
   A. Endorsed for Superintendent, Principal, and/or Supervisor of Instruction and shall indicate the specialization(s) and grade levels in which the holder may be assigned within the public schools
   B. Issued to administrators who graduate from an out-of-state IHE, or who are transferring credential from another state or country to complete the requirements for testing, if applicable, to complete the Evaluation Leadership Institute.
   C. Issued for 1 year valid until June 30 of the expiring year
   D. Three years of teaching/management experience
   E. Master's degree required

Student Support Certificates

I. School Counselor
   A. Temporary Professional Student Support Certificate for out-of-state applicants (valid 1 year, nonrenewable)

1. Issued to applicant who meets requirements for a Provisional Teaching Certificate (see Licenses for Professional Educators, II, above) and the following criteria:
   a. Master's degree in counseling from a regionally accredited IHE in a state other than West Virginia
   b. Successful completion of an accredited school counseling program
   c. GPA of 3.0

B. Initial Professional Student Support Certificate (valid 3 years)
   1. Issued to applicant who meets the following criteria:
      a. Master's degree in counseling from an accredited IHE
      b. Successful completion of an accredited school counseling program
      c. West Virginia–required Praxis exam

C. Professional Student Support Certificate (valid 5 years)
   1. Issued to applicant who meets the requirements for a Professional Five-Year Student Support Certificate:
      a. Two years of work experience (one of which must be completed within West Virginia) as a school counselor,
         and
         Six semester hours of college course work relating to public education;
         or
      b. Master's degree plus 30 Salary Classification;
         or
         Has reached 60 years of age.

D. Permanent Professional Student Support Certificate
   1. Issued to an applicant who meets the requirements for a Permanent Professional Teaching Certificate:
      a. Five years of educational work experience in the area(s) for which certification is held, including 2 years work as a school counselor (1 year must be completed within West Virginia)
         and
         Six semester hours of college course work relating to public education;
         or
      b. Master's degree plus 30 Salary Classification;
         or
         Has reached 60 years of age.

II. School Psychologist
   A. Temporary Professional Student Support Certificate
      1. Issued to applicant who meets requirements for a Provisional Student Support Certificate
      2. See I, School Counselor, A, directly above.
   B. Initial Professional Student Support Certificate (valid 3 years)
      1. Issued to applicant who completes master's degree in a field related to education from an accredited institution of higher education as defined in West Virginia Board of Education (WVBE) policy 5202, section 4.60
      2. See I, School Counselor, B, directly above.

C. Professional Student Support Certificate (valid 5 years)
1. See I, School Counselor, C, directly above.
D. Permanent Professional Student Support Certificate
1. See I, School Counselor, D, directly above.
III. Speech-Language Pathologist
A. Temporary Student Support Certificate
1. Issued to applicant who meets requirements for a Provisional Student Support Certificate
2. See I, School Counselor, A, directly above.
B. Initial Professional Student Support Certificate
1. Issued to applicant who earns a master's degree in an approved program in Speech-Language Pathology from a regionally accredited IHE
C. See I, School Counselor, C and D, directly above.
IV. Renewal of the Professional Student Support Certificate
A. Application for renewal of the Professional Student Support Certificate for School Counselor, School Psychologist, and Speech-Language Pathologist must be submitted after January 1 of the year in which the license expires.
B. The applicant for licensure must submit evidence of satisfying the following:
1. Completed 6 semester hours of appropriate college/university course work related to the public school program with a minimum 3.0 GPA
2. See Licenses For Professional Educators, V, B, above, except that requirements must be met in the 5-year period immediately preceding the date of application.
V. Professional Five-Year Student Support Certificate
A. Six semester hours of appropriate college/university course work reflecting a 3.0 GPA and related to the public school program
or
Minimum of a master's plus 30 Salary Classification
B. Two years of experience within 1 endorsement or a combination of endorsements, on the Initial Professional Student Support Certificate
C. Recommendation of superintendent
VI. Permanent Professional Student Support Certificate
A. Five years of educational experience in areas for which certification is held (1 year must be completed in West Virginia);
and
B. Master's degree related to the public school program,
or
Professional Five-Year Student Support Certificate;
and
C. Six semester hours of appropriate renewal credit reflecting a 3.0 GPA,
or
Minimum of a master's degree plus 30 Salary Classification,
or
Has reached 60 years of age;
or
D. NBPTS Certification.

Wisconsin

Educator Standards

I.   Teacher Standards: To receive a license to teach in Wisconsin, an applicant shall complete an approved program and demonstrate proficient performance in the knowledge, skills, and dispositions under all of the following standards:

   A.   The teacher understands the central concepts, tools of inquiry, and structures of the disciplines he or she teaches and can create learning experiences that make these aspects of subject matter meaningful for pupils.

   B.   The teacher understands how children with broad ranges of ability learn and provides instruction that supports their intellectual, social, and personal development.

   C.   The teacher understands how pupils differ in their approaches to learning and the barriers that impede learning and can adapt instruction to meet the diverse needs of pupils, including those with disabilities and exceptionalities.

   D.   The teacher understands and uses a variety of instructional strategies, including the use of technology, to encourage children's development of critical thinking, problem solving, and performance skills.

   E.   The teacher uses an understanding of individual and group motivation and behavior to create a learning environment that encourages positive social interaction, active engagement in learning, and self-motivation.

   F.   The teacher uses effective verbal and nonverbal communication techniques as well as instructional media and technology to foster active inquiry, collaboration, and supportive interaction in the classroom.

   G.   The teacher organizes and plans systematic instruction based upon knowledge of subject matter, pupils, the community, and curriculum goals.

   H.   The teacher understands and uses formal and informal assessment strategies to evaluate and ensure the continuous intellectual, social, and physical development of the pupil.

   I.   The teacher is a reflective practitioner who continually evaluates the effect of his or her choices and actions on pupils, parents, professionals in the learning community, and others, and who actively seeks out opportunities to grow professionally.

   J.   The teacher fosters relationships with school colleagues, parents, and agencies in the larger community to support pupil learning and well-being and acts with integrity, fairness, and in an ethical manner.

II. Administrator standards: To receive a license in a school administrator category, an applicant shall complete an approved program in school administration and demonstrate proficient performance in the knowledge, skills, and dispositions under all of the following standards:

   A.   The administrator has an understanding of and demonstrates competence in the teacher standards.

   B.   The administrator leads by facilitating the development, articulation, implementation, and stewardship of a vision of learning that is shared by the school community.

C. The administrator manages by advocating, nurturing, and sustaining a school culture and instructional program conducive to pupil learning and staff professional growth.

D. The administrator ensures management of the organization, operations, finances, and resources for a safe, efficient, and effective learning environment.

E. The administrator models collaborating with families and community members, responding to diverse community interests and needs, and mobilizing community resources.

F. The administrator acts with integrity, fairness, and in an ethical manner.

G. The administrator understands, responds to, and interacts with the larger political, social, economic, legal, and cultural context that affects schooling.

III. Pupil Services Standards: To receive a license in a pupil services category (school counselors, school social workers, school psychologists, and school nurses), an applicant shall complete an approved program and demonstrate proficient performance in the knowledge, skills, and dispositions under all of the following standards:

A. The pupil services professional understands the 10 Teacher Standards (see I, directly above).

B. The pupil services professional understands the complexities of learning and has knowledge of comprehensive, coordinated practice strategies that support pupil learning, health, safety, and development.

C. The pupil services professional has the ability to use research, research methods, and knowledge about issues and trends to improve practice in schools and classrooms.

D. The pupil services professional understands and represents professional ethics and social behaviors appropriate for school and community.

E. The pupil services professional understands the organization, development, management, and content of collaborative and mutually supportive pupil services programs within educational settings.

F. The pupil services professional is able to address comprehensively the wide range of social, emotional, behavioral, and physical issues and circumstances which may limit pupils' abilities to achieve positive learning outcomes through development, implementation, and evaluation of system-wide interventions and strategies.

G. The pupil services professional interacts successfully with pupils, parents, professional educators, employers, and community support systems such as juvenile justice, public health, human services, and adult education.

License Stages for Teachers, Administrators, and Pupil Services

I. Provisional License (valid 3 years; renewable)

A. Prerequisites

1. Bachelor's degree and completion of state-approved educator preparation program

a. Officer of the institution's state-approved educator preparation program must endorse applicant.

       b.   Additional requirements/experience may be required for specific license areas.

   2.   Graduates of professional educator programs in a state or United States territory other than Wisconsin may apply for a license based on reciprocity.

   3.   Successful completion of an alternative teacher certification program operated by an alternative preparation program provider that is a nonprofit organization under section 501(c)(3) of the internal revenue code. The program must operate in at least 5 states, have been in operation for at least 10 years, and require the candidate to pass both a subject area and pedagogy test known as the Professional Teaching Knowledge exam to receive a certificate.

   4.   See Testing Requirements, below, for full details.

II. Life License is issued to an applicant who has held a provisional license and submits verification of 6 semesters of successful teaching, pupil services, or administrative experience in a school district.

III. Master Educator Life License

   A.   Mastery of Wisconsin standards in high-stakes portfolio assessment through the Wisconsin Master Educator Assessment Process (WMEAP) requiring:

      1.   Related master's degree
      2.   Demonstrated improvement in pupil learning
      3.   Assessment by Department of Public Instruction (DPI)–trained WMEAP Team
      4.   Professional contributions

     or

   B.   National Board of Professional Teaching Standards Certification
   C.   Satisfactory background check is required of all applicants.

Testing Requirements

I. Content Knowledge Proficiency demonstrated by a passing score on standardized test (Praxis II), or 3.0 GPA in content area, or proficiency in content portfolio developed by the educator preparation program

   A.   Foundations of Reading Test
      1.   Effective for applicants who apply for licensure after January 31, 2014
      2.   Elementary, special education, reading teacher, and reading specialist licenses

   B.   Contact the team at the Wisconsin Department of Public Instruction (see Appendix 1) or http://tepdl.dpi.wi.gov/licensing/wisconsin-educator-testing-requirements for qualifying scores for specific licenses.

Wyoming

General Licensure Information

I. All teachers and administrators employed in a Wyoming school district must be licensed in accordance with state law. The Wyoming Professional Teaching Standards Board (PTSB) requires all Wyoming educators to have completed an approved teacher preparation program from an accredited institution of higher education (IHE) in order to become licensed to teach in a Wyoming school district.

II. There are 2 routes to teacher licensure in Wyoming.
    A. Licensure Through Program Completion requires the completion of an educator preparation program from a regionally accredited college or university.
    B. Licensure through out-of-state work experience requires that the applicant has taught 3 out of the last 6 years in the state of licensure, including verification of full-time teaching, administrative, or other school experience for up to or including the past 10 years, signed by the respective school administrators. Please note that student teaching is not accepted as experience in this regard.

Requirements for Initial Licensure

I. To obtain initial, first-time licensure, applicants must meet all the following requirements:
    A. Complete an approved educator preparation program at a regionally accredited college or university. The program must:
        1. Include student teaching;
        2. Lead to an institutional recommendation for licensure; *and*
        3. Lead to licensure in the state where the program is located.
    B. Submit an institutional recommendation for licensure, signed by an authorized official, recommending the applicant for licensure in the applicable endorsement area(s)
    C. Submit official college transcripts documenting completion of teacher preparation program
    D. Undergo fingerprinting and complete a background check
    E. Demonstrate knowledge of the US and Wyoming constitutions either through course work or by successfully passing an exam
    F. Pass approved Praxis II exams in 2 teaching areas:
        1. Elementary Education—A passing score on Praxis II exam 5001 by passing the included tests with the following scores or better: 5002—157, 5003—157, 5004—155, and 5005—159
        2. Social Studies Composite—A passing score of 158 or better on Praxis II exam 5081/0081 "Social Studies: Content Knowledge" for grades 6–12, and 5089/0089 "Middle School Social Studies" for grades 5–8

    G. Submit a complete application packet and pay appropriate fees

II. Out-of-State Applicants

    A. All out-of-state applicants are required to submit the documentation listed below in addition to their complete application packet, fingerprint cards, institutional recommendation (if applicable), and US and Wyoming Constitutions requirements.

        1. Verification of work history for the past 6 years, signed by each of the applicant's school administrators or board chairs during that time period

        2. Copy of the applicant's current, valid teaching certificate or license from the state in which he or she taught

        3. Copy of the applicant's test scores from Praxis II exam(s) or an equivalent exam from his or her state

        4. In accordance with the National Association of State Directors of Teacher Education and Certification (NASDTEC) Interstate Agreement, PTSB may require an out-of-state applicant to complete additional requirements to obtain a Wyoming teaching license.

Endorsements by Grade/Age Level

Endorsement(s) for which an applicant qualifies will appear on the Standard License. As determined by program approval standards, the endorsement(s) will allow teachers to provide instruction in the classroom or the school personnel to provide services in the areas identified on the license. Teaching endorsements are valid at the grade level for which they are issued.

    I. Birth to Age 5: Early Childhood/Special Education

    II. Birth to Age 8 (or Grade 3): Early Childhood

    III. Birth to Age 5: Preschool Early Childhood (excluding Kindergarten)

    IV. Elementary Level K–6: art; elementary teacher; English as a second language; music; music instrumental; music vocal; reading; physical education; adapted physical education; institutional teacher, world languages

    V. Middle Level 5–8: art; English as a second language; health; language arts; mathematics; music; music instrumental; music vocal; reading; physical education; adapted physical education; science; social studies; world languages

    VI. Secondary level 6–12: agriculture; anthropology; art; biology; business; chemistry; computer science; drama; driver's education; earth science; economics; English; English as a second language; family consumer science; geography; health; history; journalism; mathematics; music; music instrumental; music vocal; physical education; adapted physical education; physical science; physics; political science; psychology; reading; social studies comprehensive; sociology; speech; trade and technical; at-risk/alternative teacher; institutional teacher; world language (Chinese, Japanese, French, Latin, German, Russian, Italian, Spanish)

    VII. K–12: art; audiology; educational diagnostician; English as a second language; health; gifted and talented; music; music instrumental; music vocal; physical education; adapted physical education; reading; institutional teacher; school nurse; world languages

    VIII. Special Education K–6/5–8/6–12/K–12: exceptional generalist; exceptional specialist—behavioral & emotional disabilities; exceptional specialist—cognitive disability; exceptional specialist—deaf and hard of hearing; exceptional specialist—learning disability; exceptional specialist—physical and health disability; exceptional specialist—visual disability

Additional School Personnel

I. School Administrator (valid 5 years)
   A. An individual who holds a standard Wyoming educator license may apply to add a school administrator endorsement to his or her license.
   B. This endorsement allows individuals to serve as an administrator or superintendent in any Wyoming school in accordance with his or her grade level of preparation.
   C. The following school administrator endorsements are offered by PTSB:
      1. District superintendent
      2. School principal
      3. Program director
   D. Requirements:
      1. Hold Wyoming licensure in a teaching or related services field
      2. Have completed an educational leadership program, from a nationally or regionally accredited college/university, that leads to an institutional recommendation in educational leadership, school principal, educational administrator, or other equivalent endorsement areas
   E. Educators who are applying concurrently for initial licensure and a school administrator endorsement must submit a complete application for Initial, First-Time Licensure and have at least 3 years of K–12 teaching or related service experience.
II. School Librarian (valid 5 years)
   A. An individual with this endorsement is eligible to serve as a school librarian in a Wyoming K–12 school.
   B. Endorsement requires completion of a program in school library science, K–12.
III. School Counselor (valid 5 years)
   A. Endorsement requires an institutional recommendation indicating completion of a master's or higher degree in school counseling.
IV. School Psychologist (valid 5 years)
   A. Endorsement requires an institutional recommendation indicating completion of a master's or higher degree in school psychology.
V. School Social Worker (valid 5 years)
   A. Endorsement requires an institutional recommendation indicating completion of a master's or higher degree in school social work.
VI. Speech Pathologist (valid 5 years)
   A. Endorsement requires an institutional recommendation indicating completion of a master's or higher degree in speech pathology.

Appendix 1

How to Contact State Offices of Certification

Alabama
Educator Certification Section
Office of Teaching and Leading
State Department of Education
5215 Gordon Persons Building
P.O. Box 302101
Montgomery, AL 36130-2101
334-694-4557 (10:00–noon,
 1:00–5:00)
www.alsde.edu/EdCert

Alaska
Alaska Dept. of Education & Early
 Development
Attn: Teacher Certification
801 West 10th Street, Suite 200, P.O.
 Box 110500
Juneau, AK 99811-0500
907-465-2831
907-465-2441 (fax)
education.alaska.gov/
 TeacherCertification
tcwebmail@alaska.gov

Arizona
Arizona Dept. of Education
 Educator Certification

Mailing Address:
Arizona Department of
 Education—Certification Unit
P.O. Box 6490
Phoenix, AZ 85005-6490

Physical Address:
Arizona Department of Education
1535 W. Jefferson St.
Phoenix, AZ 85007
602-542-4367 (8:30–4:30)
www.azed.gov/educator-certification
Certification@azed.gov

Arkansas
Office of Educator Licensure
State Dept. of Education
Four Capitol Mall, Room 106-B
Little Rock, AR 72201
501-682-4342 (8:00–4:30)
501-682-4898 (fax)
ArkansasEd.gov
Melissa.Jacks@arkansas.gov

California
Commission on Teacher
 Credentialing
1900 Capitol Avenue
Sacramento, CA 95811-4213
916-322-4974 (12:30–4:30)
www.ctc.ca.gov
credentials@ctc.ca.gov

Colorado
Department of Education
Educator Preparation, Licensing,
 and Enforcement
6000 E Evans Ave., Building #2,
 Suite 100
Denver, CO 80222
303-866-6628 (7:30–12:30)
303-866-6722 (fax)
www.cde.state.co.us/cdeprof
cdelicensing@cde.state.co.us

Connecticut
Bureau of Educator Standards and
 Certification
State Department of Education
P.O. Box 150471
Hartford, CT 06115-0471
860-713-6969
860-713-7017 (fax)
www.sde.ct.gov/sde/cert
teacher.cert@ct.gov

Delaware
Educator Licensure and Certification
Department of Education
Collette Education Resource Center
35 Commerce Way, Suite 1
Dover, DE 19904
302-857-3388 (8:00–4:30)
www.doe.k12.de.us
deeds@doe.k12.de.us

District of Columbia
Office of the State Superintendent of
 Education
Educator Quality and Effectiveness
Teaching & Learning Unit
1050 First St., NE
Washington, DC 20002
202-727-6436
osse.dc.gov/ed-credentials
osse.asklicensure@dc.gov

Florida
Bureau of Educator Certification
Department of Education
Room 201, Turlington Building
325 W. Gaines Street
Tallahassee, FL 32399-0400
800-445-6739 (in US)
850-245-5049 (outside US)
www.fldoe.org/teaching/certification
Submit email on website

Georgia
Professional Standards Commission
Educator Certification Division
200 Piedmont Ave. SE
Suite 1702, West Tower
Atlanta, GA 30334-9032
404-232-2500 (metro Atlanta and
 outside Georgia)
800-869-7775 (in-state, outside
 metro Atlanta)
www.gapsc.com
mail@gapsc.com

Hawaii
Hawaii Teacher Standards Board
Licensing Section
650 Iwilei Road, Suite 268
Honolulu, HI 96817
808-586-2600
808-586-2606 (fax)
hawaiiteacherstandardsboard.org
htsb@hawaii.gov

Idaho
Certification/Professional Standards
    Commission
State Department of Education
650 W. State St., P.O. Box 83720
Boise, ID 83720-0027
208-332-6882
208-334-2228 (fax)
www.sde.idaho.gov/cert-psc/cert/
certification@sde.idaho.gov

Illinois
ISBE Educator Effectiveness
    Division
100 North First Street
Springfield, IL 62777-0001
217-557-6763
217-524-1289 (fax)
www.isbe.net/Pages/Educator
    -Licensure.aspx
licensure@isbe.net

Indiana
Office of Educator Effectiveness and
    Licensing
Indiana Department of Education
115 W. Washington Street
South Tower, Suite 600
Indianapolis, IN 46204
317-232-9010
www.doe.in.gov/licensing
licensinghelp@doe.in.gov
Email documents: transcript@doe
    .in.gov

Iowa
Board of Educational Examiners
Grimes State Office Building
400 East 14th Street
Des Moines, IA 50319-0147
515-281-3245
515-281-7669 (fax)
boee.iowa.gov

Kansas
Teacher Licensure and Accreditation
Kansas State Department of
    Education
Landon State Office Building
900 SW Jackson Ave.
Topeka, KS 66612
785-296-2288
785-296-7933 (fax)
www.ksde.org/Agency/Division
    -of-Learning-Services/Teacher
    -Licensure-and-Accreditation

Kentucky
Education Professional Standards
    Board
Division of Certification
100 Airport Road, 3rd Floor
Frankfort, KY 40601
502-564-4606
888-598-7667
502-564-7080 (fax)
www.epsb.ky.gov
dcert@ky.gov

Louisiana
Louisiana Department of Education
Division of Educator Licensure
P.O. Box 94064
Baton Rouge, LA 70804-9064
877-453-2721 (toll-free)
www.louisianabelieves.com
Submit email at ldoe.force.com/s/
    ask-certification

Maine
Certification Office
Maine Department of Education
23 State House Station
Augusta, ME 04333-0023
207-624-6603
207-624-6604 (fax)
www.maine.gov/doe/cert
cert.doe@maine.gov

Maryland
Maryland State Department of
    Education
Certification
200 West Baltimore Street
Baltimore, MD 21201-2595
410-767-0412
866-772-8922 (toll-free)
410-333-6442 (TTY-TDD)
410-333-8963 (fax)
www.mdcert.org

Massachusetts
Department of Elementary and
    Secondary Education (ESE)
Office of Educator Licensure
75 Pleasant Street
Malden, MA 02148-4906
781-338-3000 (24/7 automated)
800-439-2370 (TTY)
www.doe.mass.edu/licensure/

Michigan
Office of Professional Preparation
    Services
Michigan Department of Education
608 West Allegan Street
P.O. Box 30008
Lansing, MI 48909
517-241-5000
www.michigan.gov/moecs
MDE-EducatorHelp@michigan.gov

Minnesota
Professional Educator Licensing and
    Standards Board
1500 Highway 36 West, Suite 300
Roseville, MN 55113
651-539-4200
mn.gov/pelsb
pelsb@state.mn.us

Mississippi
Office of Educator Licensure
Mississippi Department of
    Education
P.O. Box 771
Jackson, MS 39205-0771
601-359-3483
www.mdek12.org/OTL/OEL
teachersupport@mde.k12.ms.us

Missouri
Educator Certification
P.O. Box 480
Jefferson City, MO 65102-0480
573-751-0051
573-526-3580 (fax)
dese.mo.gov/educator-quality/
    certification
certification@dese.mo.gov

Montana
Educator Licensure
Office of Public Instruction
P.O. Box 202501
Helena, MT 59620-2501
406-444-3095
888-231-9393 (in-state toll free)
opi.mt.gov/Educators
cert@mt.gov

Nebraska
Teacher Certification Division
Nebraska Department of Education
301 Centennial Mall South
P.O. Box 94987
Lincoln, NE 68509-4987
402-471-0739
www.education.ne.gov/tcert
nde.tcertweb@nebraska.gov

Nevada
Nevada Department of Education
www.doe.nv.gov/educator
    _licensure/
license@doe.nv.gov

Office of Educator Licensure–
    Southern Nevada
9890 South Maryland Parkway,
    Suite 221
Las Vegas, NV 89183
Phone: 702-486-6458 (8:00–5:00)
Fax: 702-486-6450

Office of Educator Licensure–
    Northern Nevada
755 N. Roop St. Ste 107
Carson City, NV 89701
775-687-5980 (8:00–5:00)

New Hampshire
New Hampshire Department of
    Education
Bureau of Credentialing
Division of Educator Support and
    Higher Education
101 Pleasant Street
Concord, NH 03301-3494
603-271-2409
www.education.nh.gov/certification
cert.info@doe.nh.gov

New Jersey
New Jersey Department of
    Education
Office of Certification & Induction
P.O. Box 500
Trenton, NJ 08625-0500
609-292-2070 (8:00–4:00)
609-984-3356 (fax)
nj.gov/education/license/index.html

New Mexico
New Mexico Public Education
    Department
Attn: Licensure
300 Don Gaspar
Santa Fe, NM 87501
505-827-1436
505-827-1449 (fax)
www.ped.state.nm.us/licensure
LicensureUnit@state.nm.us

New York
Office of Teaching Initiatives
New York State Education
    Department
89 Washington Avenue, 5N EB
Albany, NY 12234
518-474-3901 (9:00–4:00, M–F)
www.highered.nysed.gov/tcert
tcert@nysed.gov

North Carolina
Department of Public Instruction
6301 Mail Service Center
Raleigh, NC 27699-6301
919-807-3310 (out of state)
800-577-7994 (in-state only)
www.NCPublicSchools.org/
    licensure/
asklicensure@dpi.nc.gov

North Dakota
Education Standards & Practices
    Board
Teacher Licensure
2718 Gateway Ave., Suite 204
Bismarck, ND 58503-0585
701-328-9641
701-328-9647 (fax)
www.ND.gov/espb/licensure
espbinfo@nd.gov

North Dakota Dept. of Public
    Instruction
600 E. Boulevard Ave., Dept. 201
Bismarck, ND 58505-0440
701-328-2260
www.nd.gov/dpi/schoolstaff/

Ohio
Office of Educator Licensure
Ohio Department of Education
25 South Front St., Mail Stop 504
Columbus, OH 43215-4183
614-466-3593
877-644-6338 (toll-free)
education.ohio.gov/Topics/
    Teaching/Licensure
Educator.Licensure@education.ohio
    .gov

Oklahoma
Teacher Certification
State Department of Education
2500 N. Lincoln Blvd., Rm. 212
Oklahoma City, OK 73105-4599
405-521-3337
www.ok.gov/sde/teacher
-certification
jeff.smith@sde.ok.gov

Oregon
Teacher Standards and Practices
Commission
250 Division St. NE
Salem, OR 97301
503-378-3586
503-378-4448 (fax)
www.oregon.gov/tspc
contact.tspc@oregon.gov

Pennsylvania
PA Department of Education
Bureau of School Leadership and
Teacher Quality
333 Market Street, 12th Floor
Harrisburg, PA 17126-0333
717-728-3224
www.education.pa.gov/Educators/
Certification
ra-edcertquestions@pa.gov

Rhode Island
Office of Educator Quality and
Certification
State Department of Education
255 Westminster St.
Providence, RI 02903-3400
401-222-8893
www.ride.ri.gov/
TeachersAdministrators/
EducatorCertification.aspx
EQAC@ride.ri.gov

South Carolina
Department of Education
1429 Senate Street
Columbia, SC 29201
803-896-0371 (8:30–1:00)
803-896-0325 (1:00–4:00)
ed.sc.gov/educators/certification
certification@ed.sc.gov
transcripts@ed.sc.gov (for emailing
transcripts)

South Dakota
Department of Education
Certification Office
800 Governors Drive
Pierre, SD 57501
605-773-3134
doe.sd.gov/certification/
certification@state.sd.us

Tennessee
Tennessee Department of Education
Office of Educator Licensing
12th Floor, Andrew Johnson Tower
710 James Robertson Parkway
Nashville, TN 37243-0377
615-532-4885
615-532-1448 (fax)
www.tn.gov/education/licensing
Educator.Licensure@tn.gov

Texas
Texas Education Agency
Educator Certification and Testing
WBT 5-100
1701 N. Congress Ave.
Austin, TX 78701-1494
512-936-8400
tea.texas.gov/Texas_Educators/
Certification/
See website for contact information

Utah
USBE Licensing
250 East 500 South
P.O. Box 144200
Salt Lake City, UT 84114-4200
801-538-7740
801-538-7973 (fax)
www.schools.utah.gov/cert

Vermont
Educator Licensing Office
Vermont Agency of Education
219 N. Main St., Ste. 402
Barre, VT 05641
802-479-1700 (7:45–4:30)
education.vermont.gov/educator
-quality/become-a-vermont
-educator
aoe.licensinginfo@vermont.gov

Virginia
Virginia Department of Education
Division of Teacher Education and
Licensure
P.O. Box 2120
Richmond, VA 23218-2120
804-225-2022
804-530-4510 (fax)
www.doe.virginia.gov/teaching/
licensure/index.shtml
licensure@doe.virginia.gov

Washington
Office of Superintendent of Public
Instruction (OSPI)
Professional Certification Office
Old Capitol Building
P.O. Box 47200
Olympia, WA 98504-7200
360-725-6400
360-664-3631 (TTY)
www.k12.wa.us/certification
cert@k12.wa.us

West Virginia
Office of Certification and
  Professional Preparation
Building 6, Suite 700
1900 Kanawha Blvd., East
Charleston, WV 25305-0330
304-558-7010
800-982-2378
wvde.state.wv.us/certification

Wisconsin
Teacher Education, Professional
  Development & Licensing
Department of Public Instruction
125 S. Webster Street
Madison, WI 53703
608-266-1027
800-266-1027
dpi.wi.gov/tepdl/licensing
licensing@dpi.wi.gov

Wyoming
Professional Teaching Standards
  Board
State of Wyoming
1920 Thomes Avenue, Suite 100
Cheyenne, WY 82002
307-777-7291
800-675-6893
307-777-8718 (fax)
wyomingptsb.com/
wyoptsb@wyo.gov

Appendix 2

Addresses for Certification Information for US Possessions and Territories

American Samoa
American Samoa Department of
    Education (Utulei)
Pago Pago, AS 96799
Phone: (684) 633-5237
Fax: (684) 633-4240
asdoetq@doe.as

**Commonwealth of the Northern
    Mariana Islands**
Jessica Estrada, Certification &
    Licensure Officer
Capitol Hill
P.O. Box 501370 CK
Saipan, MP 96950
Phone: (670) 237-3061
Fax: (670) 664-3045
www.cnmipss.org/certification-and
    -praxis/
boe.certification@cnmipss.org

Federated States of Micronesia
FSM Department of Education
P.O. Box PS 87, Palikir
Pohnpei, FM 96941
Phone: (691) 320-2609
Fax: (691) 320-5500
www.fsmcd.fm

Guam
Guam Commission for Educator
    Certification
Office: University of Guam School
    of Education, Room 105 (1st Flr)
Mail: 303 University Drive SOE
    Bldg, Room 105
Mangilao, GU 96913
Fran-Nicole Camacho, Certification
    Officer
francamacho@gcec.guam.gov
Phone: (671) 735-2554
Fax: (671) 735-2569
gcec.guam.gov

Marshall Islands
Embassy of the Republic of the
    Marshall Islands
2433 Massachusetts Avenue, NW
Washington, DC 20008
Phone: (202) 234-5414
Fax: (202) 232-3236
www.rmiembassyus.org
info@rmiembassyus.org
See also www.gooverseas.com/
    teach-abroad/marshall-islands

Palau
Emery Wenty, Director, Ministry of
    Education
P.O. Box 189
Koror, Palau 96940
Phone: (680) 488-2489/2567/4220
Fax: (680) 488-8465
palaugov.org/bureau-of-education/
ewenty@palaumoe.net

Puerto Rico
Council on Education of Puerto
    Rico
P.O. Box 19900
San Juan, PR 00910-1900
Phone: (787) 722-2121
www.ce.pr.gov

Virgin Islands
Virgin Islands Board of Education
    (St. Thomas)
P.O. Box 11900
60B, 61 and 62 Dronningens Gade
St. Thomas, VI 00801
Phone: (340) 774-4546
Fax: (340) 774-3384
www.myviboe.com/certifications/
    apply-certification
stt@myviboe.com

Virgin Islands Board of Education
    (St. Croix)
1123 King Street
Christiansted, VI 00820
Phone: (340) 772-4144
Fax: (340) 772-2895
stx@myviboe.com

**United States Department of
    Defense Education Activity**
Educator Recruitment and Staffing
DoDEA Headquarters
4800 Mark Center Drive
Alexandria, VA 22350-1400
www.dodea.edu/offices/hr/
    employment/categories/index.cfm
(571) 372-0576